ACTA UNIVERSITATIS GOTHOBURGENSIS

GOTHENBURG STUDIES IN ENGLISH 38

MOVING INWARD

A STUDY OF ROBERT BLY'S POETRY

BY
INGEGERD FRIBERG

ACTA UNIVERSITATIS GOTHOBURGENSIS
GÖTEBORG SWEDEN

Distributors:
ACTA UNIVERSITATIS GOTHOBURGENSIS
Box 5096
S-402 22 Göteborg 5
Sweden
Printed in Sweden by Holms Gårds Tryckeri, Edsbruk 1977

6 000670330

CONTENTS

PREFACE

This thesis has grown out of a general interest in American life and ideas as I have experienced them within the American society and in its literature. For awakening this interest, for endless encouragement in my early work, and for a wonderful friendship, I thank Ms. Jane Thomas, M.A., Minneapolis, Minnesota.

For encouraging me to take up graduate studies and to devote them to imagery and symbolism in American poetry, I sincerely thank Prof. Claes Schaar, Lund.

For advice and support during the actual work with the present thesis, I express my thanks to my supervisor, Prof. Erik Frykman, who has followed my work throughout, read each successive chapter of my manuscript, suggested improvements, and discussed alternative interpretations, for which I am most grateful.

For reading my whole manuscript and for discussing it - especially my Jungian interpretations - at a seminar, I express my appreciation and thanks to Fil. dr Torsten Rönnerstrand, Gothenburg.

For friendly interest and engagement in my work, I am very grateful to Harry Stessel, Fulbright Lecturer in Gothenburg, who read my whole manuscript, revised the language, and, at the same time, balanced some of my interpretations related to American history and society, and suggested other improvements.

For reading parts of my thesis and commenting on them, I thank friends and colleagues at the English Department in Gothenburg.

For valuable friendship and interest in my work, I thank the group of poets and friends of poetry I got to know during my stay in Minnesota: Prof. and poet Michael Dennis Browne who suggested several articles and poems for me to read and who served as a reference in my first contact with Robert Bly; Prof. and poet Keith Gunderson and his wife Donna who made possible my first interview with Robert Bly; James Naiden, editor of The North Stone Review, who gave me some material, otherwise not easily available; the late poet Franklin Brainard who discussed poetry with me in spite of a serious illness; and poet Louis Jenkins who shared and shares with me so generously his enthusiasm for poetry.

For allowing me an interview on the Bly family history, I extend my warm thanks to Robert Bly's cousin, Mr. Orrin Bly.

For the services rendered by the librarians at the Interlibrary Loans offices at the University of Minnesota and at the University of Wisconsin, Milwaukee, and for their willingness to try every possible way to make rare poetry publications available to me, I express my sincere thanks.

For carefully typing my final manuscript, and for the cheerfulness and friendliness shown during their work, I am very grateful to Ms. Lena Mattsson and Ms. Boel Engebrand.

For unfailing patience and invaluable support and encouragement, I lovingly thank my husband Jöran and my children Monika, Håkan, and Karin but most of all I ask their forgiveness for having neglected them and spent time away from them because of my work on this thesis. I give to Monika my special love and affection for typing all my first drafts and manuscripts.

For generous understanding of my interests and for loving support always, I express deep gratitude to my mother and my late father.

Finally, and most deeply felt, I express my gratitude to Robert Bly himself, as well as to his wife and children. They have shown invaluable generosity toward me in so many things. I thank Robert Bly for giving me time for interviews and conversations, for answering letters, and for inviting me to his home in Madison, Minnesota. I recall, with much love and appreciation, the special atmosphere of warmth and friendly hospitality that I experienced with the Bly family.

Gothenburg, March 28, 1977.
Ingegerd Friberg

INTRODUCTION

Biographical Data: Robert Bly was born in 1926 in Madison, Minnesota,
on the farm where he now lives. He has outlined his own background in an
interview:

> I went to high school here and then enlisted in the
> Navy. It was in the Navy that I met the first person I
> had ever met who wrote . . . [He] wrote the first poem
> that I had ever seen a living human being write... I was
> dazzled... astounded. . . . When I got out of the Navy
> I went to St. Olaf for a year and then transferred to
> Harvard where I graduated in 1950. . . .
>   At St. Olaf I started to write poems, and then when I
> went to Harvard I decided to be... well, to go ahead;
> to be a poet is different from writing poems. Then I lived
> by myself for about three years rather than going on
> to graduate school . . . I lived in Northern Minnesota
> for a while and then I lived alone in New York for a couple
> of years more... I got nowhere fast, but I was able to do
> a lot of reading and thinking that the poets who had stayed
> on in school were not able to do . . .[1]
>   I was married in 1955.[2] The next year I received a Ful-
> bright grant to go to Norway to translate some Norwegian
> poetry into English. In Norway I found the work of a lot
> of poets in the Oslo library... men like Pablo Neruda,
> Juan Ramon Jiménéz, Cesar Vallejo, George Trakl.
>   They were available in the Oslo library, but not in
> any American library that I had seen. It became apparent
> to me how isolationist America was in relation to Euro-
> pean and South American poets. They were well known in
> Europe, even in little countries, but totally ignored
> and unheard of in the United States. It became apparent
> that a good service could be done in the United States
> and that would be to start a magazine publishing some of
> these people in translation. I felt avenues opening into
> kinds of imagination that I sort of dimly sensed some-
> where off on the horizon, but I had never actually seen
> in words... Oh, I had seen half a line, or five lines
> dealing with this (imagery), but in the poets I've men-
> tioned you find this imagery for 20 and 50 and 80 lines
> long... Wonderful imagery, exuberance, and enthusiasm.
> If it interested me that much, it would, must, interest
> some other young poets. . . . When my wife and I came
> back from Europe in 1958 we settled in an old farmhouse.
> With William Duffy as the other editor, we put out our
> first issue.[3]

---

1   Robert Bly graduated with honors from Harvard. He was offered a teach-
    ing position, but he turned down the offer, believing that a univer-
    sity could not provide the solitude and stillness that he would need
    as a poet. He still holds this belief. He supports himself by his
    writing, his translations, and poetry readings.
2   That year Bly also took up graduate studies at the University of Iowa,
    from which he graduated with a Master's degree in 1956.
3   The Tennessee Poetry Journal (Winter, 1969), pp. 29-31.

That is how it started. Bly called his magazine <u>The Fifties</u>. It has since changed its name to <u>The Sixties</u> and now to <u>The Seventies</u>. Eleven issues have been published so far. Over the years not only poems in translation have been published in this magazine but also literary criticism and essays on poetical theories, often written by Bly himself.

<u>Presentation of Bly's Poetic Works</u>: In 1962 Robert Bly published his first book of poems, <u>Silence in the Snowy Fields</u>,[1] which was quite well received by critics and reviewers. For his second book, <u>The Light Around the Body</u>,[2] he was given the American National Book Award for Poetry in 1968. He attracted attention on this occasion by handing over the prize money to an anti-war organization called The Resistance. Some of the poems in this second book clearly showed his new engagement in social and moral issues, a fact that made the critics and the reviewers less unanimous in their appraisal of his poems. As early as 1966 Robert Bly and David Ray had organized "The American Writers against the Vietnam War" in order to "encourage writers and students to take a public stand on the war, and to encourage read-ins at all major campuses in the country," as they put it on the back cover of a volume called <u>A Poetry Reading against the Vietnam War</u>,[3] which they published that year with an introduction by Bly. It contains poems and prose pieces by American and European writers and statesmen. In 1969 and 1970 Bly published two small books of his own, <u>The Morning Glory</u>,[4] which contains descriptive prose poems, and <u>The Teeth Mother Naked at Last</u>,[5] which is one long anti-war poem. After another three years two more books of poems were published, <u>Jumping out of Bed</u> [6] and <u>Sleepers Joining Hands</u>.[7] Some of the poems in these two books are of a mystical kind conveying meditative and visionary experiences. In 1974 some prose poems that Bly had written in Cali-

---

1 Middletown, Conn., 1962. (Will henceforth be referred to in the notes as <u>Silence</u>.)
2 New York, N.Y., 1967. (Will henceforth be referred to in the notes as <u>Light</u>.)
3 New York, N.Y., 1966.
4 Santa Cruz, Calif., 1969. Revised and enlarged editions were published in 1970 by the same publisher. Another enlarged edition was published in 1975 by Harper & Row, New York, N. Y..
5 San Francisco, Calif., 1970. (Will henceforth be referred to in the notes as <u>Teeth Mother</u>.)
6 Barre, Mass., 1973. (Will henceforth be referred to in the notes as <u>Jumping</u>.)
7 New York, N.Y., 1973. (Will henceforth be referred to in the notes as <u>Sleepers</u>.)

fornia were published under the title <u>Point Reyes Poems</u>.[1] A year later
these poems were included in a new edition of <u>The Morning Glory</u>, of
which they make up section II.

In 1975 Bly's latest book, <u>Old Man Rubbing His Eyes</u>,[2] was published.
In that book various techniques and themes from earlier books seem to
come together. Some of the poems have been published before in earlier
books or in literary magazines. A line is sometimes changed or added,
which may give the poem a new dimension, but, otherwise, this book
serves more as a confirmation of the patterns that are traceable in his
earlier production than as a herald of new horizons in Bly's poetry.

Bly also wants to strengthen the influence in the U.S.A. of South
American, European, and Indian poetry. He has, therefore, translated and
published poems by Pablo Neruda and Cesar Vallejo, by Georg Trakl and
Rainer Maria Rilke, by Federico Garcia Lorca and Juan Ramon Jimémez, by
Gunnar Ekelöf, Harry Martinson, and Tomas Tranströmer, by Voznesensky,
Kabir, and others. He has also edited two books of poems by other writers.
One is called <u>Forty Poems Touching on Recent American History</u>,[3] and the
other <u>The Sea and the Honeycomb, A Book of Tiny Poems</u>.[4] From my point of
view, the most interesting parts of the books translated, or edited, by
Bly are the introductions, in which he often makes general statements on
poetry and poetical theory, more particular statements on the poets he is
dealing with, and also, even if more indirectly, statements on the kind
of poetry he himself writes.

<u>Criticism of Bly's Poetry</u>: Bly's books have attracted a good deal of
attention, judging from the great number of reviews of them. Furthermore,
four Ph.D. theses about his poetry have been submitted, but none of them
has been printed.[5] Anthony Piccione's Ph.D. thesis, called <u>Robert Bly and
the Deep Image</u>, was the first book-length treatment of his poetry, but it
was written as early as 1969 and, therefore, deals only with <u>Silence in
the Snowy Fields</u> and <u>The Light around the Body</u> and only with the American
editions of these two books. The British editions, which were published
in 1967 and 1968 and were considerably revised, are not mentioned at all.
However, the fact that this thesis deals with the so-called "deep image"

---

1 Half Moon Bay, Calif., 1974.
2 Greensboro, N.C., 1975. (Will henceforth be referred to in the notes
   as <u>Old Man</u>.)
3 Boston, Mass., 1970.
4 Boston, Mass., 1971.
5 They are available on special request in microfilmed copies from University Microfilms, Ann Arbor, Michigan.

gives us a clue to a conspicuous but elusive element in Bly's poetry.
It is elusive in the sense "that 'deep image' as a concept represents
a condition, a realm, of the current sensibility quite aloof from any
standard rational attempts to illuminate it."[1]

Anthony Piccione devotes Chapter I of his thesis to establishing
the relation of the "deep image" to earlier poetry. He says that "it is
T. S. Eliot's theory of the 'objective correlative' which connects the
'Symbolist and Imagist method of presentative statement' with the poetry
of 'deep image.'"[2] "Pound's concept of the image as 'an intellectual and
emotional complex in an instant of time'"[3] is also considered part of the
origin of "the current poetry of 'private experientially assimilated meaning."[4]   The special consciousness of Surrealism, traced back to Eliot,
is seen as "foreshadowing a poetry of the 'inner image,'"[5] and the poetry
of Wallace Stevens and that of Dylan Thomas are seen as different stages
in the development of a new kind of poetry, freed from traditional form
and aesthetics. Finally, in this historical review, Piccione points to
the incidental irony in the "new poets'" rejection of the poetry of Eliot
and Pound just as these two poets themselves had rejected the then-
existing tradition. Chapter II deals with definitions and explanations of
the "deep image" given both by Bly and other contemporary poets. Only
Chapter III, pp. 60-126, deals directly with Bly's poems. Chapter IV,
which is the last chapter, sees Robert Bly in relation to his contemporaries.

Jeffrey A. Justin's thesis, Unknown Land Poetry: Walt Whitman, Robert
Bly, and Gary Snyder, was submitted in 1973. As seen from the title only
part of it - one chapter - contains a direct discussion of Bly's poems.
In that chapter, called "Falling and Flying," Justin goes through Bly's
poetry in book after book in a chronological order. His method aims at
applying to the poems some of the theories that Bly has presented in his
prose essays, mostly ideas influenced by C. G. Jung and Erich Neumann.
There is a certain risk in doing that since many of the poems were written

---

1 A. Piccione, Robert Bly and the Deep Image, p. 24.
2 See Piccione, p. 3.
3 Ibid.
4 Ibid.
5 Ibid., p. 4.

before Bly seriously read any books by Jung[1] or Neumann. Although Jung is
mentioned by Bly as early as 1958,[2] the only books to which one can apply
Jung's and Neumann's ideas with any certainty, therefore, seem to me to
be The Teeth Mother Naked at Last, Jumping Out of Bed, and Sleepers
Joining Hands.

Julie H. Wosk's thesis, Prophecies for America: Social Criticism in
the Recent Poetry of Bly, Levertov, Corso, and Ginsberg, was submitted in
1974. Like Justin's work this thesis also deals only partly - one chapter
out of six - with Bly, and only with the poems in two of his books, The
Light around the Body and Sleepers Joining Hands. Wosk's approach is similar to that of Justin. Bly's prose articles are the starting-point, and
the interpretations of the poems are based on ideas and theories presented
in them.

Frances K. Sage's thesis, Robert Bly: His Poetry and Literary Criticism, submitted in 1974, is the second book-length work written about
Robert Bly, and, like Piccione's thesis, it deals mainly with the image.
As may be seen from the title, she uses the same approach as Justin and
Wosk, which means that she concentrates on the relationship between Bly's
theories and his poems. In Chapter I she gives a survey of the history of
the image, attempting to relate Bly's use of the image - the "deep image" -
to the everyday use of the word "image" and to the literary use of it, as
represented by different poets such as Pound, Yeats, Lorca, Robert Kelly,
and the Surrealist poets. She defines the "deep image" as "the concrete
shape arising out of the unconscious,"[3] or as "the linguistic rendering
of the product of association."[4]

Chapter II, called "Inwardness and the Deep Image," deals with
themes in Bly's poems. A general statement of themes introduces a theoretical discussion exemplified by some of Bly's poems. Some images are
stated as carriers of these themes, but the function of the images within
the poems is not examined. Chapter III deals with "Protest Poetry." As in
Chapter II Sage goes from preconceived themes to single poems, employing

---

1 In a letter of May 18, 1975, to the present writer, Bly says, "I didn't
   seriously read Jung until around 1970." In a letter of Nov. 30, 1976,
   he states, "I began reading Jung around 1961, and the last few years
   have read him steadily and enthusiastically." (This letter, also, is to
   the present writer.)
2 Robert Bly, "Five Decades of Modern American Poetry," The Fifties,
   1(1958), p. 37.
3 Sage, p. 62.
4 Ibid.

INTRODUCTION

the poems as illustrations of these themes, which are supposed to express Bly's opinions and interests. On the whole the chapter is more of a theoretical discussion than a detailed examination of poems.

Chapter IV, "The Image and Technique," analyses the structure, the diction, the syntax, and the rhythm of the poems. Sage concludes, "While there is a relationship among the image and the short poem, narrative form, language, syntax, rhythm, and the prose poem, there is none between the images and the overall structure of Bly's major books."[1] Chapter V, "The Image and Energy," deals only with Bly's prose essays and contains a theoretical discussion of ideas expressed in those.

Chapter VI states the final conclusion: Two strands have been discerned in Bly's poetry, the news of the human and the news of the universe. Sage sees these strands as incompatible. I think that if she had attempted to approach the long composite poem "Sleepers Joining Hands" as something more than an autobiographical poem, she would have comprehended Bly's exposition of the individual human being's encounter with universal forces - the whole exposition given in Jung's terminology of the individuation process.

What Justin, Wosk, and Sage have in common is that they start from Bly's theories as presented in his prose articles and as expressed in interviews. They explain these theories and then apply them to his poems. Furthermore, they take it for granted that the image - as I see it, a collective word used for descriptive, metaphoric, and symbolic elements in Bly's poetry - is always a "deep image," which means that an image is brought up from the unconscious. As far as I can see, it is not really possible to judge whether the origin of an image is subjective or objective. What we can judge is the source, or the subject matter, of the image, and its function within the poem. The subject matter can frequently be seen as related to the outside world, that is to Bly's own surroundings, what I have called "The Minnesota Heritage," and to the society he has grown up in, its history and present condition, which I deal with mostly in the chapter called "Our Earthly Existence," and to concepts, ideas, archetypes, and myths that Bly has become acquainted with through an extensive reading of psychoanalytic and mythological literature, something I have endeavored to show in the chapters called "The Voyage of the Unconscious" and "The Lady of the House."

---

1 Sage, p. 172.

As to the functioning of the images within the poems one has to go to
the poems themselves - not to Bly's theories - and try to see as objectively as possible how they function within particular poems. From
patterns thus established, possible thematic conclusions can be drawn and
parallels with his theories can be seen. With the theories of Bly and his
critics as a starting-point one gets caught in a circle that via the poem
leads back to the theory.

When my discussions and the discussions of Justin, Wosk, and Sage
touch upon the same ideas and when our views coincide, it is due not to
any influence but to the inherent closeness of our subjects. It is also
due to the fact that in some inevitable cases we use the same secondary
sources, but since our approaches go in opposite directions, our discussions are clearly independent of each other. Only very obvious interpretations are similar.[1]

Many definitions of "deep image" poetry have been offered and comments, on Bly's poetry in particular, have been given by poets and critics
in books and magazines. According to Stephen Stepanchev's definition in
his book American Poetry Since 1945[2] the deep image, or, as he calls it,
the subjective image, "refers to a concrete particular that has attracted
and operates in a context of powerful feelings and associations in the
unconscious of the poet and evokes a similar context in the unconscious
of the reader when it appears in an imaginatively conceived and ordered
poem."[3] Under the heading "The Subjective Image"[4] Stepanchev deals mainly
with Robert Bly's and James Wright's poetry. He discusses the relationship
of this new poetry to earlier poetry, and says about Robert Bly, James
Wright, William Duffy, Robert Kelly, and Jerome Rothenberg:

> They rejected the objective image of the Imagists of
> 1910 and championed the subjective image or the image
> freighted with unconscious elements, in the fashion of
> the Surrealists. Although they denied any influence from
> the Charles Olson-inspired groups. . . , they were in
> general agreement with them that traditional metrics of
> the accent-counting variety were unsatisfactory in sug-
> gesting American space, time, and experience; they con-
> curred in the opinion that new organizations of sounds,
> in free forms, were essential for the continuing vital-
> ity of American poetry. But they disliked what they

---

1 In fact, the theses of Justin, Wosk, and Sage were not made available
   to me until I had finished my manuscripts for the four main chapters
   of my thesis. I have, however, added footnotes in cases where our
   interpretations partly coincide.
2 New York, N.Y., 1965. (Edition used: Harper Colophon, New York, N. Y., 1967.)
3 Stepanchev, p. 177.
4 Ibid., pp. 175-187.

regarded as the bareness of much American verse and
complained about the diffuse, prosaic quality of most
of the work of their contemporaries. They were deter-
mined to avoid these defects in their own verse by
concentrating on the image, for they felt that a poem
lived in its imagery. And they began a campaign
against abstraction by urging other poets to read
the masters of modern French and Spanish poetry,
those who had written wildly and had looked inward
without fear or shame, poets like Rimbaud and Lorca.[1]

Stepanchev's final conclusion to this chapter, however, seems to me somewhat premature, based more on Bly's prose statements and theories than
on an analysis of the poems in the one book of his that had been published
at that time. I agree with him, though, that Bly's "poetic voice is clear,
quiet, and appealing,"[2] but it does not seem to me to be "evident that
Robert Bly's theory and practice cohere."[3]

Donald Hall in the introduction to the Penguin edition of his anthology Contemporary American Poetry[4] makes a statement about Robert Bly's
and Louis Simpson's poetry which has attracted much attention:

> One thing is happening in American poetry, as I see
> it, which is genuinely new, and so new that I lack
> words for it. In lines like Robert Bly's:
>
> In small towns the houses are built right on the
> ground;
> The lamplight falls on all fours in the grass.
>
> or Louis Simpson's:
>
> These houses built of wood sustain
> Colossal snows,
> And the light above the street is sick to death,
>
> a new kind of imagination seems to be working. The vo-
> cabulary is mostly colloquial but the special quality
> of the lines has nothing to do with an area of dic-
> tion; It is quality learned neither from T. S. Eliot
> nor William Carlos Williams. This imagination is irra-
> tional yet the poem is usually quiet and the language
> simple; there is no straining for apocalypse and no
> conscious pursuit of the unconscious. There is an in-
> wardness to these images, a profound subjectivity. Yet
> they are not subjective in the autobiographical manner
> of Life Studies or Heart's Needle, which are con-
> fessional and particular. This new imagination reveals
> through images a subjective life which is general,
> and which corresponds to an old objective life of

---

1 Stepanchev, pp. 175-176.
2 Ibid., p. 187.
3 Ibid.
4 Edited by Donald Hall (Penguin Books, 1962).

shared experiences and knowledge.[1]
. . . What I am trying to describe is not a school
or a clique but a way of feeling and I believe they
have grown by themselves from the complex earth of
American writing and American experience.[2]

Cleanth Brooks questions the newness of this imagination in his
article "Poetry Since 'The Waste Land.'"[3] He sees it as the same kind of
imagination that we find in poems by the Romantic poets, especially
Wordsworth:

For it was the split between the subjective and the
objective - the chasm between the life of the emotions
and attitudes within the poet and the universe outside
him - that so much troubled the Romantic poets. The
poetry of Wordsworth and the criticism of Coleridge
are dominated by the attempt to bridge this chasm. It
would be tidings indeed to learn that the American
poets of the 1950's had finally spanned it.
Such tidings might signal an end to the waste-land
experience, for if men could find in their own subjective life something that corresponds to what Mr. Hall
calls the 'old subjective life of shared experience'
then they would have reestablished a rapport with
nature and restored the community of values, the loss
of which wasted the land. The quickening rain for
which the protagonist in "The Waste Land" yearned
would at last have begun to fall. The prospect is
exciting, but I remain skeptical.[4]

In 1967 Ronald Moran and George Lensing published an answer to
Cleanth Brooks's article. The title "The Emotive Imagination: A New departure in American Poetry"[5] indicates their stand. They see Cleanth Brooks's
skepticism as a sign of the inadequateness of the New Criticism, a sign
of "the real need for critical readjustment to the unique qualities of
the emotive imagination at work,"[6] and they mention the "emotive imagination" as "a new and original poetic technique,"[7] which demands as much of

---

1 This "old objective life" refers to the Jungian term "the collective
   unconscious" - "a realm of the psyche that is common to all mankind"
   [Frieda Fordham, An Introduction to Jung's Psychology (Penguin Books,
   1953), p. 23].
2 Contemporary American Poetry, pp. 24-25.
3 The Southern Review, I, 3 (1965), pp. 487-500. Later included in Cleanth
   Brooks, A Shaping Joy; Studies in the Writer's Craft (London, 1971),
   pp. 52-65.
4 Cleanth Brooks, p. 500.
5 The Southern Review, III, 1 (1967), pp. 51-67.
6 Moran and Lensing, p. 52.
7 Ibid., p. 64.

the reader as of the poet. It implies "understanding through feeling
rather than through chartered and structured intellectuality."[1] I find it
difficult, however, to see this technique as new and original, especially
when later in the article Moran and Lensing see this kind of poetic technique as "rooted in the hard realities of the present."[2] The similarity
to Romantic poetry presents itself, although that is exactly what the two
writers of the article deny. It seems to me that Hall's statement and
Moran's and Lensing's article have in common with Stepanchev's appraisal,
mentioned above, an over-estimation of Bly's theories about the kind of
images he wanted American poets to employ, theories that Bly had expressed
in The Fifties. They make great efforts to apply these theories to Bly's
poems as well as to poems written by poets who worked or had worked in
close relationship with Bly, without realizing, or wanting to admit, that
several of the poems in, for example, Silence in the Snowy Fields were
written spontaneously as expressions of the poet experiencing his surroundings and not as pieces to fit neatly into a system of ideas. Louis
Simpson saw the difference between poetry and theory, although he seems
to me to pass his judgement indiscriminately: "So, at the same time that
Bly's new magazine The Fifties spoke of neglected 'avantgarde' traditions
in Europe, South America and China, it was furiously American, printing
poems that spoke of American earth, farm landscapes and highways. It was
a curious, and at times awkward, combination of eclectic theorizing and
local colour."[3]

In 1970 G. A. M. Janssens, Nijmegen, brings up the same issue in his
article "The Present State of American Poetry: Robert Bly and James
Wright."[4] After a close discussion of several poems by Bly and Wright, he
concludes with a comment on the essays by Brooks and by Moran and Lensing:

> My purpose has been to illustrate the limitations of
> the approach of both essayists. Cleanth Brooks com-
> pared the technique of composition of the new poets
> to Wordsworth's technique in the Lucy poems and found
> that it was essentially the same. His point was well-
> taken – it could as easily have been illustrated by
> a comparison with some other poets, e.g. Blake – but
> it seemed automatically to absolve him from a serious

---

1 Moran and Lensing, p. 53.
2 Ibid., p. 67.
3 Louis Simpson, North of Jamaica (New York, N. Y., 1972), p. 209.
4 English Studies, 51 (1970), pp. 112-137.

consideration of the possible merits of the individual poets. Ronald Moran and George Lensing on the
other hand, tried so eagerly to promote the newness
of the 'emotive imagination' that they made wholly
insupportable claims. Their effort of vindication
was laudable, but they clearly bit off more than
they could chew. [1]

Finally Janssens takes his own stand, declaring that Robert Bly's and
James Wright's "poetry has shown new possibilities of expressing how it
feels to be alive in the United States today. Their achievement has been
my subject."[2] What is most valuable in Janssens's article is that he
focuses more on the actual poetry than on the poetical theory.

In an effort to clarify his statement Donald Hall revised the "Introduction" to the second and enlarged edition of his Contemporary American
Poetry. He expresses himself more clearly and more carefully. Instead of
saying that he lacks words to express this newness, he defines it and
applies it to American poetry only. He sees in it "a quality that is closer to the spirit of Georg Trakl or Pablo Neruda" than to T. S. Eliot or
William Carlos Williams "but it is not to be pigeon-holed according to
any sources."[3] The inwardness is what he still emphasizes most strongly:

> There is an inwardness to these images, a profound
> subjectivity. . . .
>   The movement which seems to me new is subjective
> but not autobiographical. It reveals through images
> not particular pain, but general subjective life.
> This universal subjective corresponds to the old
> objective life of shared experience and knowledge.
> People can talk to each other most deeply in images.
> To read a poem of this sort, you must not try to
> translate the images into abstractions. They won't
> go. You must try to be open to them, to let them
> take you over and speak in their own language of
> feeling. It is the intricate darkness of feeling
> and instinct which these poems mostly communicate.
> The poems are best described as expressionist:
> like the painter, the poet uses fantasy and dis-
> tortion to express feeling.[4]

Donald Hall does not openly turn against the "New Criticism," nor does he
really join forces with Moran and Lensing in their conscious effort to
prove the existence of a "new departure" in American poetry. In his advice

---

1 Janssens, pp. 136-137.
2 Ibid., p. 137.
3 Contemporary American Poetry (ed. Donald Hall), 2nd rev. ed. (Penguin
   Books, 1972), p. 32.
4 Ibid., pp. 32-33.

INTRODUCTION

to the reader on how to approach these poems he is closer to
G. A. M. Janssens than to the other essayists mentioned above.

In his article "Inward to the World: The Poetry of Robert Bly"[1]
William Heyen advocates the same point of view, that it is best to concentrate on the poems themselves. First he admits that for several years
he disliked what Bly had done in Silence in the Snowy Fields: "How, in
the age of Eliot, could he write poems that defied serious inquiry and
involved explication?"[2] Not until he realized that "Bly is free from the
inhibitions of critical dictates many of us have regarded as truths,"[3]
did he find a rewarding way of approaching Bly's poetry. He had to realize that Bly "manages in fact to write poems that are themselves sus-
pensions of the critical faculty,"[4] and that "the poems had to become
what they are."[5]

Paul Lacey in his book The Inner War[6] deals with the relationship
of form and content in the poetry of five contemporary American poets:
Anne Sexton, William Everson, James Wright, Robert Bly, and Denise
Levertov. In the introductory chapter he stresses, among other aspects,
newness and inwardness in modern American poetry:

> As they come into their full power, the poets of
> the 1960s and 70s make us know that we are in a new
> time, with new themes and metaphors, new aesthetics,
> new attempts to speak of the world we know.
> . . .
> The poetry considered here reflects three emphases
> found widely in American poetry in the 1960s: a pre-
> occupation with the inner world of the psyche and its
> relation to the world of everyday existence; a re-
> valuation of the imagination as the faculty of dis-
> covery and creation; and a blurring of lines which
> have separated the poem from such other kinds of
> writing as notebook, diary, documentary, history, or
> confession.[7]

Lacey seems to be in main concurrence with G. A. M. Janssens and William
Heyen when he renounces Eliot and Joyce but recommends a study of the
Romantics as a way to an understanding of the new poets.

In his chapter on Bly - "The Live World"[8] - Lacey first discusses
Bly's poetical theories as they are presented in The Sixties, 8. There

---

1 The Far Point, 3, pp. 42-50.
2 Heyen, p. 43.
3 Ibid.
4 Ibid.
5 Ibid.
6 Philadelphia, Penn., 1972.
7 Lacey, pp. 2-3.
8 Ibid., pp. 32-56.

Bly stresses the importance of knowing well both the outer and the inner
world, "The Dead World and the Live World."[1] Lacey then explores how Bly
in his poetry,[2] within the force field of the image, relates the outer and
the inner world to each other. This seems to be an approach employed by
several of Bly's critics.

   In a recent book, Out of the Vietnam Vortex,[3] James F. Mersmann
examines war poems by four American poets: Allen Ginsberg, Denise Levertov, Robert Bly, and Robert Duncan. In his chapter on Bly, "Robert Bly:
Watering the Rocks,"[4] Mersmann states that "Bly's interest has always
been with content rather than form, and life rather than 'art.'"[5] The
main part of the chapter deals with pairs of images signifying inwardness and outwardness, the unconscious and the conscious mind, feminine
and masculine forces. These aspects, as dealt with by Mersmann, have
proved essential in any appraisal of the main body of Bly's poetry.

   In this summary of criticism on Bly's poetry I have pointed to a
serious attempt in Piccione's thesis to see the origin of Bly's poetry
in Eliot's and Pound's revolt around 1920, as well as to a complete sever-
ing of all bonds between this so called "new poetry" and the poetry of
earlier schools and traditions as stated by, for example, Donald Hall,
Ronald Moran, and George Lensing, and to the middle stand of more cau-
tious critics. Most of Bly's critics and reviewers agree on the importance of imagery in his poetry. Therefore, I have referred also to
Sage's attempt to relate Bly's use of the image to that of, for example,
Pound, Yeats, and Lorca in her survey of the use of imagery. The critics' and reviewers' preoccupation with Bly's poetical theories is also
striking. One has to be skeptical, however, as to the value of some of
these appraisals, especially when newness is discussed. Since the critics in applying Bly's theories - even if redefined by them - are pre-
occupied by particular ideas of poetry, they often make claims which
cannot be justified, for instance, their reading of inwardness into
early descriptive poems or Hall's claim to have found a new imagination
in the line: "The lamplight falls on all fours in the grass." To me this

---

1 The title of an essay by Bly in The Sixties, 8 (Spring, 1966), pp. 2-7.
2 Included in Lacey's discussion are Silence, Light, The Morning Glory,
   and Teeth Mother.
3 Lawrence, Kansas, 1974.
4 Mersmann, pp. 113-157.
5 Ibid., p. 116.

INTRODUCTION

line - both in form and content - forms a parallel to the line: "The fog comes on little cat feet" in Carl Sandburg's Imagist poem "Fog."[1]

As I see it, Bly as a poet is strongly and originally individual, but at the same time, to a certain degree, influenced not only by the Romantics and by the American tradition but also by the Surrealists and other modern movements. My main impression is that his poetry originates in his material surroundings but develops into an expression of an inner experience which he conveys in a subjective choice of imagery, which in his more recent poems I see as freighted with unconscious elements.

Aims of the Present Work: My approach will be through the imagery, which in Bly's poetry I give a wide sense of meaning, letting it include descriptive elements, metaphors, symbols, archetypes, and myths. I intend to sort out what I see as conspicuous and representative elements and concepts that recur in Bly's poems, and I hope to outline patterns of subject matter and technique by showing how the same element, or concept, can be used on different levels in different kinds of poems - poems ranging from personal to public ones, from simple descriptive to visionary ones, from poems where the direction of the meaning of the verbal structure is mainly outward to poems where the direction of meaning is wholly inward. As I see it, this is all done through the use of imagery on different levels of objectivity and subjectivity, or different levels of consciousness. In spite of multiple attempts at definitions and explications of the "subjective" or "deep" image and of the "new imagination" poetry given by the poets themselves and by their critics, to which I have made selective references above, I have found that the inherent elusiveness of the material I am working with obliges me to state also that my aim is to outline patterns as I experience them in Bly's poetry, and not mainly to prove the existence of a generally valid interpretation. I doubt that an attempt at an objectively valid interpretation of contemporary poetry with origins as subjective as Bly's would yet be meaningful. Furthermore, in the course of my discussions and analyses of imagery I hope to outline thematic patterns and to arrive also at conclusions concerning Bly's connections with the American poetical tradition and with European schools of poetry, such as the Romantics, the Symbolists, the Imagists, and the Surrealists.

---

1 Carl Sandburg, Complete Poems (New York, N.Y., 1950), p. 33.
2 Cf. Northrop Frye, Anatomy of Criticism (Princeton, N. J., 1957), p. 74.

As seen from the above statement of aims, I have chosen neither to start from what seems to be the general meaning of Bly's poetry, nor from his poetical theories, but to follow certain conspicuous entities in his poems, and in doing so map out patterns. In the course of my discussions I will, however, refer to his prose articles when parallels can be seen and when references, therefore, can be justified as complements to my interpretations.

I. THE MINNESOTA HERITAGE

In my study of recurring words and concepts in Bly's poems I intend
to select poems included in his books as well as poems published only in
literary magazines or not published at all. In this chapter I shall deal
mainly with what I see as descriptive poems. Bly very seldom, however,
offers absolutely pure descriptions. His careful choice of words in
picturing the outer world may to some readers suggest inner experiences
or reveal symbolic meanings.

My starting-point is Silence in the Snowy Fields. The introductory
poem, "Three Kinds of Pleasures"[1] illustrates to some extent Bly's technique. We find in it the metaphor of movement which serves as a framework for many minor and major entities of his poetry. The "I" used here,
as well as in many other poems, seems really to refer to the poet, to
Bly himself. In his prose writings he mentions with contempt the poet who
hides behind a persona: "It is imagined that when the poet says 'I' in a
poem he does not mean himself, but rather some other person . . . The poem
is conceived as a clock which one sets going."[2] He speaks with admiration
of a poet whose presence "as a living figure" is noticable in his poems:
"I mean here much more than the mere grammatical first person: I mean the
pervading presence of the poet who simultaneously shares in the processes
of life and reveals some of its meaning through his actions."[3] He restates
the importance of the poet's own true experience: "The Japanese say, Go to
the pine if you want to learn about the pine. If an American poet wants to
write of a chill and foggy field, he has to stay out there, and get cold
and wet himself."[4]

In "Three Kinds of Pleasures" the poet describes what he sees while
driving toward Chicago, probably from Minnesota, through the states of
Wisconsin and Illinois. Place names are mentioned in this poem, as well
as in several others, a kind of American regionalism which Bly has in
common with Robert Frost and Carl Sandburg. The landscape presented is an

---

1 Silence, p. 11.
2 Robert Bly, "A Wrong Turning in American Poetry," Choice: A Magazine of
   Poetry and Photography, 3 (1963), p. 37.
3 Crunk (except in one case, Crunk is the pseudonym for Robert Bly, accor
   ding to Bly himself), "The Work of Gary Snyder," The Sixties, 6 (1962),
   p. 27.
4 Robert Bly, "The First Ten Issues of Kayak," Kayak, 12 (1967), p. 49.

ordinary one, outlined by "those dark telephone poles," "the gray sky,"
and "the snowy fields." The trees in the winter fields are black, the
weeds are stiff, and the stubble in the picked cornfields is brownish.
The landscape appears dark and barren; the snow is white only in the
wheeltracks of the combine. But although it is a barren landscape, it
contains movement and suggestions of life. Human qualities are given to
the trees and the snow. The telephone poles "lift themselves" and "leap
on the gray sky," "the darkness drifts down," there is a light to be
seen in the barns, and "the bare trees" are "more dignified than ever,/
Like a fierce man on his deathbed." Finally, the expression "a private
snow" suggests that individuality can be given also to an inanimate thing.

Thus, Bly, in the making of the poem, moves through its landscape,
starting in the open spaces enclosed by the sky and the fields of the
first stanza, narrowing it down in the second stanza to the fields and
the wheeltracks in order to introduce a personified landscape in the last
stanza. The movement of the poet becomes the backbone of the poem to
which the descriptive elements – snow, fields, trees, barns – are attached.
These elements are found in some of Bly's poems as governing images, as
carriers of themes and symbolic meanings. Thus, this first poem of Bly's
first book of poems provides a certain frame of reference. Four of its
items – movement, the snow, the field, and the barn – will be considered
in this chapter.[1]

Movement: A Basic Pattern

In "Driving toward the Lac Qui Parle River"[2] the idea of movement is
suggested even in the title. The poem is very similar to "Three Kinds of
Pleasures." The poet is traveling by car at dusk – in Minnesota this time
– and he describes his sense perceptions and feelings. Description and
mood merge:[3]

> .I
> I am driving; it is dusk; Minnesota.
> The stubble field catches the last growth of sun.
> The soybeans are breathing on all sides.
> Old men are sitting before their houses on carseats
> In the small towns. I am happy,
> The moon rising above turkey sheds.

---

1 A numerical count of nouns in Bly's poems has shown these nouns to be
   among the predominant ones.
2 Silence, p. 20.
3 Cf. Janssens, p. 121.

It is an hour of stillness but also of life and change in which nature
takes part. This is conveyed through the verbs: "breathing," "catches,"
"rising." In the second stanza the movement of traveling and the sound of
crickets break the stillness:

                                    II
            The small world of the car
            Plunges through the deep fields of the night,
            On the road from Willmar to Milan.
            This solitude covered with iron
            Moves through the fields of night
            Penetrated by the noise of crickets.

The verbs "plunges," "moves," and "penetrated" effect the change, while
the poet is confined to "the small world of the car" surrounded by darkness. In the third stanza, however, the stillness returns and the perspective opens up again:

                                   III
            Nearly to Milan, suddenly a small bridge,
            And water kneeling in the moonlight.
            In small towns the houses are built right on the ground;
            The lamplight falls on all fours in the grass.
            When I reach the river, the full moon covers it;
            A few people are talking low in a boat.

Now the stillness of small town Minnesota, described in the first stanza,
is deeper and reveals a life in which water and light are endowed with
human qualities. Lines 2, 3, and 4 suggest a closeness between humans and
their surroundings, between animate and inanimate,[1] that points to a surrealistic view of life, or as Anna Balakian says, "a more total comprehen-
sion of the unity of the universe."[2] Lacey sees two worlds described in the
poem: "the larger world of living,"[3] where "animate and inanimate objects
change places or lend their natures to one another,"[4] and the closed independent world of the car"[5] which is "a place of retreat to solitude."[6] "The
car plunging into the deep fields of night becomes the inner world of man
penetrating into the deepness of nature, and nature in turn plunges into
the 'solitude covered with iron,' for the car is 'penetrated by the noise

---

1 Cf Paul A. Lacey, The Inner War, p. 39.
2 Anna Balakian, Surrealism: The Road to the Absolute (Dutton Paperback,
   rev. ed., 1970), p. 23.
3 Lacey, p. 40.
4 Ibid., p. 39.
5 Ibid., p. 40.
6 Ibid.

of crickets.'"[1] This interchange of movement and sound results in the last
stanza in a oneness of inner and outer harmony. In the poet's mind "the
world of nature and the world of men, of human conversation and natural
beauty, are one."[2]

"Driving through Ohio"[3] shows a formal resemblance to "Three Kinds
of Pleasures" and "Driving toward the Lac Qui Parle River" in that each
is divided into three numbered parts or stanzas, and that place names are
important. At a closer reading, however, one sees that only the outer
framework is the same. Movement is not very important; instead the adjec-
tive "white" dominates the description. In the first stanza the white
tourist home impresses me as clean but impersonal. The room is stereo-
typical "with National Geographics on the table." In the second stanza
the whiteness of the barns and of the painted trunks of the cottonwood
foreshadows the atmosphere of death associated with the phrase "the
widow's coast." From vantage points on top of houses widows might be supposed to look for their sailor husbands who will not return from "the
dangerous Atlantic." Thus, we are prepared for the description of "the
white cemeteries" adding to "the sense of death" in the last stanza:

> Now we drive north past the white cemeteries
> So rich in the morning air!
> All morning I have felt the sense of death;
> I am full of love, and love this torpid land.
> Some day I will go back, and inhabit again
> The sleepy ground where Harding was born.

The repetition of the words "slept" and "sleepy" in the poem is con-
sistent with the atmosphere created by the word "white." The sleepiness
refers to humans as well as to the country, and in the second stanza it is
paralleled in the torpid joy. Even the river is slow and muddy, and the
cottonwood with its unnatural color has connotations of deadwood. In the
third stanza the country actually turns into the land of the dead, both
literally and figuratively; in the poet's mind the cemeteries represent
"the torpid land" - "the sleepy ground" - of historic America, to which
he wants to return.

The basic pattern of movement through the landscape is mentioned
only in the title of the poem and in the last stanza and it is of no real

---

1 Lacey, p. 40.
2 Ibid., p. 41.
3 Silence, p. 33.

importance in the description of the land. However, there seems to be
movement on another level: the poet moves from descriptive to metaphoric poetry.

In the short poem "Driving to Town Late to Mail a Letter"[1] movement,
simultaneous with the perception of a landscape, again results in a statement of feelings. The poet is alone, and he renders his experience of the
town at night:

> It is a cold and snowy night. The main street is
>   deserted.
> The only things moving are swirls of snow.
> As I lift the mailbox door, I feel its cold iron.
> There is a privacy I love in this snowy night.
> Driving around, I will waste more time.

In this poem, too, actual movement is mentioned but is literally unimport-
ant . There is, however, a movement between contrasts that strikes the
reader. The mention of the coldness of the snowy night in general and of
the iron of the mailbox in particular makes the expression of love and
contentment unexpected. The reality of the snow and the cold is employed
by the poet to serve as a contrasting setting for what he feels to be
the inherent significance of the situation: a privacy and solitude that
harmonizes with his state of mind. This poem seems to end in much the
same way as "Three Kinds of Pleasures"[2] and "Driving toward the Lac Qui
Parle River."[3] In all three Bly moves within his Midwestern landscape,
presenting it to us in visual and tactile images, but at the end of each
poem he has brought us to a point at which the landscape suggests something beyond its objective existence: the outer scene and the inner world
of the poet meet. Piccione refers to this poem as an example of the attention Bly pays to "the 'minimal' regions."[4] "It is what it is. It is set
in a private experience to which the poet brings his special feeling of
'privacy.' . . . It is a happy moment intensely focussed upon itself, in
terms of the poet's personal joy with the 'minimal.' If we have expected
more ambitious things of a poem, if we feel it is a waste of otherwise
valuable time, we have missed the point."[5]

In "On the Ferry across Chesapeake Bay"[6] the movement is obviously

---

1 Silence, p. 38.
2 See above, pp. 16-17.
3 See above, pp. 17-19.
4 Piccione, p. 116.
5 Ibid., pp. 116-117.
6 Silence, p. 35. See also below, p. 48, and p. 82.

both on a natural and on a symbolic level, more so than in the poems discussed so far. On the natural level we have the poet as a passenger on
the ferry, describing the sea in visual imagery. The "orchard of the sea,"
the "whitecaps," the "deep green sea," and "the strange blossoms of the
sea" make an impressionistic impact akin to that emanating from Renoir's
painting "The Wave." But the waves are also powerful symbols of man's
journey toward death; they are "silent speakers" from the grave. As the
sea falls back into itself, so the body must travel toward nothingness,
not because it wants to enjoy the beauty and forcefulness of the scenery
but because it must march on. Very similar to this poem, but at the same
time very different, are the last two stanzas of "Images Suggested by
Medieval Music."[1] The sea voyage in this poem is not a basic pattern, it
is definitely a symbol. It is a voyage of the music lover, a joyful
voyage, as opposed to the meaningless ploughing toward death in "On the
Ferry across Cheasapeake Bay."

> As I listen, I am a ship, skirting
> A thousand harbors, . . .

Bly may have had Walt Whitman's "Passage to India" in mind when expressing his "joy of trackless seas." Thus, for the poets and all lovers of
the arts

> The voyage goes on. The joy of sailing and the open
> sea!

I will mention, without a detailed discussion, two more poems based
on the concept of movement. The early unpublished poem "A Missouri
Traveller Writes Home: 1830"[2] is a long narrative about a group of white
men traveling by boat on the Missouri through Indian country, in which
the Indians are seen "always walking Western banks,/ Faced toward full
sun," while the white men in the end "start to westward through the heavy
grass." It is a traditional poem with conventional symbolism. The traveler encounters death – a wounded, dying bear – and in the end he himself goes westward – toward death.

I see "The Traveller"[3] as an absolute contrast. The persona of this
poem moves in a surrealistic dream world:

1 Silence, p. 44.
2 Robert Bly, Steps toward Poverty and Death, unpublished MA thesis (the
  Univ. of Iowa, 1956), pp. 19-21. Sage refers to a printed version of
  this poem with the title "A Missouri Traveller Writes Home: 1846"
  (p. 105 of her thesis).
3 Audience, 8:3 (Winter, 1962), p. 70.

> The traveller goes through the world
> Riding on the bark of a tree.
> He walks in the city streets, meditating
> Like the fleece of a sheep,
> Or rides for hours on busses,
> With a tree growing from the sole of his foot.
> Alone at last he floats in his room,
> His face surrounded with leaves;
> And he carries inside
> Six tiny grains of mustardseed
> And the seeds of wild strawberries;
> and beneath his shirt the loaf of bread
> Baked on the stormy day
> When the Roman Empire ended at last.

The laws of Nature are violated in this world. The boundaries of time are broken down. The traveler is age-old, and he carries life inside him. This poem, so different from the other poems written at the same time, shows the poet of the new imagination at work. The persona exists in different realities, experiencing everything at all times, his energy transgressing laws and boundaries. The poem seems to contain examples of associative leaping, something for which Bly praises Spanish poets such as Antonio Machado and Juan Ramon Jiménez ten years later in an essay called "Spanish Leaping."[1] Even before the poem starts, the poet himself has taken a leap, or, as Bly puts it in another essay: "The poet's ecstatic energies have conquered the weight of the world before the poem begins."[2] He develops the same idea in a third essay, "Looking for Dragon Smoke," in which he gives an historic review of associative leaping beginning: "In ancient times,'in the time of inspiration,' the poet flew from one world to another, 'riding on dragons,! as the Chinese said."[3] Thus, movement becomes the flight of the poet's imagination also.

The concept of movement frequently occurs in Bly's poetry. Through the examples mentioned, I want to point to its existence as a framework and basic pattern in Bly's early poems, where it plays a narrative, a descriptive, as well as a symbolic and surrealistic role. Bly continues to employ this basic pattern in poems of various kinds. Therefore, it will recur in my discussions all through this thesis.

---

1 Robert Bly, "Spanish Leaping," The Seventies, 1 (1972), pp. 16-21.
2 Robert Bly, "American Poetry: On the Way to the Hermetic," Books Abroad, Vol. 46, No. 1 (Winter, 1972), p. 22.
3 Robert Bly, "Looking for Dragon Smoke," The Seventies, 1 (1972), p. 3.

The Snow: Descriptive Element and Metaphor

In his review of Silence in the Snowy Fields, Charles Simmons mentions some of the frequently recurring elements in Bly's poems: "There are almost no people in Mr. Bly's world. It is as if the earth had been depopulated by a deadly cloud, which left only him, an animal or two, and the dessicated remains of once growing vegetation. Things are beyond rotting here; all is glistening snow, abandoned farms and houses, harbors at dawn, pure skies, barren fields of fallen grasses seen at night."[1] The snow is noticed by several reviewers. Kevin Crossley-Holland says, for instance, "Robert Bly, who hails from the Middle West, is also primarily concerned with the natural world: with snow and the silence it breeds, with the lakes of Minnesota, with pheasants, split-tail swallows and loons."[2]

In 24 out of the 77 poems in the American editions of Bly's first two books we find the word "snow," It is an important element in his descriptive poems, not as a framework like the concept of movement, but more as a carrier of added meanings. Bly suggests this in an early poem, "The Man Who Waits for Divine Love,"[3] in which he says,

> . . .
> "But snow is more than shelter," you once said.
> "It is a world with its own private way
> Of looking at all things." . . .

Snow is a positive force. Love and snow are compared in this early poem:

> . . .
> Our love grew with winter, came like snow.
> . . .

It also protects life:

> . . .
> I gaze upon that church where even now
> The winter altars lie with asphodels,
> And where beneath these swelling drifts of snow
> The tendrils slowly move within the straw,
> Thinking, though we do nothing, the winter dies;
> This is a miracle. . . .

---

1 Charles Simmons, "Poets in Search of a Public," The Saturday Review (March 30, 1963), p. 48.
2 Kevin Crossley-Holland, "On the Natural World," Books & Bookmen, Vol. 12 (May, 1967), p. 24.
3 MA thesis, p. 3.

"Snow is strange in Bly," says John Logan in his review of <u>Silence</u> <u>in the Snowy Fields</u>. "In his work snow is associated primarily neither with death nor with purity as it is so often in poetry. Rather it is associated with positive change, with achievement."[1] The positive change brought about by the shelter-giving snow is the climax in "Approaching Winter."[2] The poem describes an autumn. Each stanza contains one or two lines of factual description followed by one or two lines of metaphoric language. Most conspicuous in stanzas I, II, and III are the personifying verbs animating the harvested corn and, still more, the ears that were not noticed and, therefore, left behind:

I
September. Clouds. The first day for wearing jackets.
The corn is wandering in dark corridors,
Near the well and the whisper of tombs.

II
I sit alone surrounded by dry corn,
Near the second growth of the pigweeds,
And hear the corn leaves scrape their feet on the wind.

III
Fallen ears are lying on the dusty earth.
The useful ears will lie dry in cribs, but the others,
            missed
By the picker, will lie here touching the ground
            the whole winter.

IV
Snow will come, and cover the husks of the fallen ears
With flakes infinitely delicate, like jewels of a
            murdered Gothic prince
Which were lost centuries ago during a great battle.

The harvested corn is dry and dead, but the unpicked corn is in touch with earth, with life, and snow will come and cover up the scene of decay and death. The comparison between snowflakes and jewels, lost centuries ago, places the dying corn in a timeless perspective. The associative leap in this poem is between the snowflakes of the present and the jewels of centuries ago.

The snow has a similar role in "Romans Angry about the Inner World."[3] The captive woman, who knows about the life of inwardness, is tortured to death by the Roman executioners, who represent the life of outwardness. The efficient outer world - like the useful dry corn - seems to be on the

---

1 John Logan, "Poetry Shelf," <u>The Critic</u>, Vol. XXI (Dec., 1962 - Jan., 1963), p. 85.
2 <u>Silence</u>, p. 19. (In the British edition the title is "Sitting in a Cornfield.")
3 <u>Light</u>, p. 9. See also below, p. 180, for further interpretation.

winning side. But then the snow comes, covers and transforms what has
been discarded, considered dead, and rolled onto the ground:

> What shall the world do with its children?
> There are lives the executives
> Know nothing of,
> A leaping of the body,
> The body rolling - and I have felt it -
> And we float
> Joyfully on the dark places;
> But the executioners
> Move toward Drusia. They tie her legs
> On the iron horse, "Here is a woman
> Who has seen our mother
> In the other world!" Next they warm
> The hooks. The two Romans had put their trust
> In the outer world. Irons glowed
> Like teeth. They wanted her
> To assure them. She refused. Finally they took burning
> Pine sticks, and pushed them
> Into her sides. Her breath rose
> And she died. The executioners
> Rolled her off onto the ground.
> A light snow began to fall
> And covered the mangled body,
> And the executives, astonished, withdrew.
> The other world is like a thorn
> In the ear of a tiny beast!
> The fingers of the executives are too thick
> To pull it out!
> It is like a jagged stone
> Flying toward them out of the darkness.

The snowfall is the turning-point. After the snow has done its work, the
scene changes. The executives, mentioned in the second line as ignorant
of a joyful inner life, have replaced the Roman executioners; they have
become aware of their involvement in a complex situation. Anthony Libby
sees the presence of the executives as an implicit comparison between
imperial Rome and "neo-imperialist" America.[1] The fear of the inner world
is the same in today's male-oriented American society as it was in the
Roman empire.

In "Hatred of Men with Black Hair"[2] the theme is similar. Everything that threatens the established order of a rational society is a
target for hatred and hostility. The symbol of the threat in this case
is "men with black hair," i.e. the Indians and the Vietnamese.[3] Employing

---

1 Cf. Anthony Libby, "Robert Bly Alive in Darkness," The Iowa Review,
   3/3 (Summer, 1972), p. 85.
2 Light, p. 36.
3 Cf. Mersmann, pp. 123-124.

"a type of allegorical surrealism,"[1] Bly describes the various manifestations of this hatred, and in the last stanza he introduces the snow as a
preserver of what is kept in the dark:

> I hear voices praising Tshombe, and the Portuguese
> In Angola, these are the men who skinned Little Crow!
> We are all their sons, skulking
> In back rooms, selling nails with trembling hands!
>
> We distrust every person on earth with black hair;
> We send teams to overthrow Chief Joseph's government;
> We train natives to kill Presidents with blowdarts;
> We have men loosening the nails on Noah's ark.
>
> The State Department floats in the heavy jellies near
>   the bottom
> Like exhausted crustaceans, like squids who
>   are confused,
> Sending out beams of black light to the open sea,
> Fighting their fraternal feeling for the great
>   landlords.
>
> We have violet rays that light up the jungles at night,
>   showing
> The friendly populations; we are teaching the children
>   of ritual
> To overcome their longing for life, and we send
> Sparks of black light that fit the holes in the
>   general's eyes.
>
> Underneath all the cement of the Pentagon
> There is a drop of Indian blood preserved in snow:
> Preserved from a trail of blood that once led away
> From the stockade, over the snow, the trail now lost.

In the deep unconscious of the American psyche this hatred is lodged, and
it is there as a silent excuse for carrying on wars.[2] Lacey reads the
last stanza as a summary of American history: "the Pentagon, a symbol for
irrational, evil power to people who share Bly's political views, stands
like an altar over the sacralizing drop of blood, the saint's relic from
which it takes its strength. The religion is the worship of power - of
business, righteousness, and stones."[3]

The snow, as it covers, also reveals a primeval darkness. Silence in
the Snowy Fields ends in the darkness of a snowstorm. The poem "Snowfall
in the Afternoon"[4] conveys the winter darkness of a late afternoon which
turns into a mystical darkness, in which the barn with its valuable load

1 Piccione, p. 96.
2 Cf. below, Chapter IV, the interpretation of "Teeth Mother."
3 Paul A. Lacey, The Inner War, p. 46. Cf. the poem "The Busy Man Speaks,"
   in Light, p. 4.
4 Silence, p. 60.

of corn moves, and finally becomes a symbolic general darkness:

I

The grass is half-covered with snow.
It was the sort of snowfall that starts in late
                afternoon,
And now the little houses of the grass are
                growing dark.

II

If I reached my hands down, near the earth,
I could take handfuls of darkness!
A darkness was always there, which we never noticed.

III

As the snow grows heavier, the cornstalks fade farther
                away,
And the barn moves nearer to the house.
The barn moves all alone in the growing storm.

IV

The barn is full of corn, and moving toward us now,
Like a hulk blown toward us in a storm at sea;
All the sailors on the deck have been blind for many
                years.

The darkness of the snow possibly carries several different meanings. It
might stand for the blindness of the human mind, for the darkness of the
human situation, or for death, the end of all life toward which man's
movement tends.[1] The idea that the darkness of the snow suggests death
is derived partly from the fact that for the British edition of Silence
in the Snowy Fields Bly changed the order of the poems, so that the book
starts with morning and newly awakened life and ends with afternoon and
the darkness of winter. D. J. Hughes sees "Snowfall in the Afternoon"
as perhaps the most successful illustration of Bly's way of developing
a poem: "Bly's characteristic development is to begin a poem with a
simple narrative or descriptive donnée and then proceed, through modula-
tions more or less subtle to an overwhelmed, even apocalyptic end. . . .
The poem moves forward, weighty and gathering, and the last line wounds."[2]
Silence in the Snowy Fields, considered as a whole, seems to conform to
a similar pattern, at least as the order of the poems stands in the final
edition.

    Snow is convincingly associated with death in "The Executive's
Death,"[3] the introductory poem in The Light around the Body. The snow in

---

1   See below, p. 43, for an additional commentary.
2   D. J. Hughes, "The Demands of Poetry," The Nation (Jan. 5, 1963), p. 17.
3   Light, p. 3.

this case serves as a link in a chain of images of coldness and height
designating a loneliness that is felt both in life and death:

> . . . high in the air, executives
> Walk on cool floors, and suddenly fall:
> Dying, they dream they are lost in a snowstorm in
> mountains,
> On which they crashed, carried at night by great
> machines.
> As he lies on the wintry slope, cut off and dying,
> A pine stump talks to him of Goethe and Jesus.
> . . .

In an earlier version of this poem, called "Merchants Have Multiplied,"[1]
the same thing is said in only one line:

> In the high air, executives walk in the snow
> that leads to death.

The snow leading to death is in the life of the modern man who is caught
in the business world; it is more than just part of the dying man's
dreams. In "Suddenly Turning Away"[2] the snow is part of a similar chain
of associations of coldness, in this case evoking an atmosphere of hostility:

> Someone comes near, the jaw
> Tightens, bullheads bite
> The snow, moments of intimacy waved away,
> Half-evolved antennas of the sea snail
> Sink to the ground.
> The sun
> Glints on us! But the shadows
> of not-love come.
> It cannot be stood against.
> And we suffer. The gold discs
> Fall from our ears.
> The sea grows cloudy.

The bullhead - a fish that survives out of water if on ice or snow -
becomes the symbol of man's inclination to turn toward unfriendliness
and anger instead of warmth and love in a situation when relationships
are disturbed. Thus, the snow becomes the unnatural element of disappoint-
ment and non-love. Human suffering, symbolized in the loss of the gold
discs - a token of nobility in, for example, the Inca tribe - becomes the
outward sign of non-communication and estrangement. Human contact becomes
difficult to establish: "The sea grows cloudy."

---

1 Chelsea, 8 (Oct., 1960), p. 64.
2 Light, p. 18.

In "Unrest"[1] the snow is part of the landscape that modern man is
struggling through like the Knights of Charlemagne,[2] and again snow and
darkness are associated; the darkness of the Middle Ages becomes that of
our own age. Humanity is traveling backward:

> . . .
> Charlemagne, we are approaching your islands!
>
> We are returning now to the snowy trees,
> And the depth of the darkness buried in snow, through
>   which you rode all night
> With stiff hands; now the darkness is falling
> In which we sleep and awake - a darkness in which
> Thieves shudder, and the insane have a hunger for snow,
> In which bankers dream of being buried by black stones,
> And businessmen fall on their knees in the dungeons of
>   sleep.

This criticism of modern society is particularized to criticism of individuals at the end of the poem, as may be seen in the preceding quotation.
The darkness of the age has become that of the individual mind.

Insanity and snow are juxtaposed also in "Sleet Storm on the Merritt
Parkway."[3] In this poem the chain of image associations leading up to the
snow metaphor is logically continuous. The poem starts in the poet's immediate surroundings with a description of the landscape he observes from
his car:

> I look out at the white sleet covering the still
>   streets
> As we drive through Scarsdale -
> The sleet began falling as we left Connecticut,
> And the winter leaves swirled in the wet air after
>   cars
> Like hands suddenly turned over in a conversation.
> Now the frost has nearly buried the short grass of
>   March.
> . . .

This cold and frosty landscape brings to the poet's mind "the many comfortable homes stretching for miles" in this area. The description of
the homes, however, features words associated with a certain coldness:
"polished floors," "white curtains," and "flagons of black glass." Therefore, the irony of the line

---

1 Silence, p. 25.
2 According to Robert Bly in an interview, April 13, 1973, conducted by
   the author.
3 Light, p. 25.

What a magnificent place for a child to grow up!

is not surprising. The consequences are well prepared for:

> And yet the children end in the river of price-fixing,
> Or in the snowy field of the insane asylum.

The word "yet" is needed only to sustain the irony of the preceding line. The poem could very well have ended here, but instead the poet's thoughts return to the actual scene of the sleet storm for a moment as if to gain strength and support for a final statement pertaining to the negativism and confusion of the whole nation:

> The sleet falls - so many cars moving toward New York -
> Last night we argued about the Marines invading
>   Guatemala in 1947,
> The United Fruit Company had one water spigot for 200
>   families,
> And the ideals of America, our freedom to criticize,
> The slave systems of Rome and Greece, and no one agreed.

However, not only the children growing up surrounded by the coldness of materialism are threatened by the "snow." The snow in "Asian Peace Offers Rejected without Publication"[1] indicates a living death. Man has "something inside." If he allows it "to be buried in snow," then he is not human any longer:

> . . .
> Men like Rusk are not men:
> They are bombs waiting to be loaded in a darkened
>   hangar.
> . . .
>
> Lost angels huddled on a night branch!
> The waves crossing
> And recrossing beneath,
> The sound of the rampaging Missouri,
> Bending the reeds again and again - something inside us
> Like a ghost train in the Rockies
> About to be buried in snow!
> Its long hoot
> Making the owl in the Douglas fir turn his head ...

In "Looking at New-Fallen Snow from a Train"[2] the different roles of the snow seem to be brought together in one poem. The snow is part of the setting, but at the same time it covers up things softly, it creeps in and rests everywhere, even "on the doorsills of collapsing children's

----

1 *Light*, p. 30.
2 Ibid., p. 45.

houses." The poet uses the snow most effectively, however, as a background for a scene of sudden death in the city and for the surrealistic scene of a man lying down to sleep with the birds of prey and carrion – surrounded by manifestations of life energy[1] – waiting for him. The snow as a descriptive element and as a metaphor in this poem seems to work in both positive and negative contexts, or fields of force. It works a positive change in man's surroundings as it softens and covers every object. But its relation to death and silence is obvious. It is nourished by the dying man's breath. The snow is a shroud for everything that is empty, rotting, collapsing, everything that lies down to sleep:

> Snow has covered the next line of tracks,
> And filled the empty cupboards in the milkweed pods;
> It has stretched out on the branches of weeds,
> And softened the frost-hills and the barbed-wire rolls
> Left leaning against a fencepost –
> It has drifted onto the window ledges high in the peaks
> > of barns.
>
> A man throws back his head, gasps
> And dies. His ankles twitch, his hands open and
> > close,
> And the fragment of time that he has eaten is
> > exhaled from his pale mouth to nourish the
> > snow.
> A salesman falls, striking his head on the edge
> > of the counter.
>
> Snow has filled out the peaks on the tops of rotted
> > fence posts.
> It has walked down to meet the slough water,
> And fills all the steps of the ladder leaning against
> > the eaves.
> It rests on the doorsills of collapsing children's
> > houses,
> And on transformer boxes held from the ground
> > forever in the center of cornfields.
>
> A man lies down to sleep.
> Hawks and crows gather around his bed.
> Grass shoots up between the hawks' toes.
> Each blade of grass is a voice.
> The sword by his side breaks into flame.

It is not very surprising that snow has become an integral part of the work of a poet from Minnesota. For Bly the snow is part of life; it

---

1 See below, Chapter II, p. 107, about the grass growing between the toes of the hawks, and Chapter IV, p. 182, about the grass and the sword as symbols of inner energy.

often turns his thoughts inward into himself and opens up new vistas for him, as in "Watering the Horse,"[1] where the perception of the snow flake turns into an experience of illumination:

> How strange to think of giving up all ambition!
> Suddenly I see with such clear eyes
> The white flake of snow
> That has just fallen in the horse's mane!

Since the poem as a whole conveys a joyful tone of satisfaction, I conclude that "strange" here has the less common meaning of "wonderful" and not its usual meaning of "foreign." Therefore, the first line probably means that the poet has already given up ambition, or that, at least, he has decided to do so. Seeing the snowflake he realizes that once he made that decision, his senses became more open and ready to register silent little things that add to the beauty of life.

Several critics have commented on this poem. They all agree that it records an "instant of clarity."[2] Paul Lacey, furthermore, points to parallels with Oriental poetry:

> This poem . . . can serve as an example of how the oriental simplicity of [Bly's] poetry reveals the inner world. Like a haiku, it does not lead us through the steps of a meditation, but distills the meditation into its conclusion and confirms it by the clarity of image which follows upon it. . . .
> Clear sight follows insight; thought, emotion, sight become a single experience, an enlightenment, anchored in the vivid perception of a white flake of snow in a horse's mane."[3]

Piccione sees the first line as a negative statement. Therefore, I conclude that he reads "strange" as meaning "foreign", which makes his interpretation contrary to mine. He feels that disparate elements - the giving up of ambition and the experience of the revelation - are being reconciled in the poem.[4] I see the revelation as a confirmation and an intensification of the renouncing of ambition. Janssens relates this poem to Bly's own statement about "the haiku, 'in which the words reach at the same instant to the life inside the brain and the life outside.'

---

1 Silence, p. 46.
2 Mersmann, p. 122. Short comments by Sage and Justin bring up similar points: "To free the mind is to start to see " (Sage, p. 67); "Giving up the competitive affairs of the city life means returning to nature " (Justin, p. 104).
3 Lacey, pp. 38-39.
4 See Piccione, p. 119.

The fusion of the two is achieved in 'Watering the Horse.'"[1] This, however, seems to be also true of Bly's descriptive poems that mirror a
state of mind.[2]

The word "snow" does not occur very frequently in Bly's later books.
In Jumping out of Bed it occurs in three poems in roles similar to those
mentioned above. In "Some November Privacy Poems"[3] - a series of four
short poems - the snow accentuates the oldness of nature and earth as
it covers the boulders:

* * *

> How marvellous to look out and see
> the boulders
> that have been gloomy since the earth began
> now with a faint dusting of snow.

* * *

In the title poem, "Jumping out of Bed,"[4] snow and silence are juxtaposed
just as in the title of Bly's first book. The snow symbolizes the silence
of inwardness.[5] In "Six Winter Privacy Poems"[6] the snow is mentioned four
times. Its main role is as a descriptive element, but as the whole setting of the sequence takes on symbolic overtones, the snow becomes part
of an imaginative landscape, as in poem 2:

> My shack has two rooms; I use one.
> The lamplight falls on my chair and table,
> and I fly into one of my own poems -
> I can't tell you where -
> as if I appeared where I am now,
> in a wet field, snow falling.

The theme of privacy connected with the snow, as in "Driving to Town
Late to Mail a Letter,"[7] recurs in "The Night Journey in the Cooking Pot"[8]
in Sleepers Joining Hands:

---

1 Janssens, p. 122.
2 See, for example, above, pp. 17 and 19-20.
3 Jumping, p. 13. (Although Jumping is not paginated, I refer to its
   poems as if it were, counting the first title page as number 1.) Cf.
   below , p. 79.
4 Jumping, p. 43.
5 See below, pp. 106-107 and 125, for quotation and a fuller analysis
   of the poem.
6 Jumping, p. 45. For a full analysis of the poem, see below pp. 125-128.
7 See above, p. 20.
8 Sleepers, pp. 59-63.

> . . .
> The snow begins falling.
> A winter privacy is before us,
> winter privacy,[1]
> . . .

In another line in this poem the snow is given a role in a statement about the poet's experience of his unconscious:[2]

> I love the snow, I need privacy as I move,[3]

The snow is also part of the landscape that, in the shape of a shaman, he imagines himself to be moving in.[4] That the snow belongs to a border zone between what is known and what is covered up and, therefore, not fully known, seems to be inherent in its associations with privacy and silence. In "The Night Journey in the Cooking Pot" the region that is not fully known is the place for the rebirth experience, for which different images are used:

> . . .
> Who is it that visits us from beneath the snow?
> Something shining far down in the ice?
> Deep in the mountain the sleeper is glad.[5]
> . . .

The "sleeper," the hero on his quest, returns to ordinary life as a visitor from the unknown region.[6]

Thus, Bly's use of the snow pertains to various areas of life: it is characteristic of the Minnesota landscape during a large portion of the year, and as such it suggests shelter and love; covering, preserving, and transforming; darkness and death; privacy and silence.

The Field: Descriptive Element and Metaphor

Southwestern Minnesota, where Bly grew up and where he now lives, is very rich farm land. The fields, extending for miles, impress the visitor with their rich black soil in the spring, with their deep green growth in the summer, with their abundant harvests or their vast emptiness in

---

1   Sleepers, p. 60.
2   See below, p. 156.
3   Sleepers, p. 59.
4   See below, pp. 112–113, and p. 156, for quotation and further commentary.
5   Sleepers, p. 61.
6   See below, pp. 158–159.

the fall, and with their immense whiteness in the winter. The farm with
its several buildings - the barn and the silos often at quite a distance
from the farmhouse - is a community in itself, growing out of, and dependent on these spacious fields. This is the world of many of Robert Bly's
poems. Ralph J. Mills says, "The environment in which Mr. Bly lives and
which fills his poetry is one selected for artistic as well as personal
reasons, or so it must appear. Though the Minnesota farmland was apparently the place where he grew up, he obviously made a definite choice,
a meaningful one with regard to his work, in returning there."[1]

The Minnesota fields mostly appear as part of the setting through
purely descriptive phrases like "the picked cornfields," "the snowy
fields," "the winter fields," "an open field," "the stubble fields," and
"the cornfield in the moonlight," but sometimes Bly "moves on from the
natural detail to the larger meaning."[2] In "Summer, 1960, Minnesota"[3]
the first stanza with its landscape of "hot beanfields" and "sturdy
alfalfa fields" is a stepping-stone to the description of the "inscape"
of stanza two:[4]

I

After a drifting day, visiting the bridge near Louis-
berg,
With its hot muddy water flowing
Under the excited swallows,
Now, at noon
We plunge through the hot beanfields,
And the sturdy alfalfa fields, the farm groves
Like heavy green smoke close to the ground.

II

Inside me there is a confusion of swallows,
Birds flying through the smoke,
And horses galloping excitedly on fields of short grass.

. . .

Here the poet tells us explicitly that he is describing his inner world,
but more often we have to sense this ourselves. He transfers his feelings
to the landscape, the poet becomes one with his outer world and outward
things live his inner life. "The proud and tragic pastures" in "With Pale

---

1 Ralph J. Mills, Jr., "Four Voices in Recent American Poetry." The
   Christian Scholar (Winter, 1963), pp. 342-343.
2 Roderick Nordell, "From the Bookshelf: A Poet in Minnesota,"
   The Christian Science Monitor, LV (Jan. 23, 1963), p. 9.
3 Silence, p. 31.
4 See below, pp. 53-54, for an analysis of the whole poem.

Women in Maryland"[1] and the "sunny field" in "Afternoon Sleep"[2] reflect
the poet's mood rather than the state of the fields. In "Solitude Late
at Night in the Woods"[3] the phrase "the trapped fields" aids by contrast
in bringing out the feeling of oneness with Nature and of the joy and
limitless freedom that the poet experiences while walking "in the trees",
"in the bare woods."

The "bare, pioneer field" in "At the Funeral of Great-Aunt Mary"[4]
recreates for us the emotional barrenness, the callousness, of many
modern Americans who are afraid of being emotionally upset if they have
to witness the lowering of the casket into the earth. This is brought
out in the last stanza, which stands in telling contrast to the speech
of the minister in the preceding stanza:

> . . .
> The minister tells us that, being
> The sons and daughters of God,
> We rejoice at death, for we go
> To the mansions prepared
> From the foundations of the world.
> Impossible. No one believes it.
>
> III
> Out on the bare, pioneer field,
> The frail body must wait till dusk
> To be lowered
> In the hot and sandy earth.

The poet's non-belief becomes the focus and turning-point of the poem.
The "bare, pioneer field" is a field of death both literally and metaphorically. This could be said also about the fields in "Fall"[5] where
the atmosphere of harvest time – the color of the sky and the sound of
the wind through the cornfield – reminds the farmer of death.[6] A clearly
metaphorical use is made of the field in the phrase "the snowy field of
the insane asylum" in "Sleet Storm on the Merritt Parkway,"[7] where it
is associated with stretches of cold uniformity both in the hospital
itself and in the human mind.

---

1 Silence, p. 32.
2 Ibid., p. 43. (Called "Waking from an Afternoon Sleep" in the British
   edition.) See below, p.122, for quotation and further interpretation.
3 Ibid., p. 45. See below, p. 87, for quotation and further interpretation.
4 Silence, p. 34. See also below, p. 86.
5 Ibid., p. 18. (Called "October Evening in Minnesota" in the British ed.
6 See below, pp. 41-42, for quotation and further interpretation.
7 Light, p. 25. See above, pp. 29-30, for quotation and further interpretation.

Finally, in Bly's surrealistic poems the fields belong in the created
world of the poem but express realities we know. In "Those Being Eaten by
America"[1] the fields become a world sad about America:

> . . .
>
> That is why these poems are so sad
> The long dead running over the fields
>
> The mass sinking down
> The light in children's faces fading at six or seven
>
> The world will soon break up into small colonies of the
>   saved

The slender hope expressed at the end of this poem becomes despair in
"The Fire of Despair has been Our Saviour,"[2] although the title suggests
a saving power in despair itself, in the forces pulling us down. The empty
autumn field with its dry cornleaf cannot show the poet his way. It becomes a symbol of modern world where man is lost, abandoned, left behind:

> . . .
>
> This autumn, I
> Cannot find the road
> That way: the things that we must grasp,
> The signs, are gone, hidden by spring and fall, leaving
> A still sky here, a dusk there,
> A dry cornleaf in a field; where has the road gone? All
> Trace lost, like a ship sinking,
> Where what is left and what goes down both bring despair.
> Not finding the road, we are slowly pulled down.

The field as descriptive element and metaphor belongs mainly in Bly's
earlier poems. In Jumping out of Bed and Sleepers Joining Hands it does
occur but less frequently. In "Chrysanthemums"[3] the poet turns the fields
into a kind of stage for his own performances:

> 1.
> Tonight I rode again in the moonlight!
> I saddled late at night.
> The horse picked his way down a dead-furrow,
> guided by deep shadows.
>
> 2.
> A mile from the yard the horse rears,
> glad. How magnificent to be doing nothing,
> moving aimlessly through a nighttime field,
> and the body alive, like a plant!
>
> . . .

---

1 Light, p. 14. See also below, p. 51.
2 Ibid., p. 48. See also below, pp. 53, 54-55.
3 Jumping, p. 21.

This use of the field also serves to emphasize a mystic union with nature
which the poet feels in solitude, as in "After Long Busyness":[1]

> I start out for a walk at last after weeks at the desk.
> Moon gone, plowing underfoot, no stars; not a trace of
>   light!
> Suppose a horse were galloping toward me in this open
>   field?
> Every day I did not spend in solitude was wasted.

In "Thinking of 'The Autumn Fields'"[2] - Bly's version of a Chinese
poem - the fields, mentioned only in the title, are put to a philosophic
use; they are symbolic in a conventional way and stand for a man's life
span. The poet has reached the peak of his life:

> Already autumn begins here in the mossy rocks.
> . . .
>
> How easy to see the road the liferiver takes!
> . . .
> In the second half of life a man accepts poverty and
>   illness;
> praise and blame belong to the glory of the first
>   half.
> Although cold wind blows against my walking stick,
> I will never get tired of the ferns on this mountain.
> . . .

In Sleepers Joining Hands the fields are always used metaphorically,
although the same vocabulary is used as in earlier poems. The poems in
this book are journeys of the mind; they are voyages into the unconscious.
In "Water Under the Earth"[3] the unconscious is presented as the "circle
of the fire" and as the "unused fields," both phrases suggesting a closed
area containing energy. Furthermore, both terms are used by Jung and his
followers to designate both the psyche as a whole and the unconscious.
In their terminology the circle is the symbol of wholeness and the field
is a place where latent energy is ordered and stored.[4]

In the long title poem, which in fact consists of four separate
poems, the fields have the same meaning, i.e. they are part of the inner
landscape that the persona on his individual quest passes through. In
the first of these four poems, "The Shadow Goes Away,"[5] the fields are
his own life as it appears in his memories and dreams, cluttered with

---

1 Jumping, p. 23.
2 Ibid., p. 9.
3 Sleepers, pp. 6-7.
4 See below, p. 129, for quotation and references.
5 Sleepers, pp. 53-55.

fragments of past experiences, and with personal relationships:[1]

> . . .
> I fall asleep, and dream I am working in the fields....
> Now I show the father the coat stained with goat's
> blood....
> The shadow goes away,
> we are left alone in the father's house.
> I knew that.... I sent my brother away.
> . . .

The third of these poems, "The Night Journey in the Cooking Pot,"[2]
describes an inner experience, the actual rebirth experience. At the end
of the poem, however, "the burial fields," seen as part of a chain of
circumstances in the ordinary world, participate in bringing the poet
back to ordinary consciousness. At the moment when he feels most free,
when he decides "that death is friendly," the feeling of bonds and limitations crashes in on him:[3]

> . . .
> I fall into my own hands,
>   fences break down under horses,
> cities starve, whole towns of singing women carrying
>   to the burial fields
>   the look I saw on my father's face,
> I sit down, again, I hit my own body,
> I shout at myself, I see what I have betrayed.
> What I have written is not good enough.
> Who does it help?
> I am ashamed sitting on the edge of my bed.

In the last of these four poems, "Water Drawn Up Into the Head,"[4]
the inner quest is expressed in terms of a falling asleep and a rejoicing,
a going away and a coming back, and a losing of oneself "in the curved
energy." It seems therefore probable that "the husky soybean fields" at
the beginning would signify an unconscious that the conscious part of the
psyche glimpses:[5]

> . . .
> I am passive, listening to the lapping waves,
> I am divine, drinking the air,
> consciousness fading or sweeping out over the husky
>   soybean fields like a revolving beacon
>   all night,
> . . .

---

1 See also below, pp. 146- 147, for further commentary.
2 _Sleepers_, pp. 59-63.
3 See also below, pp. 163-164, for further commentary.
4 _Sleepers_, pp. 64-67.
5 See below, p. 165, for a full quotation and a further commentary.

Thus, the fields are part of the special universe that the meditator, the quest hero, the poet of the unconscious, enters, experiencing everything:[1]

> . . .
>
> Sometimes when I read my own poems late at night,
> I sense myself on a long road,
> I feel the naked thing alone in the universe,
> the hairy body padding in the fields at dusk....
>
> . . .

As may be seen in the preceding pages the field concept does not always dominate the poems in which it occurs. All the same, its importance for a full understanding of the individual poem is unquestionable. This is the reason for my decision to select "the field" for separate discussion but still not to enter into any detailed analyses. Most of the poems mentioned in this chapter will also be discussed in other contexts below, as indicated in the footnotes.

The Barn: Descriptive Element and Metaphor

Robert Bly believes in the old occult saying, "Whoever wants to penetrate more deeply into the invisible has to penetrate more deeply into the visible,"[2] a saying he has chosen as an epigraph for The Morning Glory. The barn, an ingredient in Bly's visible surroundings, serves as such in some descriptive poems but has been endowed with special meanings in others.

In "Barnfire during Church,"[3] one of Bly's earliest poems, the barn is the center of interest; it is important to the Minnesota farmer as the storage for his wealth, the corn. Even the Sunday service at Church is abruptly broken off when the barn catches fire:

> And as we spoke the Nicene Creed we were called out
> To fight the barn afire
> And here the summer's corn is born again
> In reformation into air.

It is everybody's concern to put out the fire:

> The children cry and call
> And throw their snowballs in the fire; . . .

---

1 See below, pp. 167- 168, for a full quotation and a further commentary.
2 The Morning Glory (Unless it is otherwise indicated, I am quoting the 2nd edition.), p. 7.
3 The Paris Review (Spring, 1953), p. 27; also MA thesis, p. 12. (Only this later version, which is slightly different, has the title mention above.)

Still, the main point of this early poem seems to be for the poet to re-
create in words the spectacle of the fire:

>   . . .   the barleys burn;
>   The walls are folding; burning rust and gold
>   the loft hangs fire in air; the straw and chaff
>   Burn black the timid dampness of the night
>   And churn the ancient wall-stones to a dust.

In The Morning Glory, a book containing mainly descriptive prose
poems, a barn is the object of description in "Walking on the Sussex
Coast,"[1] but the poem also brings out the sheltering security of it at
night:

>   I love this stone barn. The ground around is
>   green, springy, rolling over into the ocean. . . .
>   The straw on the ground is fresh and yellow from
>   tumbled bales. . . . How lovely to flop down here,
>   our sides touching other cows, protected from sea-
>   wind by stone walls that will later become the
>   color of the night. We know that at dawn we can look
>   out the open door and see the green hills again!

Probably the same feeling of security filled the poet with pleasure
when he saw "the lights in the barns" on his way to Chicago in "Three
Kinds of Pleasures."[2] That is also what makes "the cows stand around the
barn door" in "Fall,"[3] a narrative and descriptive prose poem in Silence
in the Snowy Fields:

>   . . .
>   The dusk has come, a glow in the west, as if seen
>   through the isinglass on old coal stoves, and the
>   cows stand around the barn door; now the farmer looks
>   up at the paling sky reminding him of death, and in
>   the fields the bones of the corn rustle faintly in
>   the last wind, and the half moon stands in the south.
>   Now the light from barn windows can be seen through
>   bare trees.

The barn and "the lights from barn windows" stand out in warm and friendly
contrast to a world otherwise filled with the animals' fear of the dark -
brought out also in the line about "the chickens, huddling near their
electricity"[4] - and the farmer's fear of death. This farmer seems to have
much in common with the old man in Robert Frost's "After Apple-Picking."[5]

---

1   The Morning Glory, p. 17.
2   Silence, p. 11. See also above, p. 17.
3   Ibid., p. 18. See also above, p. 36.
4   From the first sentence of the poem. Cf, also below, p. 110 and p. 186,
    where a similar line in "Teeth Mother" is mentioned.
5   Robert Frost, The Complete Poems, (London, 1951), pp. 88-90.

Both see the world "as through a glass darkly," both sense the closeness
of death, and somehow they both seem to say, "I am overtired / Of the
great harvest I myself desired."[1] Bly's farmer, however, can still take
satisfaction in "the lights from barn windows," although "seen through
bare trees." Again, Bly conveys an inner state of mind through details
from his outer world.

In a review of Bly's poetry Louis Simpson says, "The life we share
with animals and saints is the source of poetry."[2] To examplify this he
quotes "Love Poem,"[3] in which the barn is one of the objects in the poet's
surroundings that his love embraces:

> When we are in love, we love the grass,
> And the barns, and the lightpoles,
> And the small main streets abandoned all night.

In a similar way in "Driving through Ohio"[4] "the white barns leaning into
the ground" are part of the "torpid joy" the poet shares with his land.

So far we have seen the barn associated with wealth, with security,
light, and love. In "Awakening"[5] it is associated with darkness; one of
the central images is the barn as a container of darkness. The first
stanza is filled with surrealistic imagery conveying a state of mind in
between sleep and wakening:

> We are approaching sleep: the chestnut blossoms in
>   the mind
> Mingle with thoughts of pain
> And the long roots of barley, bitterness
> As of oak roots staining the waters dark
> In Louisiana, the wet streets soaked with rain
> And sodden blossoms, out of this
> We have come, a tunnel softly hurtling into darkness.

This stanza leads up to the image of the tunnel, signifying a condition
of sleep and dreams, which on the other hand denotes an inner wakening, as
may be seen in several of Bly's poems. The second stanza also deals with
a condition that is undergoing change, the moment before a storm:

---

1 Robert Frost, The Complete Poems, p. 89.
2 Louis Simpson, "Poetry Chronicle," The Hudson Review (Spring, 1963),
   p. 138.
3 Silence, p. 41. See also below, p. 82 and p. 102.
4 Ibid., p. 33. See also above, p. 19.
5 Ibid., p. 26.

The storm is coming. The small farmhouse in Minnesota
Is hardly strong enough for the storm.
Darkness, darkness in grass, darkness in trees.
Even the water in wells trembles.
Bodies give off darkness, and chrysanthemums
Are dark, and horses, who are bearing great loads
             of hay
To the deep barns where the dark air is moving from
             corners.

The barn in this stanza corresponds to the tunnel in the first stanza.
Both are containers of a positive darkness into which you sink as you
do in sleep and as the hay does, sheltered from winter storms. In the
third stanza the in-between state is life downtown in a big city:

Lincoln's statue, and the traffic. From the long past
Into the long present
A bird, forgotten in these pressures, warbling,
As the great wheel turns around, grinding
The living in water.
Washing, continual washing, in water now stained
With blossoms and rotting logs,
Cries, half-muffled, from beneath the earth, the
             living awakened at last like the dead.

The images used to describe life in this stanza are like those in the
first, in which blossoms and water suggest the movement of the mind into
sleep, which means an awakening of the unconscious. Thus, in the last
stanza we see ordinary life in a similar condition. "We are all asleep
in the outward man,"[1] is the epigraph of Silence in the Snowy Fields.
The container of darkness in this stanza is the earth itself - a grave
maybe. Man has to die to the outer world, to sink into himself, to effect
an inner awakening. Movement into darkness, toward one's inner self, is a
recurring idea in Bly's poetry.

Bly's first book, Silence in the Snowy Fields, ends with the poem
"Snowfall in the Afternoon,"[2] which closes with the image of a
barn, filled with life-sustaining corn, that moves in the darkness of a
snowstorm. It provides a powerful image of the human situaiton as Bly
sees it. We are all surrounded by the darkness of a storm. The barn -
the earth with its resources - is our saviour, but those who sail the
ship of rescue have been blind for many years.

The barn occurs only in three poems in The Light around the Body,
and it is not the governing image in any of them. It is dark in "Melan-

---

1 Quotation from Jacob Boehme.
2 Silence, p. 60. See above, pp. 26-27, for quotation and further commentary.

cholia,"[1] dark like the mood of the poet who is attending a funeral. It
is abandoned in "Three Presidents,"[2] and it is being covered with snow
in "Looking at New-Fallen Snow from a Train."[3] I think it is significant
for The Light around the Body that it has hardly any room at all for the
barn, and that when it does occur, there are no friendly lights in its
windows. This book contains much social and political criticism. Bly
feels that America has turned away from friendly things. "All the sailors
on deck have been blind for many years."[4]

In Bly's later books we find the barn in only one poem, "The Night
Journey in the Cooking Pot," and it refers to the barn where Christ was
born. However, even this barn, the symbol of our salvation, is surrounded
by hostility. Herod orders the Christ child killed. In the same way in
our modern society the child within us is killed:

> . . .
>
> The barn doors are open. His breath touches the manger
>   hay
> and the King a hundred miles away
> stands up. He calls his ministers.
> "Find him.
> There cannot be two rulers in one body."
> He sends his wise men out along the arteries,
> along the winding tunnels, into the mountains,
> to kill the child in the old moonlit villages of the
>   brain.[5]
>
> . . .

Experience must take the place of innocence.[6]

The night journey that the visit to Christ's birthplace is part of
is very different form the Midwestern journey we started out on at the
beginning of this chapter. The poet's mind takes in the world around him
and then moves in any direction. There is continuous movement along an
endless road where limits of time and space do not seem to exist. In the
next chapter the concepts of place and time, among others, will take us
to new domains in Bly's poetry. In the poems discussed above the descriptive element has been dominant. From now on social engagement, vision,
and meditation will take its place.

---

1 Light, p. 41.
2 Ibid., p. 19.
3 Ibid., p. 45. See above, pp. 30 - 31, for quotation and interpretation
   of the whole poem.
4 Silence, p. 60. See also above, pp. 26-27 and 43.
5 Sleepers, p. 62
6 For an interpretation in the terms of an inner quest see above, pp.
   161-162.

II. OUR EARTHLY EXISTENCE

Much of Robert Bly's poetry is rooted in his home region, the Midwest, but the perspective widens, and in this chapter I hope to show
that what he really deals with is life in general. Therefore, I intend
to study place, time, and life energy – the basic elements of our earthly
existence. In the discussion above of recurring elements in Bly's poetry
I mentioned the idea of transition and a breaking down of barriers. Such
ideas were employed by the Surrealist poets in France, especially in
their handling of the concepts of place and time. Anna Balakian in her
discussion of André Breton states that "Time has acquired a new flexi-
bility"[1] and "Space has been endowed with a wider scope."[2] As seen from
this quotation, she even goes so far as to use the word "space," which
suggests no limitations, instead of the more specific and concrete word
"place." She also argues that the Surrealists' technique, applied in
their handling of place and time, was influenced by the Romantics. Commenting on Gérard de Nerval she says, "It is with a shock that we waver
from the past to the present, from the real to the unreal, from the visible to the invisible as the narrative flows on."[3] In the introduction
to her more recent book Surrealism: The Road to the Absolute she searches
for "surrealistic tremors in the most recent poetry,"[4] and she offers
poems by Robert Bly as examples of a type of poetry that suggests "surrealist motivation and sources."[5] In studying place, time, and life
energy in Bly's poems I will try to examine the validity of this sugges-
tion by observing how he handles these elements and what meanings he con-
fers upon them.

The Concept of Place

Among the words denoting place in Robert Bly's poetry I have chosen
to discuss "the road." There are other alternatives, but I want to deal
with some of those in other contexts. I have, for instance, discussed
"the field" under the heading of "The Minnesota Heritage," as this word
comes from the poet's everyday surroundings and occurs more often in personal poems about inner and outer experiences than in poems of more gen-

---

1 Anna Balakian, The Literary Origins of Surrealism (New York, N. Y.,
   1947), p. 19.
2 Ibid.
3 Ibid., p. 35.
4 Anna Balakian, Surrealism: The Road to the Absolute, p. 24.
5 Ibid., p. 25.

eral significance. The words "sea" and "lake," as well as other words denoting water, will be dealt with in Chapter III under the heading of
"The Voyage of the Unconscious." The word "road," however, as well as its
synonyms, occurs all through Bly's poetry and has been given many different roles. Bly's handling of this word seems to me representative of his
handling of words denoting place in general.

The word "road" is employed with about the same frequency all through
Bly's poetry. In <u>Silence in the Snowy Fields</u> it is conspicuous as it is
contained in one of the titles of the subdivisions in both the American
and the British editions. The American edition has three subdivisions,
the last being "Silence on the Roads." This title, both in phrasing and
in meaning, is parallel to the title of the book. It brings out the quality of stillness and solitude in the open spaces of the Midwestern landscape, something that seems invaluable to the poet.[1] The British edition
has five subdivisions, the first being "We Know the Road." In the changing
of the titles, as well as in the rearranging of the poems, I see a development toward a larger inclusiveness of scope and meaning and toward a
deepened confidence on the part of the poet. In the title "We Know the
Road" the wider scope is suggested by the use of "we" which implies less
emphasis on silence and solitude than the titles of the subdivisions in
the American edition do, where these words occur in two out of three
titles. The deepened confidence is, of course, in the word "know." The
larger scope of meaning in the word "road" is easily seen in the poem
"After Working"[2] in which the whole phrase, "We know the road," occurs;
the road turns into a symbolic road leading into the future:

---

1 A line in "Roads" (<u>Old Man</u>, p. 49), a poem in Bly's latest book, confirms this observation. This short descriptive poem is of nearly the
   same type as those included in <u>Silence in the Snowy Fields</u>:

        "Roads"
        "in memoriam"

        Last night, full moon.
        The snowy fields, the roads silent and alone.
        Clods rose above the snow in the plowing west,
        like mountain tops, or chest of graves.

2 <u>Silence</u>, p. 51.

MOVING INWARD

A Study of Robert Bly's Poetry

by

Ingegerd Friberg

Dissertation for the Degree of Doctor of
Philosophy to be publicly examined in English
with due permission of the Philological Section
of the Faculty of Arts, University of Göteborg,
on Tuesday, May 31st, 1977, at 1.15 p.m. in
the Department of English, Room 237, Lundgrens-
gatan 7, Göteborg.

I
After many strange thoughts,
Thoughts of distant harbors, and new life,
I came in and found the moonlight lying in the room.

II
Outside it covers the trees like pure sound,
The sound of tower bells, of water moving under the ice,
The sound of the deaf hearing through the bones of their
            heads.

III
We know the road; as the moonlight
Lifts everything, so in a night like this
The road goes on ahead, it is all clear.

The confidence expressed in the final stanza is reached through inner
and outer observations. Via images of sound the moonlit landscape is turned
into the poet's future life road. The moonlight, which finally renders
the symbolic meaning of the road, gradually comes to life. In the first
stanza it is described as "lying in the room." The second stanza starts
in the same descriptive manner: "Outside it covers the trees." However,
the rest of stanza II, with its images of sound for the moonlight, is
startling. These lines put Bly side by side with the impressionist
painters who wanted light and colors to be more than just visual. Renoir
said, "I want a red to be sonorous, to sound like a bell."[1] The moonlight
in Bly's poem finally turns into a strong force that "Lifts everything;"
it dispels shadows and doubts from both the outer and the inner roads.
The use of synaesthesia in creating powerful images was used, for example,
by the Surrealists in France. Anna Balakian discusses it with reference to
Pierre Reverdy[2] and she quotes a translation of Paul Eluard's "Nous
Sommes," which contains a phrase with an image parallel to Bly's:

And sleep from joy at the sound of the sun.[3]

The word "road" does not always contain symbolic overtones. In three
descriptive poems, "Three Kinds of Pleasures,"[4] "Driving toward the Lac
Qui Parle River,"[5] and "Driving North from San Francisco"[6] the road is
simply part of the scenery described by the poet as he moves through the
landscape. But since so often he directs his observations both outward
and inward at the same time, there is not always a distinctive border-

---

1   Encyclopedia of Painting (New York, N. Y., 1970), p. 414.
2   Balakian, Surrealism: The Road to the Absolute, p. 113.
3   Ibid., p. 162.
4   Silence, p. 11. See also above, pp. 16-17.
5   Ibid., p. 20. See also above, pp. 17-18.
6   Poetry, CIV:6 (Sept., 1964), pp. 366-367.

line between objects and symbols, between a real and a symbolic place.
In "On the Ferry across Chesapeake Bay"[1] the road is the distance he
travels not just on a specific journey but also on his journey through
life. In this poem the poet's confidence seems shaken, or rather, he has
probably not yet reached the confidence expressed in "After Working."
The poem was written in the early 50's after he had spent some time
alone in New York. He is searching for a meaning in life:

> Having accomplished nothing, I am travelling somewhere
>   else

So far he cannot see his life road leading anywhere, but he knows he
must move on:[2]

> . . .
> For though on its road the body cannot march
> With golden trumpets - it must march -
> And the sea gives up its answer as it falls into
>   itself.

Also in "After Drinking All Night with a Friend, We Go Out in a Boat
at Dawn to See Who Can Write the Best Poem"[3] the actual movement of the
boat becomes symbolic at the moment that it is described:

> . . .
> I am like you, you dark boat,
> Drifting over water fed by cool springs.
> . . .

The drifting is without direction; there is no goal clearly seen toward
which the poet moves, although he discerns meaning in everyday experiences - in what makes up his everyday world:

> . . .
> A few friendships, a few dawns, a few glimpses of grass,
> A few oars weathered by the snow and the heat,
> So we drift toward shore, over cold waters,
> No longer caring if we drift or go straight.

This sense of drifting along the life road, trying to find direction
and a meaning in life, develops into a feeling of homelessness at the end
of Silence in the Snowy Fields and into despair in Bly's second book
The Light around the Body. In "Silence"[4] the fall has come and the poet

---

1 Silence, p. 35.
2 See also above, pp. 20-21, and below, p. 82.
3 Silence, p. 56.
4 Ibid., p. 59.

feels lost, wandering without direction among doorposts and cars. The
sloth inside his body holds him back, away from the sunny places, unable
to accept kindness which is expressed in the image of stones wandering
like himself. Everything on the long roads of life seems to be wandering,
experiencing the same homelessness as the poet:

> . . .
>
> Something homeless is looking on the long roads -
> A dog lost since midnight, a small duck
> Among the odorous reeds,
> Or a tiny box-elder bug searching for the window pane.
> Even the young sunlight is lost on the window pane,
> Moving at night like a diver among the bare branches
> silently lying on the floor.

In "Come with Me"[1] removed Chevrolet wheels "howl with a terrible
loneliness," burst tires lie "abandoned on the shoulders of thruways,"
and "those roads in South Dakota that feel around in the darkness..." do
not lead anywhere, do not save us from homelessness. As several critics
point out, this poem starts with an invitation to the reader to feel the
despair of the roads of modern America:

> Come with me into those things that have felt this
> despair for so long -

The idea of invitation is even more clear in the British edition of The
Light around the Body, in which the poem opens the book. Paul Zweig senses "a prophetic ring, inviting the reader to shape the poem into a meditation."[2] If it is meant to be a meditation on the horrors of reality done
in order to deepen our social awareness, I can agree with Zweig. However,
I find it difficult to notice any "prophetic ring" in the poem. It gives
a picture of reality, of life in a materialistic society, in terms of
thruways and roads. Lisel Mueller sees as the theme of the poem "the human
longing for wholeness [applied] to the collapse of America the Beautiful,
the displacement of the dream by the nightmare."[3] The human longing for
wholeness, as I see it, is not to be found in the actual poem, but rather
in the poet's effort to write the poem, and maybe it is this longing that
turns Zweig's thoughts toward meditation as a remedy in a world of "collapsed bodies, that tried and burst, / And were left behind." Perhaps he

---

1 Light, p. 13
2 Paul Zweig, "A Sadness for America," The Nation (March 25, 1968),
   p. 418.
3 Lisel Mueller, "Five Poets," Shenandoah, XIX (Spring, 1968), p. 71.

had read the early version of the poem in which Bly talks about "collapsed souls, who tried and burst,"[1] a line that suggests a spiritual collapse rather than a material one.

The metaphor of the roads in South Dakota is important also in "The Current Administration"[2] as the symbolic setting for American society, which in this poem is toiling in its business world of diamonds and Cadillacs, and existing in an atmosphere of ideas imported form the Old World:

> 2
> Snow fell all night on a farmyard in Montana.
> And the Assyrian lion blazed above the soybean fields.
> The last haven of Jehovah, down from the old heavens,
> Hugged a sooty corner of the murdered pine. Arabic
>   numerals
> Walked the earth, dressed as bankers and sportsmen,
> And at night diamonds in slippers invade our sleep.
> Black beetles, bright as Cadillacs, toil down
> The long dusty road into the mountains of South Dakota.
>   . . .

The name of South Dakota probably has the special role of calling to mind unbearable heat in the summer, severe cold in the winter, and endless highways surrounded by emptiness and space, with The Badlands and Mount Rushmore as possible destinations for the traveler.

The word "road" also functions as a setting or stage in several other poems with varying themes. In some political poems it serves as the stage of disintegration, war, and chaos. In "Watching Television"[3] we witness the disintegration of both the body and the mind:

> Sounds are heard too high for ears,
> From the body cells there is an answering bay;
> Soon the inner streets fill with a chorus of barks.
>
> We see the landing craft coming in ,
> The black car sliding to a stop,
> The Puritan killer loosening his guns.
>
> Wild dogs tear off noses and eyes
> And run off with them down the street -
> The body tears off its own arms and throws them into
>   the air.
>
> The detective draws fifty-five million people into his
>   revolver,
> Who sleep restlessly as in an air raid in London;
> Their backs become curved in the sloping dark.

---

1 Poetry, CIV:6 (Sept., 1964), p. 365.
2 Light, p. 22.
3 Ibid., p. 6.

> The filaments of the soul slowly separate:
> The spirit breaks, a puff of dust floats up,
> Like a house in Nebraska that suddenly explodes.

The word "street" here - instead of "road" - aids in creating the city atmosphere of demoralizing TV programs, and simultaneously functions as a symbol for the inner and outer scene of activity. A different version of this poem has an anti-war touch in its second stanza. The barren battlefields of World War I - presented as roads and streets - seem fitting backgrounds for the murderous adventures of American TV programs:

> We see on tape the treeless roads in the Argonne,
> The streets for whom there is no afterlife,
> The Puritan killer loosening his guns.[1]

Harsh criticism of his own society also is voiced by Bly in "Those Being Eaten by America"[2] where the roads have a function similar to that of the fields later in the poem.[3] Beings, already torn apart, run away along these roads in hopeless protest:

> The cry of those being eaten by America,
> Others pale and soft being stored for later eating
>
> And Jefferson
> Who saw hope in new oats
>
> The wild houses go on
> With long hair growing from between their toes
> The feet at night get up
> And run down the long white roads by themselves
>
> . . .

The Gothic atmosphere of this surrealistic world, which stands out the more starkly in that it is being contrasted to the hopeful innocence of Jefferson's America,[4] drives everything that is alive into protesting madness:

> . . .
>
> The dams reverse themselves and want to go stand alone
>   in the desert
> Ministers who dive headfirst into the earth
> The pale flesh
> Spreading guiltily into new literatures
>
> . . .

---

1 Choice: A Magazine of Poetry and Photography, Vol. 3 (1963), p. 111.
2 Light, p. 14.
3 See above, p. 37.
4 Wosk points to the same contrast on page 55 of her thesis. See also below, p. 100.

What the "eating" in this poem refers to is not clear, and it does not
really matter whether it is associated with weaker nations being eaten by
wars outside America, or with groups being exploited within the country.
In other poems the target of Bly's criticism is unmistakeable. Anti-war
poems, for example, form a large part of The Light around the Body. In
some of these the atrocities of war are enacted on the roads, as in "War
and Silence,"[1] in which the disintegration scenes in the third and fourth
stanzas are seen against the background of a Negro's homelessness, the
silence of nature, and the lies of bishops in the first two stanzas:

> The bombers spread out, temperature steady
> A Negro's ear sleeping in an automobile tire
> Pieces of timber float by saying nothing
> *
> Bishops rush about crying, There is no war,
> And bombs fall,
> Leaving a dust on the beech trees
> *
> One leg walks down the road and leaves
> The other behind, the eyes part
> And fly off in opposite directions
> *
> Filaments of death grow out.
> The sheriff cuts off his black legs
> And nails them to a tree

This poem with its apt surrealistic overtones was written during the Vietnam War, but Bly had made known his anti-war attitude as early as the
Korean War, as his "Choral Stanza"[2] testifies. Written in a more traditional style it is a prayer for peace, ascending form a stage of war and
death, and again this stage is seen in terms of streets:

> For peace and peace the prayers ascend
> From tongues in darkness sung to tongues in light
> In death
> In turbulence of death
> The bodies broken in the Asian streets
> To float in peace
> I've seen the bodies broken in the Asian streets
> The blood comes down like rain
> And bones like hail
> Dear God, we have abundant death.

To give an historical poignance to his criticism of American society
the poet makes the streets of Detroit of the early nineteenth century the

---

1 Light, p. 31. See also below, p. 90.
2 The Paris Review (Summer, 1953), p. 79.

setting for "Andrew Jackson's Speech."[1] In giving in to the rich, the poor
workers of Detroit have broken faith with the spirit of the Revolution:

> . . .
>
> "The poor have been raised up by the Revolution.
> Washington, riding in cold snow at Valley Forge,
> Warned the poor never to take another husband."
>
> His voice rose in the noisy streets of Detroit.

Comparing his own time with the Middle Ages and the Ice Age in "The
Fire of Despair Has Been Our Saviour,"[2] Bly sees causes of despair all
through history. However, he sees hope in despair. As the black branches
of autumn trees promise spring, so is there salvation in despair. In the
Middle Ages it was hard to find; it was like "the hidden joy of crows."[3]
In the Ice Age the coldness of death made man cry out in agony before he
could find his way out of "the snowbound valley." For the poet the present
time is "autumn" and he looks for signs of a road leading through despair
to despair's saving force:

> . . .
>
> This autumn, I
> Cannot find the road
> That way: the things that we must grasp,
> The signs, are gone, hidden by spring and fall, leaving
> A still sky here, a dusk there,
> A dry cornleaf in a field; where has the road gone? All
> Trace lost, like a ship sinking,
> Where what is left and what goes down both bring despair.
> Not finding the road, we are slowly pulled down.

The signs to be seen are of no help; they all just bring despair, and "we
are slowly pulled down."[4] But that is the moment when the poet, unawares,
turns toward the saving force. Nothing in the outside world can give direction and meaning, so we have to let go and submit to being pulled down.
The pattern of turning outward first, then inward, and finally being
pulled down, is more clear in "Summer 1960, Minnesota"[5] in which the
first stanza describes the outer landscape, the second stanza the poet's
inner world,[6] and the third stanza the actual fall into darkness:

---

1 *Light*, p. 24.
2 Ibid., p. 48.
3 Cf. "The crow shall find new mud to walk upon" in "Where We Must Look
   for Help," *Silence*, p. 29, and below, p. 81.
4 Cf. above, p. 37.
5 *Silence*, p. 31.
6 Cf. above p. 35.

III
Yet, we are falling,
Falling into the open mouths of darkness,
Into the Congo as if into a river,
Or as wheat into open mills.

What the descent into darkness means we cannot tell directly from these
two poems. A comparison with "Awakening," however, seems to point to ideas
found also in that poem: "Man has to die to the outer world, to sink into
himself, to effect an inner awakening."[1] Despair brings us to the point
at which we are pulled on to the road of inwardness. An unpublished early
version of "The Fire of Despair Has Been Our Saviour" was called "The Man
Who Sees the Hill of Despair from Afar."[2] It contains no road metaphor at
all. Neither is there any "I" in the poem, and the last line of the final
version is missing. A second version[3] has the same title as the final version, and the road metaphor is introduced, but the final line is still
missing:

. . .

This autumn, instants
Of despair are deep
And hard to find for us, for in the woods at the end
Of roads is despair, yet the things that we must grasp,
The signs of the road are gone, hidden by spring and
          fall, leaving
A still sky here, a dusk there,
A dry cornleaf in the field; all
Trace lost, like a ship sinking,
Where what is left and what goes down both bring despair.

In this version the descent, or the fall into darkness, never takes place,
but, instead, in the first four lines of the last stanza the poet's search
for roads leading into despair is clearly spelled out, while the saving
force in despair is suggested only in the title. The second and final versions are closer to each other than the early version is to either of
those. That version seems more surrealistic since the comparison with the
Middle Ages and the Ice Age is not made clear, and thus the logic of the
poem is harder to find. On the other hand, this makes the reason for the
despair more overwhelming and immediate, so that the final image - "The
world is a ship sinking" - carries greater outward force:

---

1   Above, p. 43.
2   MA thesis, p. 17.
3   The Paris Review (Spring, 1958), p. 123.

. . .

```
        The instant of agony
        Is deep and hard to find for us, harder
        Than those others, for the things it is our destiny
                    to grasp
        Are hidden by spring and fall, leaving
        A still sky here, a dusk there,
        A dry cornleaf in the field,
        The world is a ship sinking
        Where what is left and what goes down both bring
                    despair.
```

As I see it, this version puts greater emphasis on what brings despair
than on the saving force in the inwardness that despair may lead to.
There may not be a saving force at all. The different title also supports
this conclusion. Thus, a comparison of these three versions of the same
poem seems to reveal different degrees of outer and inner awareness. In
an interview Bly mentions this poem and its different versions: "I worked
on it about eight years. I got the first stanza done, the second stanza
done, and I could not finish the end of the third stanza. And finally, in
desperation, I put it into Light around the Body. It was ten years old
and still, the last line isn't any good. . . . What I was trying to say
is that this sensation of sorrow is very important in finding the road."[1]

Whether this poem should be classified as a personal or a political
poem is not immediately evident. The fact that it has qualities of both
types, at least when all three versions are taken into consideration,
makes it more of a political poem than it seems at first. Discussing
political poetry in an article from 1967, Bly says, "Paradoxically, what
is needed to write true poems about the outward world is inwardness."[2]
Furthermore, he defines the true political poem as a quarrel by the poet
with himself, which, like the personal poem, moves to deepen awareness,[3]
and it should move, as I see it, along the road searched for in this poem.

A poem called "Wanting to Experience All Things,"[4] written about ten
years later than the first version of "The Fire of Despair Has Been Our
Saviour," opens with the same situation: one does not find the road

---

1 Peter Martin, "Robert Bly: Poet on the Road Home," The Straight Creek
   Journal, 1:36 (Oct. 24, 1972), p. 11.
2 Robert Bly, "On Political Poetry," The Nation (April 24, 1967), p. 522;
   also part of "Leaping up into Political Poetry," which is the introductory essay of Forty Poems Touching on Recent American History.
3 See Robert Bly, "On Political Poetry," p. 523.
4 Light, p. 60.

through darkness to clarity and is pulled into the darkness. This poem,
however, turns visionary and ends in clarity. It is a surrealistic poem
in which everything is said by means of images, from which the movement
from blindness to light emerges forcefully:

> The blind horse among the cherry trees –
> And bones, sticking from cool earth.
> The heart leaps   .
> Almost up to the sky! But laments
> And filaments pull us back into the darkness.
> We cannot see –
> But a paw
> Comes out of the dark
> To light the road. Suddenly I am flying,
> I follow my own fiery traces through the night!

The role of the road metaphor here is much like its role in Bly's later
books; it is the poet's road, not just his life-road, but also the inward
road his mind travels in meditation or in creative moments. In "The Night
Journey in the Cooking Pot"[1] he conveys the joy he had experienced the
first time he discerned this road:

> * * *
> I float on solitude as on water... there is a road....
> I felt the road first in New York, in that great room
> reading Rilke in the womanless loneliness.
> How marvelous the great wings sweeping along the floor,
> inwardness, inwardness, inwardness,
> the inward path I still walk on,
> I felt the wings brushing the floors of the dark,
> trailing longer wings,
> the wing marks left in the delicate sand of the corridors,
> the face shining far inside the mountain.
> . . .

This road of inwardness is a road of solitude. In "The Magnolia Grove"[2]
Bly conveys the joy of solitude in Nature, a joy that seems to be as endless as the path beside the river:

> . . .
> Settling down at dusk from the dome of light
> bird voices get mingled with the river sounds.
> The path beside the river winds off into the distance.
> Joy of solitude, will you ever come to an end?

In "On a Moonlit Road in the North Woods"[3] we find the poet meditating in the solitude of nature:

---

1 Sleepers, p. 59.
2 Jumping, p. 33. This poem is a rewriting of Michael Bullock's translation of a Chinese poem in his book Poems of Solitude. Robert Bly kept
   the last line of Michael Bullock's poem as it was because he liked it
   so much and dedicated his version to Michael Bullock.
3 Jumping, p. 15. See also below, p. 94.

I sit on the forest road,
cross-legged.
I am an oyster
breathing on his own shore.

*

Cars seldom use this road.
I looked up and down,
    no car coming, none would,
perhaps for hours....

*

All day my thoughts ran on in small rivulets
near some bigger flood.
Several times water
    carried me away:
then I was a cedar twig,
    a fish scale....

*

And what does the oyster think
on this forest road?
He thinks of his earlier life,
of meeting her again.

The word "road" in this poem is not used symbolically; it stands
for an actual forest road. But what is described in the poem is the road
of meditation, which might be what the forest road refers to in the last
stanza, and which in this case leads back to man's origin: the Mother.
The theme of mother consciousness is suggested already in the first
stanza in the image of the oyster, which, according to one of Bly's
prose essays, is one of the "favorite creatures of the Mother"[1] in ancient myths. This poem takes us through the different steps on the road
of meditation.[2] The meditator sits down in the foetal position, which is
also suggested by the image of the womb-shaped oyster. Then he glances
at the world around him before turning inward. The way his thoughts go
is described in water images suggesting the unconscious, and finally he
is carried away toward the Mother: "He thinks of his earlier life, / of
meeting her again."

The long road of inwardness also leads through the joy and ecstacy
connected with the creation of poetry. In "Water Drawn Up Into the Head,"
in the part called "An Extra Joyful Chorus for Those Who Have Read This
Far"[3] the poet says that sometimes when reading his own poems late at

---

1   Robert Bly, "I Came Out of the Mother Naked," Sleepers, p. 32. See
    also below, pp. 183-184.
2   Cf. below, Chapter III, about the rebirth experience.
3   Sleepers, pp. 66-67.

night, he feels as if he were on a long road, and in a Whitmanesque catalogue we see him as all things and all beings from Beowulf fighting "the
mysterious mother" to "an eternal happiness fighting in the long reeds."[1]

As in his earlier books, however, so in his later books not all the
poems built around the road metaphor are entirely joyful. Dark qualities
make themselves felt. In "Shack Poem"[2] the insecurity of the roads calls
for meditation. These roads seem to be spiritual roads just as the Kingdom in the second stanza is of the Spirit:[3]

> 1.
> I don't even know these roads I walk on,
> I see the backs of white birds.
> Whales rush by, their teeth ivory.
>
> 2.
> Far out at the edge of the heron's wing,
> where the air is disturbed by the last feather,
> there is the Kingdom....
>
> 3.
> Hurrying to brush between the Two Fish,
> the wild woman flies on ...
> blue glass stones a path on earth mark her going.
>
> 4.
> I sit down and fold my legs....
> The half dark in the room is delicious.
> How marvellous to be a thought entirely surrounded
> by brains!

In "Hair"[4] people of the outer world - movie stars, politicians,
businessmen, royalties, generals, priests, singers - are all lost:

> . . .
>
> All those men who cannot find the road,
> who die coughing particles of black flesh onto neigh-
> boring roofs.
>
> ...

The road which those men cannot find is the road of meditation. The salvation for them is in "hair." Hair, according to Bly, stands for the
mammal, for mother consciousness, for sexual life. Men should be able
to move into the mammal part of the brain, where there is located "a
sense of community: love of women, of children, of the neighbor, the

---

1 See below, pp. 167-171, for a more detailed interpretation.
2 Sleepers, p. 8. See also below, p. 115.
3 Robert Bly in an interview conducted by the author, June 27, 1974.
4 Sleepers, pp. 10-12. See also below, pp. 199-200, for a more detailed
interpretation.

idea of brotherhood, care for the community, or for the country."[1]

"Meeting the Man Who Warns Me"[2] is not only about the need of meditation, nor only an admonition to meditation: it conveys the experience
of meditation. It becomes an under-water journey "far down the damp steps
of the Tigris," a voyage of the unconscious. The poet experiences both
light and darkness, and the voyage ends in a vision of the road ahead:

> . . .
> seeing the light given off under the door by shining
>   hair.
>
> . . .
>
> I look back, it is like the blind spot in a car.
> So much just beyond the reach of our eyes,
> what tramples the grasses while the horses are asleep,
> the hoof marks all around the cave mouth...
> what slips in under the door at night, and lies exhausted
>   on the floor in the morning.
>
> . . .
>
> When I was alone, for three years, alone,
> I passed under the earth through the nightwater,
> I was for three days inside a warm-blooded fish.
> 'Purity of heart is to will one thing.'
> I saw the road..." "Go on! Go on!"
> . . .

But seeing and traveling the road of inwardness and meditation are
not enough. The meditator, the poet, must find and bring back something
for the outer world. "In that sphere he finds strange plants and curious
many-eyed creatures which he brings back with him. This half-visible
psychic life he entangles in his language."[3] Frustration sets in, however,
when the poet cannot make the outer world understand:

> . . .
> I am on the road, the next instant in the ditch, face
>   down on the earth,
> wasting energy talking to idiots.[4]
> . . .
>
> What I have written is not good enough.
> Who does it help?
> I am ashamed sitting on the edge of my bed.[5]

---

1 Robert Bly, "The Three Brains," The Seventies, Vol. 1 (Spring, 1972),
  p. 62.
2 Sleepers, p. 56-58. See below, pp. 150-155, for a more detailed interpretation.
3 Robert Bly, "On Political Poetry." The Nation (April 24, 1967), p. 522.
4 "The Night Journey in the Cooking Pot," Sleepers, p. 62.
5 Ibid., p. 63.

Still, the final mood of the poet-traveler, of the poet-meditator, is not one of shame. At the end of the road all space is conquered; a univer sal communion takes place between those who understand "the light around the body," those whose "faces shine with the darkness reflected from the Tigris."[1]

> Hands rush toward each other through miles of space.
> All the sleepers in the world join hands.[2]

The Concept of Time

It was the significance that Bly found in the concept of time that made him rearrange his poems for the British edition of Silence in the Snowy Fields. The result of the rearrangement is a traditional frame-work in which the seasons symbolize the life-cycle, and the times of the day reflect the poet's moods. In his use of the seasons of the year and the times of the day Bly more frequently turns to "fall" and "winter" than to "spring" and "summer", and more frequently to "night" than to any other time of the day. "Dusk" and "dawn" run seconds in the use of times of the day. Thus, it seems that periods of darkness and of transi-tion from darkness to light and from light to darkness prevail in Bly's poetry. His use of the names of months also confirms this. November is mentioned more often than any other month. September comes second. Both are periods of transition from light toward darkness. In my discussion of the concept of time I will start with simple poems in which dawn and dusk bring out certain moods, and progress to poems in which the distor-tion of time and the mixing of past and present serve a special purpose, and finally to poems in which night prevails, night and darkness often being the symbols of the dark passage leading to a new life - a new dawn - thus, closing the circle.

Bly's dawn poems are often filled with joy, as is the Whitmanesque "Poem in Three Parts,"[3] the first stanza of which overflows with an en-joyment of life, of the body, and of Nature:

> Oh, on an early morning I think I shall live forever!
> I am wrapped in my joyful flesh,
> As the grass is wrapped in its clouds of green.

---

1 "Water Drawn Up Into the Head," Sleepers, p. 67.
2 Ibid. (The last two lines of the last poem of Sleepers Joining Hands).
3 Silence, p. 21.

The picture of dawn in "Getting up Early"[1] renders color and light directly as the poet sees them in the sky, in the water of the well, and over
the trees. The climax of the poem comes in stanza 3 in which the word
"dawn" occurs and a personificaiton of it is well integrated with the rest
of the poem:

> I am up early. The box-elder leaves have fallen.
> The eastern sky is the color of March.
> The sky has spread out over the world like water.
> The bootlegger and his wife are still asleep.
>
> I saw the light first from the barn well.
> The cold water fell into night-chilled buckets,
> Deepening to the somber blue of the southern sky.
> Over the new trees, there was a strange ligth in the
>   east.
>
> The light was dawn. Like a man who has come home
> After seeing many dark rivers, and will soon go again,
> The dawn stood there with a quiet gaze;
> Our eyes met through the top leaves of the young ash.

The personification of dawn brings out the poet's sensitivity and openness
toward the beauty of nature before the last stanza gives his reaction to
the fickleness of beautiful moments:

> Dawn has come. The clouds floating in the east have
>   turned white.
> The fence posts have stopped being a part of the darkness.
> The depth has disappeared from the puddles on the ground.
> I look up angrily at the light.

These two poems clearly belong to Bly's early period of personal and
descriptive poetry. A later dawn poem called "With a Naked Girl, up to
See the Spring Dawn"[2] is a poem of the same type, conveying an unmistak-
able joy through description, but it is descriptive in a surrealistic
way that tends toward mysticism. The surrealistic overtones lie in the
breaking down of barriers between the dead and the live world, and between reality and dreams:

> A flower moves in the wind by the ocean.
> A lion comes down; the sun rolls itself in smoke;
> Beyond the reefs green fire is dancing over the water.
>
> The drowned ship rises;
> The tiny shells are clinging on frond and tendril.
> The dead give out a cry of rejoicing!

---

1 *Silence*, p. 39.
2 *Kayak* 2 (1965), p. 30.

> Come to the window, sweet,
> The horse chestnut tree is in bloom.

At dawn Nature displays its fullness of life, lays open its sadness for humanity, and becomes part of the poet's emotional experience, as expressed in "Poem against the Rich":[1]

> Each day I live, each day the sea of light
> Rises, I seem to see
> The tear inside the stone
> As if my eyes were gazing beneath the earth.
> The rich man in his red hat
> Cannot hear
> The weeping in the pueblos of the lily,
> Or the dark tears in the shacks of the corn.
> Each day the sea of light rises
> I hear the sad rustle of the darkened armies,
> Where each man weeps, and the plaintive
> Orisons of the stones.
> The stones bow as the saddened armies pass.

The poet's fascination with the transitional moment is noticeable also in his descriptions of dusk. How short the duration of dusk is and how quickly the evening comes is brought out through personifying imagery in "Surprised by Evening":[2]

> . . .
>
> The evening arrives; we look up and it is there,
> It has come through the nets of the stars,
> Through the tissues of the grass,
> Walking quietly over the asylums of the waters.
>
> . . .

In "Fall" [3] the arrival of dusk turns the farmer's thoughts toward death:

> . . .
>
> The dusk has come, a glow in the west, as if seen
> through the isinglass on old coal stoves, and the cows
> stand around the barn door; now the farmer looks up at
> the paling sky reminding him of death, . . .

In "Sunset at a Lake"[4] dusk is characterized in the first lines by drowsiness and calm. But the calm becomes "inhospitable," and something in-

---

1 _Silence_, p. 27. See also below, p. 99.
2 Ibid., p. 15.
3 Ibid., p. 18. (It is called "October Evening in Minnesota" in the British edition.)
4 Ibid., p. 17.

visible rules the scene as "viscous darkness" and troubled cries make
themselves known. Even the weeds shudder from loneliness as the life-
giving forces withdraw:

> The sun is sinking. Here on the pine-haunted bank, the
> mosquitoes fly around drowsily, and moss stands out as
> if it wanted to speak. Calm falls on the lake, which
> now seems heavier and inhospitable. Far out, rafts of
> ducks drift like closed eyes, and a thin line of silver
> caused by something invisible slowly moves toward
> shore in the viscous darkness under the southern bank.
> Only a few birds, the troubled ones, speak to the darken-
> ing roof of earth; small weeds stand abandoned, the
> clay is sending her gifts back to the center of the
> earth.

Bly's dusk poems often have a sinister and ominous ring to them, as in
the uncanny description of the sunsets of the shortening fall days in
"The Clear Air of October":[1]

>   . . .
> And I know the sun is sinking down great stairs,
> Like an executioner with a great blade walking into
>   a cellar,
> And the gold animals, the lions, and the zebras, and
>   the pheasants,
> Are waiting at the head of the stairs with robbers'
>   eyes.

This is the last stanza of a poem about fall turning into winter, a poem
that is built almost entirely of images. The leaves falling are seen as
gold wings without birds, and the cold makes the water solid. Cold shadows
falling for miles, crossing lawns and the doors of Catholic churches, forebode the winter darkness which is likened to a horse riding eastward carrying a thin man with no coat. Everything in the poem is experienced through
the poet's consciousness. He introduces himself several times in phrases
like "I can see," "I can feel," and "I know." The cricket's singing
appears to give him joy at first, but then the shadows, the darkness, and
the creatures with robbers' eyes take over, and the final note seems to be
one of fear.

In three short poems, published in Epoch in 1963, dusk, or the time
when "grass darkens," influences the atmosphere noticably. "At the Ranch"[2]
is a poem ominous of evil, in which weird happenings forebode disaster,
and men on horseback are seen in distant and dark places, their identi-

---

1 Silence, p. 52.
2 Epoch, 13:1 (Fall, 1963), p. 42.

ties and their errands as dim and enigmatic as the time of the day:

> Inscriptions on gravestones mysteriously disappear.
> Many men at different places the same night
> See the same figure slipping form the stable;
> The ministers are fleeing to the mountains.
> Horsemen suddenly appear on the bluffs at dusk
> At some isolated place, far out in the dark plains.
> The sun will rise tomorrow on smoking ruins,
> Then a long ride in the country, passing under
>   ominous timbers.

In "Supper,"[1] in which the time is not only dusk but also night, the atmo
phere is one of depression:

> Grass darkens in the ditches in towns without movie
>   houses
> Where the train sweeps through still hunting for free
>   land
> And the cornstalks let out slow cries.
> The grocery man walks out at night on his lawn,
> And suddenly feels the pressure of the sky -
> The hands inside him pushing out fall back
> And he returns and eats a meal in total silence.

In "Dusk in the Sixties"[2], though the word "dusk" is mentioned only in th
title, it is related to the atmosphere of grief. Again dusk is the time
when evil forces are abroad:

> Fish dart out from under rocks that resemble human
>   faces.
> Grocers lose their buoyancy, their feathers clogged
>   with oil,
> And drown in the spring rivers. There is a terrible
>   grief
> In the small hair along the necks of men in churches:
> The grief of those shut out from the castle forever
> As night comes, and the countryside full of evil
>   knights
> On big-kneed horses....

These three poems were written during the time when Bly's social awareness was beginning to show more and more. In "The Executive's Death,"[3]
the introductory poem of The Light around the Body, the last five lines
convey a similar atmosphere by invoking a dusk filled with sighs:

---

1 Epoch, 13:1 (Fall, 1963), p. 42.
2 Ibid.
3 Light, p. 3.

> . . .
> Commuters arrive in Hartford at dusk like moles
> Or hares flying from a fire behind them,
> And the dusk in Hartford is full of their sighs;
> Their trains come through the air like a dark music,
> Like the sound of horns, the sound of thousands of
>   small wings.

In an early version of this poem, called "Merchants have Multiplied,"[1] it
is insurance men who arrive at dusk in Hartford - Hartford being the home
city of many insurance companies. This change again shows the extension of
Bly's perspective: specific nouns give way to more general terms, thus
strengthening the impact of the theme of gloom and loneliness both in
life and in death.[2]

Bly's frequent use of dawn and dusk - like his use of spring and
fall - also implies the importance of a middle state, an absence of borders and barriers. This transitional state, of significance in many poems,
is brought out in different ways, not always by the use of words denoting
time. I think that a middle state is suggested in "Old Boards"[3] in which
the poet seems to find meaning in contrasts. In the first stanza, boards,
dry and eternal, are seen on the ground, which is wet and muddy. In the
second stanza the contrast is between ocean and land and the boards serve
as mediators:

> II
> This is the wood one sees on the decks of ocean
>   ships,
> Wood that carries us far form land,
> . . .

In the final stanza the boards are likened to a man with a romantic
spirit, who lives his simple everyday life and has his own dreams at the
same time:

> III
> This wood is like a man who has a simple life,
> Living through the spring and winter on the ship of
>   his own desire.
> He sits on dry wood surrounded by half-melted snow
> As the rooster walks away springily over the dampened
>   hay.

The half-melted snow, illustrating a condition neither solid nor liquid,
and suggesting a time half-way between winter and spring, emphasizes the

---

1 Chelsea, 8 (Oct. 1960), p. 64.
2 See above, pp. 27-28, and below, pp. 174-175.
3 Silence, p. 57.

transitional stage which in this poem would refer to the situation of a
romantic who lives in a world where reality and dream blend and influence
each other, the reality being the world of the rooster and the dream
world the ocean-going ship. T. S. Eliot describes this stage in Four
Quartets:

> Between melting and freezing
> The soul's sap quivers. [1]

The creativity of this energy-loaded transitional stage is effec-
tuated in "Moving Inward at Last," [2] in which contrasts meet and bring
about a union of outer and inner life, making possible the flow of the
unconscious. The contrasts could be seen as masculine and feminine symbols, which in Bly's poetry symbolize in turn the outward and the inward
mind. [3] The bull and the mountain, the male symbols, are shut out from the
fragments of former life that are preserved in the cave, the female symbol. [4] The mediator in this case is the fire which changes everything into
water, the symbol of the unconscious:

> The dying bull is bleeding on the mountain!
> But inside the mountain, untouched
> By the blood,
> There are antlers, bits of oak bark,
> Fire, herbs are thrown down.
>
> When the smoke touches the roof of the cave,
> The green leaves burst into flame,
> The air of night changes to dark water,
> The mountains alter and become the sea.

The poem seems to me to convey ideas similar to those in Yeats's "The Second Coming." The development of outwardness is like the widening gyre
which keeps expanding until it collapses and something extraordinary
happens. Also in Yeats's poem there is a union of opposites as the beast
goes toward Bethlehem, where some kind of new life is to be born.

In "Looking at Some Flowers" [5] a fusion of light and shadow, of life
and death, reveals the beauty of the transitional stage, what Piccione
calls "the in-between experience." [6] This stage is also shown as a new

---

1 T. S. Eliot, Four Quartets (New York, N. Y., 1943),"Little Gidding,"
   ll. 11-12.
2 Light, p. 57.
3 Cf. below, p. 181.
4 See also below, p. 141, and p. 156, about the cave as a container of
   darkness.
5 Light, p. 50.
6 Piccione, p. 98.

reality, created in a union of plant and animal life, and as a domain,
alternately dry and watery, land and sea:

> Light is around the petals, and behind them:
> Some petals are living on the other side of the light.
> Like sunlight drifting onto the carpet
> Where the casket stands, not knowing which world it
>   is in.
> And fuzzy leaves, hair growing from some animal
> Buried in the green trenches of the plant.
> Or the ground this house is on,
> Only free of the sea for five or six thousand years.

Thus, "One thing is also another thing," as Bly phrases this surrealistic
idea in "Remembering in Oslo the Old Picture of the Magna Carta."[1] The fact
that any length of time may have passed since one thing was another thing
is of no importance. All times, and consequently many different events,
may be experienced at the same time; past time is present time, or as
Whitman says, "Past and present and future are not disjoined but joined."[2]
One person is also another person:

> The girl in a house dress, pushing open the window,
> Is also the fat king sitting under the oak tree,
> And the garbage men, thumping their cans, are
> Crows still cawing,
> And the nobles are offering the sheet to the king.
> One thing is also another thing, and the doomed
>   galleons,
> Hung with trinkets, hove by the coast, and in the
>   blossoms
> Of trees are still sailing on their long voyage from
>   Spain;
> I too am still shocking grain, as I did as a boy,
>   dog tired,
> And my great-grandfather steps on his ship.

A two-fold time experience is presented in a still earlier unpublished poem called "What Burns and is Consumed."[3] Negative and positive
elements balance each other and form a unit, which is represented in the
image of the tide in the third line. This theme is intensified by the reference in the same stanza to Christ's denunciation of his own family. In
the second stanza the two phases of the tide, the rising and the falling,
are exemplified and experienced simultaneously as love and non-love, and
as life embittered by thoughts of death:

---

1 _Silence_, p. 30.
2 Walt Whitman, "Preface to 1855 Edition 'Leaves of Grass,'" _Leaves of Grass and Selected Prose_ (New York, N. Y., 1949), p. 460.
3 MA thesis, p. 8.

You wonder why we take so many trips.
Pausing, I fold my hands, and turn away--
I speak of vegetation and the tide--
But when December rides the mountain trees,
And breaks the seas past any strength of ships,
Now I remember Christ the crucified,
Who hurt his Mary, could not help but say
At feast: "What have I to do with thee?"
Leaving for Jerusalem. This intensity
A Baptist said was set in every knee
By that pale-headed shape behind the rise,
When life picked out the thorns form Adam's eyes.

There are peeling ferns inside Skid-Row
Gospel missions in New Orleans,
Where after twenty years, a woman weeps,
Finding a man whose hands were sealed with rings.
"Still love me?" "I do. Forget it."
He left and walked to where he sleeps
Where he eats his pork and beans from cans
And keeps a whore who has no teeth. These things
I heard. Learn them. They hold some belief.
Some day we both will die. That is another grief.
That cannot be atoned in Copley Square
With bitter kisses in the Christmas air.

Pozzo in Samuel Beckett's _Waiting for Godot_ expresses similarly, but more
poignantly, the closeness in time of life and death:

Have you not done tormenting me with your accursed time!
It's abominable! When! When! One day, is that not enough
for you, one day he went dumb, one day I went blind,
one day we'll go deaf, one day we were born, one day
we shall die, the same day, the same second, is that
not enough for you? They give birth astride of a
grave, the light gleams an instant, then it's night
once more.[1]

In Bly's poem the general setting also supports the theme: December -
Christmas time - brings the worst storms, and the poet remembers "Christ
the Crucified" instead of Christ newly born. The thought of death is
always present and makes time always one and the same, as in T. S. Eliot'
Four Quartets:

Time past and time future
What might have been and what has been
Point to one end, which is always present.[2]

In many poems the blending of times is effected by means of objects

---

1 Samuel Beckett, _Waiting for Godot_ (New York, N. Y., 1954), p. 57.
2 T. S. Eliot, _Four Quartets_: "Burnt Norton," ll. 44-46.

in the poet's surroundings used as symbols of past and present time. For
Bly, then - as for Apollinaire - the "point of departure is a factual
event or concrete detail of the color of the times."[1] In the last stanza
of "Awakening"[2] a glimpse of a city center with its traffic around a
statue of Lincoln triggers the poet's imagination.[3] However, it is not
just the starting-point that links Bly to Apollinaire in this stanza
but also the theme of life and death mingled, "blossoms and rotting
logs" staining the same water, the living and the dead partaking in the
same awakening, and the poem moving into mysticism. Apollinaire in "La
Maison des Morts" similarly combines "the two spheres of life and death,
and he allows his living and dead creatures to intermingle and coexperi-
ence not abstract but very concrete sensations."[4] In making the moments
of birth and death identical Bly apprehends time as T. S. Eliot does in
Four Quartets:

> The end is where we start from.
>
> . . .
>
> We die with the dying:
> See, they depart, and we go with them.
> We are born with the dead:
> See, they return, and bring us with them.[5]

Another early poem in which the poet's imagination is triggered by an
outer event, and in which the past and the present blend until time
stands still, is "Hearing Men Shout at Night on MacDougal Street":[6]

> How strange to awake in a city,
> And hear grown men shouting in the night!
> On the farm the darkness wins,
> And the small ones nestle in their graves of cold:
> Here is a boiling that only exhaustion subdues,
> A moiling of muddy waters,
> On which the voices of white men feed!
>
> The street is a sea, and mud boils up
> When the anchor is lifted, for now at midnight is
> there about to sail
> The first New England slave-ship with the Negroes in
> the hold.

---

1 Anna Balakian, Surrealism: The Road to the Absolute, p. 92.
2 Silence, p. 26.
3 For quotation see above, p. 43.
4 Anna Balakian, Surrealism: The Road to the Absolute, p. 91.
5 T. S. Eliot, Four Quartets: "Little Gidding," ll. 216, 228-231.
6 Silence, (British edition), p. 29, and, slightly changed, Light, p. 21.

About the circumstances around this poem Bly says,

> Before we had any children my wife and I used to go to
> New York in March every year after having spent the
> winter on the farm. We stayed at a hotel on MacDougal
> Street and 8th Street. After we had gone to bed and
> were trying to sleep, people were screaming out in the
> street, and I could distinguish between black men's
> voices and white men's voices. Black men's voices are
> richer. White men's voices are weaker. I couldn't
> sleep. I got up and wrote a poem. The voices in the
> street made me think of how the negroes first were
> brought to this country. It wasn't the Southerners
> who brought the slaves, it was the Christians in
> New England who bought them in Africa and sold them to
> the Southerners, and the slave-ship is still leaving from
> Africa because in this country there has been no develop-
> ment since that moment.[1]

The technique of catching a detail in his surroundings and associ-
ating it with an event or a person in American history, in order to break
down time barriers and launch criticism against the American society in
his own time, is used in several other poems as, for example, in "Poem
against the British":[2]

                          I
        The wind through the box-elder trees
        Is like rides at dusk on a white horse,
        Wars for your country, and fighting the British.

                          II
        I wonder if Washington listened to the trees.
        All morning I have been sitting in grass,
        Higher than my eyes, beneath trees,
        And listening upward, to the wind in leaves.
        Suddenly I realize there is one thing more:
        There is also the wind through the high grass.

                          III
        There are palaces, boats, silence among white buildings,
        Iced drinks on marble tops, among cool rooms:
        It is good also to be poor, and listen to the wind.

This poem was simply called "Wind" when it was first published,[3] a title
that stresses the weight of the main image of the poem: the real wind in
the trees and in the grass around the poet, the hostile wind blowing
against the British, probably referring to the War of Independence, and
finally a cold wind of criticism against the status symbols of a modern
society.

---

1 Interview, April 13, 1973, conducted by the author.
2 Silence, p. 28.
3 The Paris Review (Winter/Spring, 1962), p. 19.

This technique of anchoring the poem in the present, while using history to criticize modern society and modern politics, is mostly found in the earlier poems. In The Light around the Body, in which the poet's social and political engagement is all-important, we find this technique only in "At a March against the Vietnam War."[1] The poet, taking part in the march, looks down and sees feet moving. With his inner eye he sees something else moving in the darkness: "a boat, / Covered with machine guns." This darkness is the same as

> . . . that darkness among pine boughs
> That the Puritans brushed
> As they went out to kill turkeys.

Again, the simultaneous use of the present and the past conveys the idea of no change, no development since the birth of the nation, only in this case Bly is more outspoken and makes a smarting accusation:

> We have carried around this cup of darkness
> We have longed to pour it over our heads
>
> We make war
> Like a man anointing himself

However, the poems in which the harshest criticism is launched, are not anchored in the present. In "After the Industrial Revolution, All Things Happen At Once"[2] history speaks for itself, and the result is a dense poem with the familiar theme of no change, no development in the U.S.A.:

> Now we enter a strange world, where the Hessian
>   Christmas
> Still goes on, and Washington has not reached the
>   other shore;
> The Whiskey Boys
> Are gathering on the meadows of Pennsylvania
> And the Republic is still sailing on the open sea.
>
> I saw a black angel in Washington dancing
> On a barge, saying, Let us now divide kennel dogs
> And hunting dogs; Henry Cabot Lodge, in New York,
> Talking of sugar cane in Cuba; Ford,
> In Detroit, drinking mother's milk;
> Henry Cabot Lodge, saying, "Remember the Maine!"
> Ford saying, "History is bunk!"
> And Wilson saying, "What is good for General Motors..."

---

1 Light, pp. 34-35.
2 Ibid., p. 29. See also below, p. 109.

> Who is it, singing? Don't you hear singing?
> It is the dead of Cripple Creek;
> Coxey's army
> Like turkeys are singing from the tops of trees!
> And the Whiskey Boys are drunk outside Philadelphia.

Here Bly denies the reality of important historic events. The battle at
Trenton in December, 1776, never took place. "The Whiskey Insurrection"
in Pennsylvania in 1794 is only being planned. The S. S. Republic was
never rescued in 1909. Everything stands still as in Emanuel Leutze's
painting "Crossing the Delaware River." "Washington has not reached the
other shore." The politicians are the same as those of generations ago and
are involved in the same kind of politics. Henry Cabot Lodge was involved
in the Cuban War in 1898; his grandson, Henry Cabot Lodge, Jr., was
ambassador to South Vietnam during two different periods of time during
the Vietnam War. The "black angel in Washington" is Charles E. Wilson[1]
who talked, during times of unemployment, about two different groups of
workers, those who were looking for jobs and those who were waiting to
be fed, which enraged the workers. "Coxey's army" refers to an uprising
and march on Washington, D. C.,in connection with unemployment in 1894,
and readers are probably expected to recall periods of unemployment in
modern times. Charles E. Wilson, who had been President of General
Motors, always gave General Motors what it wanted. When he was criticized
for it, he used to answer, "What is good for General Motors is good for
the United States." What Bly wants to suggest is that the politicians of
our time probably would think along the same lines. History ought to
serve as a warning. If we tried, we could still hear the singing of those
killed at Cripple Creek, Colorado, during the violence attending the
strikes there in 1894 and in 1903-04.[2]

The poem "As the Asian War Begins"[3] does not really contain any historical references except for the word "conestogas," which, with its old-
fashioned connotations, effaces differences in time, reveals the antiquity of the theme stated in the first line, and makes powerful the
poet's request at the end of the poem:

---

1   Secretary of Defense in President Eisenhower's Cabinet.
2   Wosk mentions some of these historic events in her thesis but for a
    different purpose than mine: "the rationalizing words of the business-
    men and statesmen contrast with the lusty energy of the historical
    rebels" (pp. 63-64).
3   Light, p. 33.

There are longings to kill that cannot be seen,
Or are seen only by a minister who no longer believes
in God,
Living in his parish like a crow in its nest.

And there are flowers with murky centers,
Impenetrable, ebony, basalt...

Conestogas go past, over the Platte, their contents
Hidden from us, murderers riding under the canvas...

Give us a glimpse of what we cannot see,
Our enemies, the soldiers and the poor.

The conestogas contain dark secrets. In the long anti-war poem "The Teeth
Mother Naked at Last" they are symbols of lies:

* * *

The ministers lie, the professors lie, the television
lies, the priests lie....
These lies mean that the country wants to die.
Lie after lie starts out into the prairie grass,
like enormous trains of Conestoga wagons....[1]

In "Turning Away from Lies,"[2] however, the poet conveys a sense that he
has seen what is under the canvas. He understands the old language of
history and is filled with grief:

1

If we are truly free, and live in a free country,
When shall I be without this heaviness of mind?
When shall I have peace? Peace this way and peace
that way?
I have already looked beneath the street
And there I saw the bitter waters going down,
The ancient worms eating up the sky.

Here again one single word - "ancient" - obliterates differences in time.
History cannot help us. Nor is there an after-life:

2

Christ did not come to redeem our sins
The Christ Child was not obedient to his parents
The Kingdom of Heaven does not mean the next life
No one in business can be a Christian
The two worlds are both in this world

We are all members of the same society of saints and thieves, the saints,
filled with emotional energy, representing one extreme, and the thieves,

---

1 Teeth Mother, p. 10. Wosk makes similar comments on the Conestogas
   (pp. 64-65 of her thesis).
2 Light, p. 43. See below, p. 131, for an interpretation in terms of a
   rebirth experience.

as outsiders in isolation, representing the other:

> ·3·
> The saints rejoice out loud upon their beds!
> Their song moves through the troubled sea
> The way the holy tortoise moves
> From dark blue into troubled green,
> Or ghost crabs move above the dolomite.
> The thieves are crying in the wild asparagus.

The idea that there is and will be no change, that one time equals another, is implicit in the deliberate imitation of the title of a poem by Shelley[1] in "Written in Dejection near Rome."[2] Employing the idea of time standing still or repeating itself, Bly here turns against the affluent society:

> What if these long races go on repeating themselves
> century after century, living in houses painted light
>   colors
> on the beach,
> black spiders,
> having turned pale and fat,
> men walking thoughtfully with their families,
> vibrations
> of exhausted violin-bodies,
> horrible eternities of sea pines!
> . . .

Thus, through surrealistic images the poet wants to make us aware of what is happening, but what only a few notice. Those who notice will break away from the others, and two groups will be formed:

> Some men cannot help but feel it,
> they will abandon their· homes
> to live on rafts tied together on the ocean;
> those on shore will go inside tree trunks,
> surrounded by bankers whose fingers have grown long
>   and slender,
> piercing through rotting bark for their food.

The first three lines of the last section quoted seem to contain the same idea as the "small colonies of the saved" in "Those Being Eaten by America."[3] In an interview Bly comments on these lines:

> Yes, I believe that the U.S. is going to break up
> into two groups. The military-industrial problem
> is not going to be solved. We will have 10% of the
> population living in greater selfishness than any
> other human beings in history.
> . . .

---

1 "Stanzas Written in Dejection near Naples"
2 Light, p. 15.
3 Ibid., p. 14.

OUR EARTHLY EXISTENCE

> The other community, without fossil fuels,
> will be interested in charity and some kind of spiri-
> tual life. And this will probably go on for a thousand
> years.[1]

His belief that this will go on for a thousand years is also expressed in
the two poems: as "The long dead running over the fields" in "Those Being
Eaten by America" and as "long races . . . repeating themselves century
after century" in "Written in Dejection Near Rome."

The idea that the past is alive in the present and that history is a
warning is expounded in a quite early poem called "Looking Backward":[2]

> If we go back, if we walk into the old darkness,
> And find Washington brooding under the long bridges,
> We will find the dead still ablaze in the anguish of
>   the egg,
> The screams of Indians echoing in the compression
>   chambers of shells,
> Or disappearing into the tunnels of flashlights,
> Mexicans falling, and soap buried alive.
>
> Strange sugarbeets are living deep in the history
>   books,
> Sugarbeets that give blood, stones
>
> That migrate, leaving cries among the stars,
> Frozen ward-heelers crawling in the icy gutters.
> To say our history is liberty after liberty is a lie:
> We have a history of horse-beaters with red moustaches
> Knocked down by a horse and bitten.
>
> We have a history of a wife howling at a husband
> To buy more, and buy more land, later
> Rationing him to a pint of whiskey and five cigars a
>   day;
> Of land pyramided with mortgages and lost,
> Of a dark fire burning soddenly in the finger tips,
> Fingers that turn over deeds, fingers on fire,
> Fingers that would light the sky if lifted at night.

The idea of moving backwards in time is sometimes connected with a
death-wish caused by grief. In "The President about to Address the Nation
in the Eighth Year of the Vietnam War"[3] the land itself is grief-stricken:

> . . .
> America lies out flat, waiting...

---

1 Franz Allbert Richter and Lew Hyde, "An Interview with Robert Bly," *The
   Lamp and the Spine*, No. 3 (Winter, 1972), p. 64. See also above, p. 37.
2 *The Paris Review*, (Winter/Spring, 1964), p. 107. See also below,
   pp. 176-177.
3 *The Tennessee Poetry Journal*, 4:1 (Fall, 1970), p. 5.

> Badgers and mink are disappearing into their holes.
> The shores press forward into the Indian water.
> The whole continent longs to get back into the lake.
> . . .

The long poem "The Teeth Mother Naked at Last" is permeated by a similar death-wish on the part of the poet, on the part of those who understand that it is the old desire to kill that drives a rich country to carry on devastating wars. First the desire to kill is expressed in strong imagery:

> It is a desire to eat death,
> to gobble it down,
> to rush on it like a cobra with mouth open,
>
> It's a desire to take death inside,
> to feel it burning inside, pushing out velvety hairs,
> like a clothes brush in the intestines
>
> This is the thrill that leads the President on to lie
> . . .
>
> This is only the deep longing for death.
> . . .
>
> Do not be angry at the President - he is longing to
>   take in his hand
> the locks of death hair -
> to meet his own children sleeping or unborn....
> He is drifting sideways toward the dusty places[1]

Then the grief and the death-wish of those who understand are described; they wish to escape, to go backward in time:

>   IV
>
> . . .
> We all feel like tires being run down roads under
>   heavy cars.
>
> . . .
>
> I know that books are tired of us.
> I know they are chaining the Bible to chairs.
> Books don't want to remain in the same room with us
>   anymore.
> New Testaments are escaping!.... Dressed as women...
>   they go off after dark.
> And Plato! Plato... Plato wants to go backwards...
> He wants to hurry back up the river of time, so he
>   can end as some blob of seaflesh rotting
>   on an Australian beach.[2]

---

1 <u>Teeth Mother</u>, pp. 10-12,
2 Ibid., pp. 16-17.

VI

. . .

If one of those children came toward me with both
        hands
in the air, fire rising along both elbows,
I would suddenly go back to my animal brain,[1]

. . .

VII

I want to sleep awhile in the rays of the sun slanting
        over the snow.
Don't wake me.
Don't tell me how much grief there is in the leaf with
        its natural oils.
Don't tell how many children have been born with stumpy
        feet
all those years we lived in Augustine's shadow.[2]

This death-wish is part of a Surrealist mysticism; it is what Ihab Hassan in his book The Dismemberment of Orpheus calls "the Orphic unity of man and nature, life and death"[3] or "the Orphic impulse among Surrealists."[4] Marcel Raymond describes the same mysticism as "a deep nostalgia, and a desperate regret at the impossibility of going back to the 'source' where potentialities exist side by side without excluding one another, to the chaos preceding all determination, to the central, anonymous, and infinite focus of universe, . . ."[5]

Thus, both in the desire to kill and in the poet's death-wish there is an evasion of reality. But when man is actually face to face with death, as is the sergeant from North Carolina in the first part of "The Teeth Mother Naked at Last," there is no escape, neither to "the past-tunnels,"[6] into which he looks at the moment of death, nor to any afterlife, because "the mansions of the dead are empty."[7] At the moment of death, time is narrowed down to "now" and "there is hardly time for good-bye."[8] In this long anti-war poem Bly wants to lay bare the forces that drive human beings to carry on wars. He wants to show us the part of our unconscious where these forces lodge, i.e. he wants to show us the "teeth-mother" - also called the "death-mother"[9] - "naked at last."

---

1 Teeth Mother, p. 20.
2 Ibid., p. 21. See below, Chapter IV, for an interpretation of the whole Teeth Mother poem.
3 Ihab Hassan, The Dismemberment of Orpheus (New York, N. Y., 1971), p. 73.
4 Ibid., p. 74.
5 Marcel Raymond, From Baudelaire to Surrealism, (University Paperback, London, 1970), p. 268.
6 Teeth Mother, p. 6.
7 Ibid.
8 Ibid.
9 Cf. below, Chapter IV.

The poet's first step in this stripping bare is to focus our attention
on the "now" of horrible warfare and then to keep referring to it all
through the poem as a contrast to the dishonest lives of politicians
and the escapist dreams of philosophers. Thus, in this poem, as in others
travels in time serve the purpose of bringing us back to here and now,
and of showing us how history repeats itself "again and again."

> Let us drive cars
> up
> the light beams
> to the stars...
>
> And return to earth crouched inside the drop of sweat
> that falls again and again
> from the chin of the Protestant tied in the fire.[1]

The notion of the past within the present, the union of all times,
is in evidence in many of Bly's poems, be they personal, political, or
visionary. This union is sometimes conveyed through symbols. In "Sitting
on Some Rocks in Shaw Cove, California"[2] a bird brings the poet a message
from long ago, just as in Pablo Neruda's poem "Letter to Miguel Otero
Silva, in Caracas."[3] Neruda says,

> . . .
> Have you ever spent a whole day close to sea birds,
> watching how they fly? They seem
> to be carrying the letters of the world to their
>   destinations.
> The pelicans go by like ships of the wind,
> other birds go by like arrows, carrying
> messages from dead kings, viceroys,
> . . .

In Bly's poem the poet spends a day in a cliff-hollow, surrounded by
fossils and furry shells, aware of the breathing of the sea and the
spiritual life of the rocks. Then the messenger comes:

> . . .
> A bird with long wings comes flying toward me in the
> dusk, pumping just over the darkening waves. He has
> flown around the whole planet, it has taken him centu-
> ries. He returns to me the lean-legged runner laughing
> as he runs through the stringy grasses, and gives back
> to me my buttons, and the soft sleeves of my sweater.

---

1   <u>Teeth Mother</u>, p. 22.
2   <u>The Morning Glory</u>, p. 19.
3   <u>Neruda and Vallejo: Selected Poems</u>. (Ed. Robert Bly) (Boston, 1971),
    p. 119.

In other poems other things and creatures in Nature awaken the poet's
feelings of affinity with times bygone as in "Some November Privacy
Poems": [1]

* * *

> How marvellous to look out and see
> the boulders
> that have been gloomy since the earth began
> now with a faint dusting of snow.

* * *

and in "A Doing Nothing Poem": [2]

> After walking about all afternoon
> barefoot,
> I have grown long and transparent....
> ... like the seaslug
> who has lived along doing nothing
> for eighteen thousand years!

Thus, the influence of the past on our lives must be seen as an
essential element in Bly's poems. In "Water Under the Earth"[3] we see this
influence as "a faint glow in the dead leaves." Modern man tries hard to
get rid of his past:

> . . .
> I see how carefully I have covered my tracks as I
>   wrote,
> how well I brushed over the past with my tail.
> . . .

But the past is everywhere:

> . . .
> I enter rooms full of photographs of the dead.
> . . .
>
> I see faces looking at me in the shallow waters
> where I have thrown them down.
> Mother and father pushed into the dark.
> . . .
>
> I have piled up people like dead flies between the
>   storm window and the kitchen pane.
> So much is not spoken!
> . . .

But it is there in the unconscious and makes possible a union felt through
"all distance and time":

---

1 *Jumping*, p. 13.
2 Ibid., p. 41.
3 *Sleepers*, pp. 6-7. See also below, p. 98.

. . .
That shows how close I am to the dust that fills the
            cracks on the ocean floor,
how much I love to fly alone in the rain,
how much I love to see the jellyfish pulsing at the
            cold borders of the universe.

. . .

There is a consciousness hovering under the mind's
            feet,
advanced civilizations under the footsole,
climbing at times up on a shoelace!
It is a willow that knows of water under the earth,
I am a father who dips as he passes over underground
            rivers,
who can feel his children through all distance and
            time!

The past, the content of the unconscious, is

. . .

What cannot be remembered and cannot be forgotten,
the chaff blowing about my father's feet.[1]
. . .

The nigth is the time when the unconscious is most strongly felt:

I dream that I cannot see half of my life.
I look back, it is like the blind spot in a car.
So much just beyond the reach of our eyes,
what tramples the grasses while the horses are asleep,
the hoof marks all around the cave mouth...
what slips in under the door at night, and lies exhausted
            on the floor in the morning.[2]
. . .

This is, of course, nothing new. The myth of the night-journey is old and
much has been written about it.[3] As I have already mentioned, Bly uses
night more often than any other time of the day. The word "night" occurs
approximately 120 times in his poems, while "dusk" and "dawn," taken
together as one concept representing the trasitional moments of the day,
occur only approximately 50 times.

        One very simple night poem is a recent one, called "Pulling the
Boat up among Lake Reeds."[4] Night's meaning is its most obvious one in
this poem: night is darkness. But the darkness of night reminds the poet

---

1   "Meeting the Man Who Warns Me", Sleepers, p. 57.
2   Ibid.
3   See footnotes below, p. 128.
4   Kayak, 28 (1972), p. 54.

of other darknesses and becomes the main metaphor of the poem, at the
same time containing three disparate moments, thus making the poem
surrealistic:

> Here inside the reeds there is such thick dusk.
> Night comes first here at the shore,
> while it is still day out on the lake.
> How many other darknesses it reminds me of!
> - the moment after a child is born,
> blood pouring from the sheep's neck,
> the rocket climbing to the moon.

In "Hearing Men Shout at Night on MacDougal Street" the darkness of the
night holds dark secrets of the Puritan New Englanders.[1] In "A Man Writes
to a Part of Himself"[2] night is the time of silence and bareness; it is
almost a void:

> . . .
> Forgive me, your husband,
> On the streets of a distant city, laughing,
> With many appointments,
> Though at night going also
> To a bare room, a room of poverty,
> To sleep among a bare pitcher and basin
> In a room with no heat -
> . . .

A void is also what the dove finds in "Where We Must Look for Help":[3]

> The dove returns: it found no resting place;
> It was in flight all night above the shaken seas;
> . . .

These are the first lines of one of Bly's earliest poems, written at about
the same time as "On the Ferry Across Chesapeake Bay."[4] Both poems seem
to convey an uncertainty on the part of the poet.[5] The dove, the bird that
Noah sends from the ark, the traditional messenger bird, returns without
bringing any signs of life from the void. Instead, it is the crow, a bird
of carrion, that finds new possibilities in the muddy ground of the void:

> . . .
> The crow, the crow, the spider-colored crow,
> The crow shall find new mud to walk upon.[6]

---

1 See above, pp. 69-70.
2 Silence, p. 36. See below, pp. 175-176, for further interpretation.
3 Ibid., p. 29.
4 Ibid., p. 35.
5 Cf. above, pp. 20-21 and p. 48.
6 Cf. also above, p. 53. Cf. Lacey, pp. 41-42.

These last two lines of the poem thematically parallel two important
lines in "On the Ferry Across Chesapeake Bay":

> For though on its road the body cannot march
> With golden trumpets - it must march -

Both poems convey the urge to survive - physically and spiritually - an
urge felt by a young man and poet in a tough world. In many poems, though
the void of the night actually means a fully positive experience as in
"Love Poem"[1] where the poet - as Surrealist poets and painters often do -
allows his joyful love to suffuse common objects and circumstances in his
surroundings, in this case even the emptiness of the nigth. The privacy
of the snowy night is also precious to the poet as expressed in "Driving
to Town Late to Mail a Letter."[2]

However, above all, night is the time when mysterious things beyond
our control happen in the world of perception and in our unconscious.
Strange sounds are heard:

> . . . : the resonance of night
> Returned its grunts and whistlings on the air.[3]
> . . .

Birds that are seldom seen are heard, sounding like human voices - wise
or mad:

> . . .
> Owls talk at night, loons wheel cries through lower waters,[4]
> . . .

Dark creatures appear:

> We spent all day fishing and talking.
> At last, late at night, I sit at my desk alone,
> And rise and walk out in the summery night.
> A dark thing hopped near me in the grass.[5]
> . . .

This poem might be seen as a forerunner to "In Danger from the Outer
World."[6] At a poetry reading,[7] Bly explained the background of this latter
poem. He had read about a couple in Africa that kept a chimpanzee in a
cage. One night they heard insistent chattering from it but did not in-

---

1   Silence, p. 41. Cf. also above, p. 42, and below, p. 102.
2   Ibid., p. 38. Cf. also above, p. 20.
3   "A Missouri Traveller Writes Home: 1830", MA thesis, p. 20.
4   "Meeting the Man Who Warns Me", Sleepers, p. 56.
5   "Late at Night during a Visit of Friends," Silence, p. 58.
6   Light, p. 47.
7   In St Paul, Minnesota, on May 2, 1974.

vestigate. In the morning they found the chimpanzee dead in its cage,
killed by a python. The chimpanzee had seen the snake coming and tried
to warn other living beings. For Bly the snake in the night

> Moving over the hills on black feet,
> Living off the country,
> Leaving dogs and sheep murdered where it slept;

symbolizes the outer world bringing death to our souls if we are neg-
ligent. If we do not notice how this

> . . . shining thing, inside, that has served us well
> Shakes its bamboo bars –
> It may be gone before we wake...

This poem illustrates well the quotation from Jacob Boehme which is the
motto for this section of the book:

> O dear children, look in what a dungeon we are lying,
> in what lodging we are, for we have been captured by
> the spirit of the outward world: it is our life, for
> it nourishes and brings us up, it rules in our marrow
> and bones, in our flesh and blood, it has made our
> flesh earthly, and now death has us. [1]

The same theme is carried a little further in "Hurrying Away from the
Earth"[2] in the next section of the same book of poems. In rearranging
the poems for the British edition Bly placed this poem and "In Danger
from the Outer World" in the same section, both under the motto just
quoted. "Hurrying Away from the Earth" is filled with utter despair. The
night is dark and sinister. The only way to get away from the night,
the outer world, seems to be through death or madness:

> . . .
>
> Some men have pierced the chest with a long needle
> To stop their heart from beating any more;
> Another put blocks of ice in his bed
> So he would die, women
> Have washed their hair, and hanged themselves
> In the long braids, one woman climbed
> A high elm above her lawn,
> Opened a box, and swallowed poisonous spiders....
>
> The time for exhortation is past. I have heard
> The iron chairs scraping in asylums,
> As the cold bird hunches into the winter
> In the windy night of November.
> . . .

---

1 Light, p. 39.
2 Ibid., p. 54.

Anna Balakian in <u>The Literary Origins of Surrealism</u> discusses man's
"imprisonment on earth"[1] as a theme in Baudelaire's poetry. Time and place
are mentioned as "two of the controlling factors of nature,"[2] or as the
two elements of which this earthly prison is built - and man struggles
to break down the prison walls. Baudelaire's conclusion is similar to
Bly's: "The only way to cheat time and place, the only way to defy nature
is through the voyage into the infinite, the voyage to Death."[3] But that
death represents the unknown comes as an afterthought in Baudelaire's
poems, and so it does in the Bly poem just quoted. People do not want to
find out the secrets of the night "wheeling [a] dark wheelbarrow / All
about the plains of heaven:"[4] "Men cry when they hear stories of someone
rising from the dead."[5] They dare not find out what is in "the casket of
the sun,/ And the moon's coffin."[6]

In other night poems, less dark than "Hurrying Away from the Earth,"
night holds alternatives for those who do not want to be captured by or
remain in the prison of the outer world. The alternatives are dream and
meditation, and they are conveyed in terms of the "night journey." We
find this type of night poem in three of Bly's books. In <u>Silence in the
Snowy Fields</u> the night journey of the dream ends in joy and new life.[7]
In <u>The Light around the Body</u> the joy of the night journey is juxtaposed
with images of death.[8] In <u>Sleepers Joining Hands</u> meditation takes us on
voyages into the unconscious;[9] we lose ourselves "in the curved energy."[10]
However, as there are many other elements involved in these poems, I intend to deal with them in a special chapter.

I do not think that a discussion of the seasons of the year would
be of any additional value. The seasons do not occur so often as the
times of the day, and when they do occur, they are employed in a similar
way. Also, the seasons of the year are mentioned in connection with other
concepts and metaphors. Winter, for example, is related to the snow-
metaphor and autumn to the field-metaphor. Furthermore, autumn and spring
are transitional periods of time. Summer is very seldom used - only once

---

1 Balakian, <u>The Literary Origins of Surrealism</u>, p. 48.
2 Ibid.
3 Ibid., p. 51.
4 <u>Light</u>, p. 54.
5 Ibid.
6 Ibid.
7 See, for example, below, pp. 138-139.
8 See, for example, below, pp. 142-144.
9 See, for example, below, pp.145- 168.
10 <u>Sleepers</u>, p. 65.

is it employed in an interesting way. The phrase "summer's insanity" in
"A Caterpillar on the Desk"[1] seems to be another of Bly's surrealistic
combinations of disparate words and concepts, whereby he breaks down
barriers and creates new realities. (Of course, it could also be seen
as a transferred epithet, but I would call that a mere coincidence; conventional poetical figures are not important in Bly's poetry.) I have
used the word "surrealistic" many times in the analyses above, and we
have seen from Bly's handling of place and time that his poetry is related to Surrealism, but still, I would not call his poems Surrealistic.
In many of them he employs surrealistic techniques - not even new with
the Surrealists - to support his themes. Surrealism is for Bly one of
his creative tools, not an art for its own sake.

My next approach to Bly's poems will be through metaphors representing life energy within the setting of place and time that we have
just moved through.

The Concept of Life Energy

In many of Bly's poems Nature plays a more important role than
people do. A flow of life energy, frequently made manifest in plant
and animal life, permeates his poetry and can be experienced through
such images as trees, plants, blossoms, birds, and crickets. In a poem
called "Night"[2] several living and growing things are brought together
in an atmosphere of joy and rest to celebrated a life of which death is
seen as an integral part. The forces pulling downward toward earth are
felt by all creatures, and they intuitively give obedience to earth
in return for life-giving energy:

> I
> If I think of a horse wandering about sleeplessly
> All night on this short grass covered with moonlight,
> I feel a joy, as if I had thought
> Of a pirate ship ploughing through dark flowers.
>
> II
> The box elders around us are full of joy,
> Obeying what is beneath them.
> The lilacs are sleeping, and the plants are sleeping,
> Even the wood made into a casket is asleep.

---

1 The Morning Glory, p. 23.
2 Silence, p. 55.

III
The butterfly is carrying loam on his wings;
The toad is bearing tiny bits of granite in his skin;
The leaves at the crown of the tree are asleep
Like dark bits of earth at its root.

IV
Alive, we are like a sleek water beetle,
Skating across still water in any direction
We choose, and soon to be swallowed
Suddenly from beneath.

Lacey's interpretation of the poem[1] emphasizes the vitality gained through an interplay between surface and depth. This interplay operates on a symbolic level in Bly's more recent poems referring to the conscious and the unconscious parts of the human psyche.

In many of Bly's early poems trees are mentioned, but in most instances as parts of the background, as in "Three Kinds of Pleasures,"[2] in which they add darkness, bareness, but also dignity to the scene:

II
The darkness drifts down like snow on the picked corn-
            fields
In Wisconsin: and on these black trees
Scattered, one by one,
Through the winter fields -
. . .

. . .   III
The bare trees more dignified than ever,
Like a fierce man on his deathbed.[3]
. . .

In "At the Funeral of Great-Aunt Mary"[4] the greenness of the trees outside the church window constitutes a background of life in this world in sharp contrast to the minister's message of mansions being prepared for us in another world. In most cases, however, the trees at some point step out of their static role and become symbols. In "Hunting Pheasants in a Corn-field"[5] this process is evident: the poet is strangely drawn toward a willow tree alone in a field. The reason for this is a Baudelairean corre-

---

1 See Paul A. Lacey, The Inner War, p. 41. See also below, p. 95.
2 Silence, p. 11. See also above, p. 17.
3 See below, p. 87.
4 Silence, p. 34. See also above, p. 36.
5 Ibid., p. 14.

spondence between this tree and his inner mind:

IV
The mind has shed leaves alone for years.
It stands apart with small creatures near its roots.
I am happy in this ancient place,
A spot easily caught sight of above the corn,
If I were a young animal ready to turn home at dusk.

Often correspondences are expressed in similes as in "Three Kinds of
Pleasures" in which the tree is likened to "a fierce man on his deathbed" which conveys dignity in a most eloquent form, dignity in spite of
complete divestiture. In that poem the tree is compared to a man, while
in "Solitude Late at Night in the Woods"[1] tenor and vehicle have exchanged roles and the body is likened to a tree:

I
The body is like a November birch facing the full moon
And reaching into the cold heavens.
In these trees there is no ambition, no sodden body,
          no leaves,
Nothing but bare trunks climbing like cold fire!

II
My last walk in the trees has come. At dawn
I must return to the trapped fields,
To the obedient earth.
The trees shall be reaching all the winter.

III
It is a joy to walk in the bare woods.
The moonlight is not broken by the heavy leaves.
The leaves are down, and touching the soaked earth,
Giving off the odor that partridges love.

As the trees are striving upward and touching the soaked earth at the
same time, so man is trapped in his outer life and belongs to "the obedient earth," but still rejoices. The personifying verbs - "reaching,"
"climbing" and "touching" - emphasize the trees as symbols of life, as
holders of energy like the human body. In a prose poem recently published,
"Standing under a Cherry Tree at Night,"[2] tree and human being similarly
have exchanged qualities; their expressions of life energy are the same:

---

1 Silence, p. 45. Cf. above, p. 36.
2 The Morning Glory (Harper & Row, 1975), p. 26.

> The cherry branchès sway... they are arms that
> prophesy music, hands that follow the note just
> about to come. The clumps of blossoms look heavily
> down, and are women's faces, not angry with us, who
> forgive and return petals to the earth. And I too
> sway like these boughs, as if in heavy canyons,
> hardly making ground, moving upstream against tiny
> cedar twigs being turned over and over in the cloudy
> spring river coming down.
> All day I walked by the sea! I climbed down the
> cliffs at times to sit with the black mussels.
> Finally, I am back here, in the garden, where the
> night air is affectionate, the stars are a transparent
> mountain range... and I am a human being standing in
> the dark looking at the cherry branches above him
> swaying against the night sky not far from the sea!

The human being in the poem, the poet, has developed toward a freedom
that allows him to enjoy Nature and the open spaces, the stars and the
night sky, without experiencing a feeling of being trapped himself.
He is "hardly making ground." The last line seems deliberately ambiguous:
the "swaying against the night sky" could as well refer to the poet as
to the tree.

The same idea, that the trees and the whole of Nature overflow with
life energy, is expressed in "With Pale Women in Maryland."[1] The trees'
stupendous burden and the poet's overabundant love exemplify this energy
and, at the same time, illustrate Bly's technique of mixing the lines
describing nature and those describing the poet's mood. The close relationship of everything that is and has been alive becomes the theme of
the poem:

> With pale women in Maryland,
> Passing the proud and tragic pastures,
> And stupefied with love
> And the stupendous burdens of the foreign trees,
> As all before us lived, dazed
> With overabundant love in the reach of the Chesapeake,
> Past the tobacco warehouse, through our dark lives
> Like those before, we move to the death we love
> With pale women in Maryland.

Bly ends the poem by speaking of a death out of which new life comes.
Death and darkness are natural parts of life in his poems; therefore
what stands for life often holds darkness:

---

1 _Silence_, p. 32. Cf. above, pp. 35-36.

Darkness, darkness in grass, darkness in trees[1]

Also in poems of social criticism the tree is an important symbol, although more of the community than of life in general. In the second stanza of "Unrest"[2] man is presented as a baboon playing:

> But the baboon whistles on the shores of death –
> Climbing and falling, tossing nuts and stones,
> He gambols by the tree
> Whose branches hold the expanses of cold,
> The planets whirling and the black sun,
> The cries of insects, and the tiny slaves
> In the prisons of bark:
> Charlemagne, we are approaching your islands!

Modern man is not human any longer. He has experienced a regression. Coldness is what the branches of the social tree hold for him. The universe is chaos and even the sun, the source of warmth, has turned black. When trees are used as metaphors in poems of social criticism it is sometimes in terms of deformity, and this fits well into the scene of death or disintegration, also expressed by the metaphors of snow or of the road. In "The Executive's Death"[3] a "pine stump" talks to the executive who lies "cut off and dying," the irony in this situation being that although both are "cut off" the pine stump will continue to live.

In "A Dream of Suffocation"[4] mental paralysis in modern life is symbolized by a branch in a show window: the branch is painted white and is gripped by a stuffed baby alligator that is keeping away from the dry leaves on the floor. Everything is artificial and false in this show window. The poem's opening lines, and several other images in the poem, suggest a cause of this sterile life. The world of business, the world of logic,[5] has a devastating influence on life:

> Accountants hover over the earth like helicopters,
> Dropping bits of paper engraved with Hegel's name.
> Badgers carry the papers on their fur
> To their den, where the entire family dies in the night.

---

1 "Awakening," Silence, p. 26. Cf. also above, pp. 42-43.
2 Ibid., p. 25. Cf. also above, p. 29.
3 Light, p. 3. Cf. also above, pp. 27-28, and below, p. 108.
4 Ibid., p. 8.
5 Cf. below, pp. 177-178, where this poem is interpreted in terms of male and female consciousness.

> A chorus girl stands for hours behind her curtains
> Looking out at the street.
> In a window of a trucking service
> There is a branch painted white.
> A stuffed baby alligator grips that branch tightly
> To keep away from the dry leaves on the floor.
>
> The honeycomb at night has strange dreams:
> Small black trains going round and round –
> Old warships drowning in the raindrop.

In this poem the painted branch and the dry leaves express a general absence of life.

Desiccation of the sources of life is conveyed by the image of the "darkness of dying grass, and yellow willow leaves" in "Listening to President Kennedy Lie about the Cuban Invasion."[1] This points to a more specific ebbing of life, which takes the form of "a bitter fatigue, adult and sad," and is caused by attitudes of cynicism and indifference that shake the individual's confidence in life. The individual feels the supports giving in:

> There is another darkness,
> A darkness in the fences of the body,
> And in moles running, and telephone wires,
> And the frail ankles of horses;
> Darkness of dying grass, and yellow willow leaves;
> There is the death of broken buttonholes,
> Of brutality in high places,
> Of lying reporters,
> There is a bitter fatigue, adult and sad.

In "War and Silence"[2] the beech trees are covered with dust when the bombs fall. Their greenness can no longer be seen. Instead one of the trees becomes a death tree, a place for self-crucifixion in despair:

> . . .
>
> Filaments of death grow out.
> The sheriff cuts off his black legs
> And nails them to a tree

In "The Teeth Mother Naked at Last" war means death to the life tree:

---

[1] Light, p. 16. Cf. also below, p. 107.
[2] Ibid., p. 31. See above, p. 52, for quotation and further interpretati

. . .
The Marine battalion enters.
This happens when the seasons change,
This happens when the leaves begin to drop from the
                trees too early
"Kill them: I don't want to see
anything moving."

. . .

Hamilton saw all this in detail:
"Every banana tree slashed, every
cooking utensil smashed, every
mattress cut."[1]

. . .

When somebody dies the life tree is wounded and everything alive is
influenced:

. . .

                4
There is a wound on the trunk,
Where the branch was torn off.
A wind comes out of it,
Rising, swelling,
Swirling over everything alive.[2]

Whether this wind brings more death or new life, we do not know, but we
do know that a wounded tree can live on. It can be a symbol of new possibilities as in "A Home in Dark Grass."[3] As the seasons change (1st stanza),
a tree loses its leaves but it does not die; it draws new energy from its
roots. So a man should be able to live a second life, as Cervantes did
after having been captured by the Moors, and as Dillinger did, who, like
Bonny and Clyde, left conventional society to live his own life:

. . .

We did not come to remain whole.
We came to lose our leaves like the trees,
The trees that are broken
And start again, drawing up from the great roots;
Like mad poets[4] captured by the Moors,
Men who live out
A second life.

---

1 Teeth Mother, pp. 7-8. Cf. also below, p. 187.
2 The last stanza of "Melancholia," Light, p. 42. See also above, pp. 43-
   44, where this poem is mentioned, and below, p. 203.
3 Ibid., p. 44.
4 Robert Bly has informed me that he intended the reading "the mad poet"
   instead of "mad poets."

> That we should learn of poverty and rags,
> That we should taste the weed of Dillinger,
> And swim in the sea,
> Not always walking on dry land,
> And, dancing, find in the trees a saviour,
> A home in dark grass,
> And nourishment in death.

The life that Bly describes at the end of the last stanza is a life
close to the life-sustaining energies lodged in Nature, symbolized by
trees and grass, and lodged in the unconscious, symbolized by the sea.
The individual leading such a life would become an outcast from conventional society, which would imply a symbolic death to the world, but a
death that means spiritual nourishment and strength. This interpretation
seems supported by the original title of the poem: "Poem in Praise of
Solitude."[1]

In a very early poem the sorb is described as a death tree that
finally brings salvation. The poem was called "Departure" when it first
appeared as part of Bly's MA thesis in 1956. Two years later, in a slightly different version, it was published in The Paris Review under the title
"The Sorb is the Tree of Thor, Who Hung Nine Days Wounded."[2] Thus Bly
emphasized the importance of the tree as a symbol, in this poem a symbol
in turn of Life in general, of Death, and of Salvation, which means that
it is given the significance of both the world tree of pagan myths and
the cross of Christian beliefs:

> Out of the jetty slip the dark bark rides,
> As I more leave, each day, the man-leafed tree,
> Hearing the Norse tell how they sail the sea.
> Each day I see the ropes between us cut,
> "A ship for safety, must have one plank sorb,"
> As the Norse say, "The Hanged Man died on sorb."
> I leave no man but from all men I part,
> Setting forth gently on the boiling water,
> Not more alone, but less; as the Norse say,
> "Thor died on sorb; the sorb is Thor's salvation!"

Bly might have derived the idea for this poem from the 138th stanza of
Havamal, which tells how Odin (not Thor) hung wounded for nine nights on
the world tree Yggdrasill:

---

1 Poetry, CIV:6 (Sept., 1964), p. 368.
2 The Paris Review, (Autumn/Winter, 1958/1959), p. 26.

```
Veit ek at ek hekk
vindga meiði á
nætr allar nío,
geiri undaðr
ok gefinn Oðni,
siálfr siálfom mér,
á þeim meiði,
er manngi veit,
hvers hann af rótom renn.¹
```

In Bly's poem the tree becomes the cross, while the hero, thinking of
Thor, develops into a "world-renouncer,"² a name used by Joseph Campbell
for heroes who leave human society.³

In a short poem, "Watching Fall Dust Inside Sheds"⁴ - not published
in any book - the trees and the grass feel the dying and the beginning
over again of the wind and the sun (3rd stanza), while the poet himself
has experienced this in terms of the night journey (2nd stanza):

```
The motes dance in the sun
With slow and grave steps
Like those who dance for the birth
Of a prince in a huge castle.

I have slept in heavy waters.
My body is sailing
On the river of the fish,
Born over and over again!

Wife come out into the sunlight.
Here is the wind falling and beginning again
In the chilled leaves of the trees,
And sunlight in pools at the roots of the grass.
```

When the poet lives a life of privacy, he feels a closeness to the life
hidden in Nature:

---

1 I know that I hung
   on the windy tree
   for nine nights long,
   by spear wounded
   and given to Odin,
   myself to myself,
   on this tree,
   of which no man knows,
   from what roots it runs.
2 See Joseph Campbell, The Hero with a Thousand Faces (Princeton Univ.
   Press, Princeton, N. J., Paperback ed., 1972. First ed., 1949), pp. 354-
   356.
3 See below, p.130.
4 The Beloit Poetry Journal, 14:1 (Fall, 1963), p. 42. See also below,
   p. 176.

* * *

Mist: no one on the other shore.
It may be the trees I see have consciousness
and this desire to weep comes from them.[1]

* * *

At a winter dawn pine trees seem the most fitting symbols of life:[2]

. . .

A winter privacy is before us,
winter privacy,   ,
the vast halls inside the heads of animals
lie before us, the slow
breaking of day, warm blood moving, moving,
and immense pine trees.[3]

Settling down into his privacy and turning inward the poet feels a joy,
which is described in images from nature:

* * *

For the first time in months I love the dark.
A joy pierces me, it arrives like a runner,
a radio signal from inside a tree trunk,
a smile spreads over the face, the eyes fall.[4]

. . .

In moments of meditation the poet identifies with parts of the tree,
for instance:

. . .

Several times water
   carried me away:
then I was a cedar twig,
   a fish scale....[5]

. . .

In creative moments he wants to become one with the trees:

. . .

Suddenly I love the dancers, leaping
in the dark, jumping
into the air, and the singers and dancers and leapers!
I start to sing, and rove around the floor,
singing like "a young Lioun"

I want to rise far into the piney tops[6]

. . .

---

1 From "Some November Privacy Poems," _Jumping_, p. 13.
2 It should be noticed that pine trees are used by Jung and his followers
   as symbols of individual life. See M.-L. von Franz, "The Process of
   Individuation," _Man and His Symbols_ (ed. by C. G. Jung and M.-L. von
   Franz), (New York, N. Y., 1964), p. 162.
3 "The Night Journey in the Cooking Pot," _Sleepers_, p. 60.
4 Ibid.
5 From "On a Moonlit Road in the North Woods," _Jumping_, p. 15. See also
   above, pp. 56-57.
6 "The Night Journey in the Cooking Pot," _Sleepers_, p. 61.

The tree with its root system hidden in the ground is a traditional symbol for life and is, of course, a fitting symbol for the mind, including both the conscious and the unconscious parts of it:

. . .

> There is a consciousness hovering under the mind's feet,
> advanced civilizations under the footsole,
> climbing at times up on a shoelace!
> It is a willow that knows of water under the earth.[1]

. . .

We find a similar idea in "Night":[2]

. . .

> The box elders around us are full of joy,
> Obeying what is beneath them.

. . .

The "tree line" becomes the border line between the conscious and the unconscious in "Waking from an Afternoon Sleep."[3] This image is not used in the early version of the poem published in the American edition,[4] in which the poet, instead of coming "down from sleep above the tree line," descends "from the mountains of sleep." This change may be seen as a sign of a conscious development in the direction of inwardness.

Trees really comprise a psychic wood in "Johnson's Cabinet Watched by Ants."[5] The forest described in this poem is the setting for a kind of nocturnal witches' Sabbath or devil's mass at which the ministers and the department heads are imagined to appear as their genuine selves without the disguises of pretence which they have to wear during the day:[6]

1

> It is a clearing deep in a forest: overhanging boughs
> Make a low place. Here the citizens we know during
>   the day,
> The ministers, the department heads,
> Appear changed: the stockholders of large steel com-
>   panies
> In small wooden shoes: here are the generals dressed as
>   gamboling lambs.

---

1 "Water under the Earth," Sleepers, p. 7.
2 Silence, p. 55. Cf. above, pp. 85-86.
3 Silence (British edition), p. 44.
4 Silence, p. 43. See below, p. 122, for quotation and further interpretation.
5. Light, p. 5.
6 Cf. Nathaniel Hawthorne's "Young Goodman Brown," Selected Tales and
   Sketches (New York, N. Y., 1950), pp. 108-122.

2
```
Tonight they burn the rice-supplies; tomorrow
They lecture on Thoreau; tonight they move around the
          trees,
Tomorrow they pick the twigs from their clothes;
Tonight they throw the fire-bombs, tomorrow
They read the Declaration of Independence; tomorrow
          they are in church.
```

The poem is a good illustration of Bly's handling of place and time. The
first lines seem to describe an ordinary forest, but soon it becomes
clear that the description has another dimension: the forest of trees
functions as a symbol of man's dark thoughts and his true self. In the
third stanza the perspective really opens up, as the devil's mass is
placed in a timeless and universal context. An old tree marks the place;
the beings singing old Etruscan songs and celebrating tyranny cease to
be human; they become earthbound creatures, ants and toads:

3
```
Ants are gathered around an old tree.
In a choir they sing, in harsh gravelly voices,
Old Etruscan songs on tyranny.
Toads nearby clap their small hands, and join
The fiery songs, their five long toes trembling
          in the soaked earth.
```

Specific parts of a tree symbolize certain kinds of energy. The
leaves, for example, suggest new life in several poems, such as "Return
to Solitude"[1] which deals with the night journey.[2] The final stanza conveys the newness which results from that experience:

```
. . .
Friends changed, houses moved,
Trees perhaps, with new leaves.
```

A more interesting meaning is conferred upon the leaves in "Early Spring,"
in which again they carry the motif of renewal, but a renewal brought
about by poetry:

```
I am doing nothing, so I read old poems.
Strangely twisted leaves emerge from their buds.
Tu Fu's spirit enters into the bones of old men leaving
          for battle.
I feel joy seeing old boards scattered on the new grass.
```

---

1 Silence, p. 12.
2 Cf. below, p. 138.
3 Silence (British edition), p. 50.

This is a slightly cut-down version of a poem included in The Lion's
Tail and Eyes in which it is called "Reading the Translations of
William Hung,"[1] thus suggesting a relationship between Bly's poem and
what he is reading.[2] The early version runs:

> I am doing nothing, so I read old poems.
> It is early spring. Strangely twisted leaves emerge
>   from their buds.
> Tu Fu's spirit enters into the bones of old men
>   leaving for battle.
> Walking around, I feel joy as I see old boards
>   scattered on the new grass.

The theme of renewal is brought out in three variations manifested in
three images: the leaves bursting out of their buds, Tu Fu's spirit
entering the old men, thus strengthening their courage, and the old
boards on the new grass giving the poet joy. In the first version, with
the phrase "It is early spring" actually in the poem, there is added
emphasis on the renewal that comes with the change from winter to
spring. The poem is mainly descriptive, with the phrase "walking
around" telling the reader that the poet describes what he experiences.
In the second version, where these two phrases are omitted, Bly brings
the sentence about the strangely twisted leaves close to the phrase
"I read old poems" and thus furnishes it with symbolic overtones. The
leaves stand for the poems that Bly writes after having read translations of old Chinese poems. One of these leaves is this poem. What is
directly reminiscent of a Chinese poem is the poet's statement that he
is "doing nothing," a phrase that Bly uses in three poems in Jumping
Out of Bed, which contains versions of several Chinese poems. P'ei Ti
says, for example, in "The Walnut Tree Orchard,"[3] "I soon found doing
nothing was a great joy to me." The way in which Bly calmly gives the
details of his common surroundings also seems to come from Chinese
poetry and illustrates what Robert Payne says about Chinese poets in
his introduction to The White Pony: An Anthology of Chinese Poetry:
"they delighted in the smallest things of life, and took pains to
remember the details of which life is made."[4] The line about Tu Fu,

---

1   James Wright, William Duffy, and Robert Bly, The Lion's Tail and Eyes
    (The Sixties Press, 1962), p. 38.
2   William Hung, a Chinese-American, presented Tu Fu and his poems in full
    to the Western World in Tu Fu, China's Greatest Poet (Cambridge, Mass.,
    1952).
3   Jumping, p. 17.
4   The White Pony: An Anthology of Chinese Poetry (ed. Robert Payne)
    (New York, N. Y., 1947), p. VII.

of course, directly points to Chinese poetry. Just as Tu Fu's spirit gives the old men courage, so the spirit of Tu Fu's poems infuses Bly's poem.

In "Old and Bad Memories"[1] the growth of the rose leaves and the thorns and, in the last line, the appearance of the dark rose could symbolize the way that images present themselves to a poet of inwardness:

> The slow haze of remembrance, as when smoke rises in
>   a town in autumn,
> We walk through the leafy city and find the smoke,
> And stand sadly and look at the charred thing.
> Inside us too, when we see smoke, we can follow it
> And find the charred thing. But how
> Different! There is exchange of fires,
> The fire that was within the coal returns,
> And in its bed the white ash
> Turns to rose leaves,
> And the dark ash to thorns;
> There, in its bed, lies the dark rose.

Bly, a poet of inwardness, develops his images through introspection, but as seen from many poems, an occurrence in the outside world can trigger off this inward process. In this case it is the smoke in "the leafy city" that corresponds to the "slow haze of remembrance." In "Poem in Three Parts"[2] the leaves of the box-elder tree spur the energy of the imagination:

> III
> The strong leaves of the box-elder tree,   ·
> Plunging in the wind, call us to disappear
> Into the wilds of the universe,
> Where we shall sit at the foot of a plant,
> And live forever, like the dust.

In Bly's later books, leaves are almost always presented as dry leaves, fallen leaves, or yellow leaves. Sometimes, however, they are endowed with positive qualities. This is particularly true of Sleepers Joining Hands in which the sum of our lives is seen as "a faint glow in the dead leaves"[3], and some creatures choose leaves for shelter:

---

1 Silence (British edition), p. 34.
2 Silence, p. 21. See also below, p. 139.
3 Cf. above, p. 79.

> . . .
> I am flying over the Josephine forests, where only the
>   rat builds his nest of leaves,[1]
>
> "I am the dark spirit that lives in the dark.
> Each of my children is under a leaf he chose from all
>   the leaves in the universe.[2]
> . . .

The tree itself, however, stands naked and joyful after the leaves have

fallen. Like a poet of inwardness it needs very little:

> Leaves slip down, falling through their own
>   branches.
> The tree becomes naked and joyful.
> Leaves fall in the tomby wood.
> Some men need so little, and even that I need very
>   little.
> Suddenly I love the dancers, leaping
> in the dark, jumping
> into the air, and the singers and dancers and
>   leapers![3]

Not only trees but all sorts of plants are richly endowed with

life energy in Bly's poems. This is often made clear through personifica-

tions. In "Sunset at a Lake"[4] "moss stands out as if it wanted to speak."

In "Driving toward the Lac Qui Parle River"[5] "the soybeans are breathing

on all sides." In "Approaching Winter"[6] "the corn is wandering in dark

corridors," and the poet can hear "the corn leaves scrape their feet

on the wind." In "Poem against the Rich"[7] the poet shares in

> The weeping in the pueblos of the lily,
> Or the dark tears in the shacks of the corn

something that the rich man cannot experience. In "Running over the

River"[8] "holy beings [are] stretched out to sleep inside pine needles."

Artists and poets from time to time have described their experiences

of such animations. Aniela Jaffé speaks of the secret soul of things

and says, "Kandinsky expressed the same ideas when he wrote: "Every-

thing that is <u>dead</u> quivers. Not only the things of poetry, stars, moon,

---

1 From "The Shadow Goes Away," <u>Sleepers</u>, p. 55.
2 From "Meeting the Man Who Warns Me," <u>Sleepers</u>, p. 58.
3 From "The Night Journey in the Cooking Pot," <u>Sleepers</u>, p. 61.
4 <u>Silence</u>, p. 17.
5 Ibid., p. 20. Cf. also above, pp. 17-19.
6 Ibid., p. 19. Cf. also above, p. 24.
7 Ibid., p. 27. Cf. also above, p. 62.
8 <u>Kayak</u>, 5 (1966), p. 33. See also above, p. 94, footnote 2.

but even a white trouser button glittering out of a puddle in the
street.... Everything has a secret soul, which is silent more often
than it speaks.'"[1]

Life hidden in plants is suggested in several poems of political
and social criticism. "A sprig of black seaweed," along with "shells,
a skyful of birds," is what Nature bestows on the inhabitants of the
large cities; in contrast with the city itself this appears as a great
gift to its children:

> . . .
>
> The city broods over ash cans and darkening mortar.
> On the far shore, at Coney Island, dark children
> Play on the chilling beach: a sprig of black seaweed,
> Shells, a skyful of birds,
> While the mayor sits with his head in his hands.[2]

The "sprig of black seaweed" is as fitting a symbol for modern man and
his way of "taking care" of his environment, as "new oats" for Thomas
Jefferson who believed in an agricultural America.[3] In a prose poem
called "Looking into a Tide Pool"[4] the seaweed is likened to the hands
of a religious healer, and represents healing life energy:

> It is a tide pool, shallow, water coming in, clear,
> tiny white shell-people on the bottom, asking
> nothing, not even directions! On the surface the
> noduled seaweed, lying like hands, slowly drawing
> back and returning, hands laid on fevered bodies,
> moving back and forth, as the healer sings wildly,
> shouting to Jesus and his dead mother.

In "On the Rocks at Maui"[5] the poet unites with different manifestations
of life in Nature:

> The Pacific water rushes in among the brown con-
> fident seaweed; over stones with whirl-holes the shape
> of galaxies! A black crab climbs up a searock sideways,
> like a demon listening in Aramaic.
>   I am not married, I have no parents, I wave my
> black claws and hurry over the rock, I love these with
> the seaweed clinging to them (they are stars), I am
> alone inside myself, I love whatever is like me, I
> leap out of the sea, I hold fast to a rock, no

1   Aniela Jaffé, "Symbolism in the Visual Arts," Man and His Symbols,
    p. 254.
2   "The Great Society," Light, p. 17. See below, p. 177, for a comment
    and a quotation of the whole poem.
3   See Light, p. 14, and above, p. 51.
4   The Morning Glory, p. 16.
5   Ibid., p. 34.

> night-mother can pry me loose, I think my thoughts,
> I pray all day, and the seagrass, waving, is fool-
> ish, and I sway too, I am glad no cows come and eat
> me, I withdraw into the desert and return, I never
> want, I hurry through the womb-systems at night, I
> meet shining boulders, I fail in sleep, in my dream
> people whisper to me that I have lost their friend-
> ship, I sleep next to women, I wake.

It seems that the life of a plant appears richer and deeper to the poet than human life does. In solitude and at night he feels particularly alive; he compares his body to a plant:

> . . . How magnificent to be doing nothing,
> moving aimlessly through a nighttime field,
> and the body alive, like a plant.[1]
>
> . . .

Of all growing things, except for trees, grass is mentioned most frequently in Bly's poetry. It is usually seen as something very much alive, something that brings joy, creates and holds life. The poet notices it at any time of the day, be it morning:

> I
> Oh, on an early morning I think I shall live for
>   ever!
> I am wrapped in my joyful flesh,
> As the grass is wrapped in its clouds of green.[2]

evening:

> . . .
> The evening arrives; we look up and it is there,
> It has come through the nets of the stars,
> Through the tissues of the grass,
> Walking quietly over the asylums of the waters.[3]
> . . .

or night:

> I
> It is a moonlit, windy night.
> The moon has pushed out the Milky Way.
> Clouds are hardly alive, and the grass leaping.
> It is the hour of return.[4]

---

1 "Chrysanthemums," _Jumping_, p. 21.
2 "Poem in Three Parts," _Silence_, p. 21.
3 "Surprised by Evening," _Silence_, p. 15.
4 "Return to Solitude," _Silence_, p. 12.

The poet and the grass share in the same life. In "Love Poem"[1] his love
encompasses it as well as the other things in his surroundings. In
"Images Suggested by Medieval Music"[2] the grass is employed as a simile
to express the joy the poet feels listening to music:

> II
> I have felt this joy before, it is like the harsh
>   grasses
> On lonely beaches, this strange sweetness
> Of medieval music, a hoarse joy,
>
> . . .

"Grass from Two Years,"[3] which appears to be a recent poem, shows
Bly's need to be in solitude near grass when writing poems. A full experience of the grass, like the one conveyed in this prose poem, fills
him with tremendous joy:

> When I write poems, I need to be near grass
> that no one else sees, as here, where I sit for an
> hour under the cottonwood. The long grass has fallen
> over until it flows. Whatever I am ... if the great
> hawks come to look for me, I will be here in this grass.
> I feel a warmth in my stomach being near this grass.
> Knobby twigs have dropped on it. The summer's grass
> still green crosses some dry grass beneath, like
> the hair of the very old, that we stroke in the
> morning.
>   And how beautiful this ring of dry grass is, pale
> and tan, that curves over the half-buried branch -
> the grass flows over it, and is pale, gone, ascended,
> no longer selfish, no longer centered on its mouth,
> it is centered now on the God "of distance and of
> absence," its pale blades lie near each other around
> the dry wood ... this stick that the rain has not
> cared for, and has ignored, as it fell in the night,
> on men holding horses in the courtyard, and the sun-
> light was glad that the branch could be ignored, and
> did not ask to be loved - so I have loved you - and
> the branch and the grass lie here deserted, a part
> of the wild things of the world, noticed only for a
> moment by a heavy, nervous man who sits near them,
> and feels he has at this moment more joy than any
> one alive.

In several cases the grass suggests newness. In "Evolution from the
Fish"[4] a new child is likened to new grass, a simile that is the core

---

1 Silence, p. 41. Cf. also above, p. 42 and p. 82.
2 Ibid., p. 44.
3 The Morning Glory (Harper & Row, 1975), pp. 71-72.
4 Light, p. 59.

of a poem about evolutionary changes. The new grass, as well as the newborn child, symbolizes a state of innocence with infinite possibilities
in the Jungian sense:

> The child . . . is a personification of vital forces
> quite outside the limited range of our conscious
> mind. . . . It represents the strongest, the most
> ineluctable urge in every being namely the urge to
> realize itself.[1]

The poem alternates between this original state of innocence and "the
limited range of our conscious mind"[2] - in the poem described as a marble
world - and "the urge to realize itself"[3] - expressed in sexual terms
in this poem:

> This grandson of fishes holds inside him
> A hundred thousand small black stones.
> This nephew of snails, six feet long, lies naked
>   on a bed
> With a smiling woman, his head throws off light
> Under marble, he is moving toward his own life
> Like fur, walking. And when the frost comes, he is
> Fur, mammoth fur, growing longer
> And silkier, passing the woman's dormitory,
> Kissing a stomach, leaning against a pillar,
> He moves toward the animal, the animal with furry
>   head!
>
> What a joy to smell the flesh of a new child!
> Like new grass! And this long man with the student
>   girl,
> Coffee cups, her pale waist, the spirit moving around
>   them,
> Moves, dragging a great tail into the darkness.
> In the dark we blaze up, drawing pictures
> Of spiny fish, we throw off the white stones!
> Serpents rise from the ocean floor with spiral motions,
> A man goes inside a jewel, and sleeps. Do
> Not hold my hands down! Let me raise them!
> A fire is passing up through the soles of my feet!

The first stanza encapsulates the development of the race. Man is the
grandson of fishes with a hundred thousand possibilities inside him.
The stone as the symbol for the inner center of a human being is a
Jungian idea. M.-L. von Franz speaks at length of it in a discussion of
the individuation process:

---

1 C. G. Jung and C. Kereny, <u>Introduction to a Science of Mythology</u>
   (London, 1951), pp. 123-124.
2 See quotation above.
3 Ibid.

> Perhaps crystals and stones are especially apt symbols
> of the Self because of the ",just-so-ness" of their
> nature. . . . Men have collected stones since the be-
> ginning of time and have apparently assumed that
> certain ones were the containers of the life force with
> all its mystery. . . . For while the human being is
> as different as possible from a stone, yet man's
> innermost center is in a strange and special way akin
> to it (perhaps because the stone symbolizes mere exist-
> ence at the farthest remove from emotions, feelings,
> fantasies, and discursive thinking of ego-con-
> sciousness). In this sense the stone symbolizes what
> is perhaps the simplest and deepest experience - the
> experience of something eternal that man can have
> in those moments when he feels immortal and unalter-
> able. [1]

Bly seems to be expressing a parallel idea in his mention of the small
black stones. Man is the nephew of snails and he has developed through
a furry animal state into what he is. The individual man - the new
child, the new grass - described in the second stanza, has to pass
through sensual pleasure, darkness, sleep, and isolation; only then
can he throw off the white stones of consciousness and civilization
and feel the fire of energy passing through his whole being.[2] Thus, in
this poem Bly again points to a mystical timeless union with universal
forces, arrived at by going back to the origins, and by submission both
to animalistic instincts and to the darkness of the unconscious. The
new grass seems to Bly to embody an original energy, what he calls
"the fire" in the last line of the poem.

The grass has the same role in a prose poem called "Grassblades"[3] -
it embodies life, both manifest and hidden. The treatment of grass in
this poem clearly shows the different stages in a typical Bly poem -
the steps toward inwardness - the first step being the pure description
of grass surrounded by water and ligth at dawn, the second step being
the wider perspective created by the use of similes, and the final step
being the blending of outer description and inner experience and a move
into symbolism:

> The mountain bushes move toughly in the wind.
> There has been a rain. And I love these stretches
> of new water, one or two inches deep, fifteen or
> twenty feet long, with green grass growing straight
> up out of them! The sun slanting in at late dawn makes
> little moats of light around the grass stems.

---

1 M.-L. von Franz, "The Process of Individuation," Man and His Symbols,
   p. 209.
2 Cf. below, p. 124, where I discuss the dream state in which this happens
3 The Morning Glory, p. 28.

> Each grassblade has its own molecules of light
> around it, as they say a mountain where men are
> meditating always has white clouds above, as - they
> say - the roof of the dying saint gathers white
> storks.
>   When I bend closer, the little motes of light dis-
> appear, and I can see the exstatic earthbed, the
> brown blades of grass left from last year, like ruins
> of things we never did. And a few green blades entire-
> ly underwater, joy of the man who has lived.

The energy-filled grass is the main image in "Walking in the Ditch
Grass."[1] The poet feels the blowing of the spring wind and the sweeping
of his own shoes through the grass as movements which both search for
and act out energy:

> The spring wind blows dissatisfactions
> and mad architects, two-mile long tails,
>
> and my shoes like whales
> eat the grass, sweeping through
> the grass, eating
> up the darkness.
>
> The night is windy. Sleek cows fly
> across the sky. Samson
> is angry.
> So much of women
> in this uneven grass.

In an interview[2] Bly talks about this poem and its growth into its final
form. After listing the different discarded versions of the last two
lines as 1. So much of life

> 2. So much of the future
>
> 3. So much of energy
>
> 4. So much of the past
>
> 5. So much of the present in this uneven grass

he sums up:

> I watched the progress of this. It took me six or
> eight months before I realized that, for a man
> life, future, energy, past, present can all be
> summed up in the word women. And actually that is
> what my unconscious wanted to say in the beginning
> because this whole movement of grass is very
> womanly, but I started to take male movements
> through it like this and pretty soon I wanted a male
> thing down here. Notice, I got in Samson, I got in
> a female cow here across the sky, but it is still

---

1 *Jumping*, p. 37.
2 Interview, June 27, 1974, conducted by the author.

> flying in a masculine way. Then I have Samson being
> angry and even that doesn't tell me that the crucial
> point in the whole Samson story is women. . . . What
> happens here is a continual fight with the male ration-
> alist part which continually tries to put in more
> abstract statements here at every point until finally
> it gives in and allows what really wanted to be said
> all the time: the reason a man loves to walk in the
> grass is because walking in that grass, if it is uncut
> and it is long, he receives a sense of some of the
> inner energy that is actually inside women. And this
> is a healing experience for him.[1]

Thus, the movement of this poem, as of most of Bly's poems, is a movement inward. It is representative of his poetry as a whole in its
attempt to understand what the sources of life are, and to what extent
these sources are really inside a man, and to what extent outside.

The movement inward is stated in the first line of "Jumping Out of
Bed,"[2] another poem in which grass is one of the central images:

> Coming nearer and nearer the resonating-chamber,
> the poem begins to throw itself around
> wildly,
> silent stretches of snow,
> grass waving for hundreds of miles.

Out of its inwardness the poem develops by its own force, or as Robert
Frost said, "Like a piece of ice on a hot stove the poem must ride on
its own melting."[3] The energy out of which the poem grows is presented
in two images: "silent stretches of snow" and "grass waving for hundreds
of miles," and these images as explained above,[4] can represent silence
and privacy, joy and inner growth. When a man, moving inward, becomes
aware of the ecstatic energy of silence and of inner growth, he is taken
by surprise and overwhelmed:

> We leap up from our Sadducean pillow,
> every spot is forgotten,
> our hair is crinkly and gold.

Thus, inwardness becomes a matter of waking up from a general stupor,[5]
and a matter of awareness of energy stored, and treasures hidden. Without
this awakening, the energy is as useless as the moon that shines unnoticed

---

1 Cf. Jung's "animus" and "anima" and also my discussion of male and
   female consciousness below in Chapter IV.
2 Jumping, p. 43.
3 Robert Frost, "The Figure a Poem Makes," The Complete Poems, p. 20.
4 See above, pp. 33, and 105-106.
5 Cf. below, p. 125.

and the teaspoon left behind in the car:

>The moon hovers over the drunk's hut.
>The teaspoon gleams in the trunk of the car.[1]

What this energy is, the poet does not know, but he has experienced it,
and in another poem the growing grass becomes one of the tokens of its
existence:

>. . .
>So rather than saying that Christ is God or he is not,
>it is better to forget all that
>and lose yourself in the curved energy.
>I entered that energy one day,
>that is why I have lived alone in old places.
>that is why I have knelt in churches, weeping,
>that is why I have become a stranger to my father.
>We have no name for you, so we say:
>he makes grass grow upon the mountains,
>and gives food to the dark cattle of the sea,
>he feeds the young ravens that call on him.[2]

The ebbing of the energy of life is registered in the grass also. "Drops
of cold dew on the grass"[3] are a sign of summer coming to an end. The
"darkness of dying grass, and yellow willow leaves" symbolize the fading
confidence of people in their leaders.[4]

However, the strength of the energy that is embodied in the grass
is suggested in "Looking at New-Fallen Snow from a Train."[5] Even in the
presence of death, and in between the toes of hawks, grass grows:

>A man lies down to sleep.
>Hawks and crows gather around his bed.
>Grass shoots up between the hawks' toes.
>Each blade of grass is a voice.
>The sword by his side breaks into flame.

Also in the first stanza of "In Danger from the Outer World"[6] grass,
November grass, is described as growing when the opposite would be expected:

---

1 Cf. also the Surrealist artists' fascination with "the object."
2 "Water Drawn Up into the Head," Sleepers, p. 65.
3 "Beginning Their Empire," Silence (British edition), p. 49. See also
below, p. 114.
4 "Listening to President Kennedy Lie about the Cuban Invasion," Light,
p. 16. Cf. also above, p. 90.
5 Light, pp. 45-46. Cf. also above, p. 31, and below, p. 108, and p. 182.
6 Ibid., p. 47. Cf. also above, pp. 82-83.

> This burning in the eyes, as we open doors,
> This is only the body burdened down with leaves,
> The opaque flesh, heavy as November grass,
> Growing stubbornly, triumphant even at midnight.

It should be noted, however, that the November grass in this poem, as well as the November birch in "Solitude Late at Night in the Woods,"[1] represents bodily energy.

The triumph of life energy is the climax of "A Home in Dark Grass," in which trees and "dark grass" symbolize a second life.[2] The darkness of the grass suggests a rebirth in terms of a descent into darkness, as in "Awakening,"[3] in which darkness also characterizes the trees and flowers. Thus, it is evident that the image of grass, regardless of whether it is related to newness or darkness, is life-confirming in Bly's poetry.

In contrast to the images of trees and grass the images of birds, insects, and other creatures are often connected with sound. Twice only are trees and grass given a voice, and in both instances a death scene is described. In "The Executive's Death"[4] the abating energy of the dying man contrasts with the lasting life of Nature, Art, and Spirit, and with the pine stump, Goethe, and Jesus as symbols of the energy of these life spheres:

> . . .
> As he lies on the wintry slope, cut off and dying,,
> A pine stump talks to him of Goethe and Jesus.
> . . .

In "Looking at New-Fallen Snow from a Train" each blade of grass that grows between the hawks' toes [5] "is a voice," which to me seems to speak of the persistance of life. However, most often in Bly's poems it is birds and crickets that bear audible witness to the energy that permeates our earthly existence.

The song of birds in "The Magnolia Grove,"[6] Bly's version of a

---

1 Cf. above, p. 87.
2 See above, pp. 91-92.
3 Cf. above , pp. 42-43.
4 Light, p. 3. See also above, pp. 27-28 and 89.
5 See above, p. 107.
6 Jumping, p. 33. See also above, p. 56.

Chinese poem, is part of the sunset that he is describing. The different
signs of life blend in beautiful harmony:

>   . . .
>
>   Settling down at dusk from the dome of light
>   bird voices get mingled with the river sounds.
>   . . .

In "'Taking the Hands'"[1] the singing of birds expresses an emotional
harmony experienced by somebody in love:

>   Taking the hands of someone you love,
>   You see they are delicate cages...
>   Tiny birds are singing
>   In the secluded prairies
>   And in the deep valleys of the hand.

In a haiku-like poem called "The Loon,"[2] the cry heard form far out
in the lake becomes the symbol of an unpretentious life:

>   A loon's cry rose from far out in the centre
>   Of the lake –
>   It was the cry of someone who owned very little.

In the last stanza of "Awakening"[3] a bird, forgotten among the pressures
of the city, still is warbling, and in "This World is a Confusion of
Three Worlds"[4] it is mentioned how, in a backyard on Twelfth Street in
New York, the poet hears "a chirping of birds." In "Sunset at a Lake"[5]
"only a few birds, the troubled ones, speak to the darkening roof of
earth." In these three instances the birds' voices sound in the midst
of a life of distress, which would signify the same persistance of life
as does the voice of the grass mentioned above.

In some poems the descriptive phrase of birds singing clearly serves
as an image, as in "After the Industrial Revolution, All Things Happen
at Once"[6] in which the turkeys singing from the treetops constitute a
metaphor for Coxey's army, which in the 1890's demonstrated against
unemployment. Thus, in this poem, the figure of the "turkeys . . . singing from the tops of trees" conveys the same atmosphere of complaint as

---

1   Silence, p. 42.
2   Silence (British edition), p. 20.
3   Silence, p. 26. See also above, p. 43.
4   Poetry, XCVI, April 1960, p. 31.
5   Silence, p. 17.
6   Light, p. 29. See also above, pp. 71-72.

the descriptive phrase "a few birds, the troubled ones, speak to the
darkening roof of earth"[1] would have if it were really developed into
a metaphor.

The cry of seagulls in "Riderless Horses"[2] is an ominous cry, well
prepared for in the first part of the poem. Every image conveys a sense
of displaced, unguided, or misused energy, some kind of blindness:

> An owl on the dark waters
> And so many torches smoking
> By mossy stone
> And horses that are seen riderless on moonlit nights
> A candle that flutters as a black hand
> Reaches out
> All of these mean
> A man with coins on his eyes
>
> The vast waters
> The cry of seagulls

It is not clear from the poem what this ominous cry from the seagulls is
supposed to convey, but it sounds like a warning of things going terribly
wrong. The owl is not placed in its right element, the torches give off
smoke instead of light, the horses have no riders,[3] the flame of the
candle is disturbed, and man is a corpse with coins holding his eyelids
shut, – which in its turn could mean that man is blinded by capitalism.
Thus, this poem deals with death in life, the death of the inner man.
The seagulls are aware of impending death. It is as if they feel the
same fear that the chickens do in "The Teeth Mother Naked at Last,"[4]
in which the chickens represent the natural flow of life energy that
shudders when the machines spread death:

> I
> Massive engines lift beautifully from the deck.
> Wings appear over the trees, wings with eight hundred
> rivets.
>
> Engines burning a thousand gallons of gasoline a
> minute sweep over the huts with dirt floors.
>
> The chickens feel the new fear deep in the pits of
> their beaks.
>
> . . .

---

1 See above.
2 Light, p. 58.
3 Riderless horses as an element in a dream are interpreted by M.-L.
   von Franz as instinctive drives that have got away from conscious
   control. (See Man and His Symbols, p. 170).
4 Teeth Mother, p. 5. Cf. also above, p. 41, and below, p. 186.

Bird images appear in two other instances in this poem. The shock experienced by living beings at the terror of killing is described surrealistacally:

> . . .
> A green parrot shudders under the fingernails.
> Blood jumps in the pocket.
> The scream lashes like a tail.[1]

The meaninglessness of killing and the waste of useful energy is shown:

> . . .
> Now the Marine knives sweep around like sharp-edged jets;
>   how easily they slash open the rice bags,
> the mattresses....
> ducks are killed with $150 shotguns.
>
> Old women watch the soldiers.[2]

Sleepers Joining Hands contains many bird images but only a few relate the sound of birds. "Pilgrim Fish Heads"[3] consists of images which bring out the controversies between the white American, in this case the Pilgrim, and the Indian, the original American. Everything that is damp is conspiring with the Indian and is frightening to the Pilgrim. The chickens seem to be part of the Pilgrim's world but they voice their dissatisfaction with it:

> . . .
> Outdoors the chickens squawk in woody hovels,
> yet the chickens are walking on Calvinist ground.
> . . .

In "Meeting the Man Who Warns Me"[4] the cry of birds signifies the energy of an inner state of mind. The persona of the poem sets out on a "night journey" and begins to feel the awakening of his unconscious, which is experienced in a dream and expressed in terms of water and the mother:

> I wake and find myself in the woods, far from the
>   castle.
> The train hurtles through lonely Louisiana at night.
> The sleeper turns to the wall, delicate
> aircraft dive toward earth.

1 Teeth Mother, p. 9.
2 Ibid., p. 8.
3 Sleepers, p. 17
4 Ibid., p. 56. See below, in Chapters III and IV, discussions of the night journey and the myths of the mother.

> A woman whispers to me, urges me to speak truths.
> "I am afraid that you won't be honest with me."
> Half or more of the moon rolls on in shadow.
> Owls talk at night, loons wheel cries through lower
>   waters,[1]
> fragments of the mother lie open in all low places.

One of the passages of "The Night Journey in the Cooking Pot"[2] also contains bird imagery. The first four lines of this passage are descriptive but when read as parallel to the following four lines, in which the poet sees himself as a bird, they also acquire symbolic significance:

> The crow nests high in the fir.
> Birds leap through the snowy branches
>   uttering small cries,
> The mice run dragging their tails in the new-fallen
>   snow.
>
> The old tree moves in the wind.
> Sitting I leap from branch to branch,
>   the old man calls out,
> long prayers at dawn, the deer antlers abandoned in
>   the snow.

The crow, the other birds, and the mice represent life on different levels of the life-tree, with the crow as the top bird, the successful bird, a ro it fills also in the early poem "Where We Must Look for Help."[3] The second part of this passage makes it clear that the tree is the life-tree, since its age is emphasized and the poet finds himself moving within its branche hearing - instead of the small cries of birds - the voice of a man at his prayers at dawn, and seeing tokens of former life left in the snow.[4] Thus, these eight lines describe a mystical experience in which the poet senses life in all its antiquity as it manifests itself for his inner eyes and ears when he turns inward toward the privacy he loves. His inwardness is symbolized by the snow and the sea in the preceding lines:

> I love the snow, I need privacy as I move,[5]
> I am all alone, floating in the cooking pot
> on the sea, through the night I am alone.

Probably the bird that symbolizes the poet in this instance is what Joseph Henderson in Jungian terms, calls a "symbol of transcendence."[6] Such

---

1 Cf. above, p. 82, where this line is mentioned.
2 Sleepers, p. 59.
3 Silence, p. 29. Cf. above, p. 53 and p. 81.
4 Cf. above, the discussion about snow as the preserver on p. 26.
5 See also above, pp. 33-34.
6 Joseph L. Henderson, "Ancient Myths and Modern Man," Man and His Symbol p. 151.

symbols "provide the means by which the contents of the unconscious can enter the conscious mind, and they also are themselves an active expression of those contents."[1] The poet has become a shaman, whose "power resides in his supposed ability to leave his body and fly about the universe as a bird."[2] The bird "represents the peculiar nature of intuition working through a 'medium' that is, an individual who is capable of obtaining knowledge of distant events - or facts of which he consciously knows nothing - by going into a trancelike state."[3] In this case "the deer antlers abandoned in the snow" are the signs of distant events or facts of which the shaman "consciously knows nothing."

The sound of crickets, as well as of other creatures, also forms a symbolic pattern of a flow of energy. In one of Bly's earliest poems, "What Burns and is Not Consumed,"[4] the sounds that crickets, loons, and other living beings make, are described by the poet as he experiences them in a cabin on a lake shore, probably in the North Woods in Minnesota:

> . . .
> The crickets climb rocks, clambering, stiff as crones
> Yet sing their day-old squeakings at the stones.
> . . .
> Hearing the wood-mice scamper in the eaves,
> . . .
> Hear in dreams the paddlings of the loon
> . . .

The sound of the grasshopper dominates the short poem "On a Cliff":[5]

> Reading the Master,
> I heard a grasshopper making dry sounds with his
>   wings,
> Leaping about in the wind,
> Two hundred feet above the water!

This poem has some characteristics of haiku, and like many of Basho's haikus, some of which Bly has translated, it is primarily a picture. What Bly is describing seems to be a moment which has made a deep impression on him but which probably is neither allegoric nor symbolic. In

---

1 Man and His Symbols, p. 151
2 Ibid.
3 Ibid. See also below, p. 157.
4 MA thesis, p. 2.
5 Poetry, CIV:6 (Sept., 1964), p. 367.

another poem written in the same year, "Cricket Calling from a Hiding
Place,"[1] the poet demonstrates through similes how the cricket's call,
sounding like a warning, stirs his imagination:

> He is like a boat with black sails!
> Or an old woman sitting by a redwood tree
> Warning the passersby that the tree is about to fall,
> A bell made of black tin in a Mexican village,
> Like the hair in the ear of a hundred year old man!

In "Cricket on a Doorstep in September"[2] the poet relates an incident
in which the crickets actually have a message for the poet:

> Feet without shoes on bare boards in late summer.
> Large drops of water on the grass.
> Mosquitoes rise for the last time from the grass.
> Crickets turn up on the doorstep to announce to the
> world
> They have landed on the cedar island far out in the
> sea!

The message conveyed by the crickets is that of time passing, of change
of summer turning into fall. A later version of the poem is called
"Beginning their Empire."[3] It is only slightly altered, but the changes
seem important and transform it into a socially-engaged poem. In the
later version the world is described as hostile. The dew on the grass i
cold. The crickets arrive on the doorstep, which seems more intentional
than turn up, and they announce that they have captured the cedar islan
and not merely landed on it. What is described is not only the end of
summer, it is also the beginning of a new era in which human dominance
ends.

The sound of crickets is very much part of the scenes described in
two more poems in Silence in the Snowy Fields, and in these it seems to
carry communications between the world and the experiencing poet. In
"Driving toward the Lac Qui Parle River"[4] "the noise of crickets" pene-
trates the solitude of the car, and in "The Clear Air of October"[5] the
poet feels the joy of the crickets singing. In "The Busy Man Speaks"[6]

---

1 Kayak, 1 (Autumn, 1964), p. 31. The poem is included in Old Man (p.
   under the title "A Cricket in the Wainscoting." The phrasing of the
   later version is more carefully done, but the changes do not affect
   the meaning or the structure.
2 Ibid.
3 Silence (British edition), p. 49.
4 Ibid., p. 20. Cf. also above, p. 18.
5 Ibid., p. 52. Cf. also above, p. 63.
6 Light, p. 4. Cf. also below, pp. 178–179, where the poem is quoted an
   interpreted.

in The Light around the Body "the mother of the night full of crickets"
is one of the images Bly uses for the kind of life that modern man
denounces in his unshakeable life of outwardness - complete in itself.

In Bly's later books it is the movements, more than the sounds, of
different creatures that disclose the energy that is flowing or stored
in them. In a descriptive prose poem called "At a Fish Hatchery in Story,
Wyoming"[1] Bly takes life energy as his main theme. Moving from narrative, through descriptive, into figurative language Bly succeeds in
creating a world in which the pulsation of life energy is of primary
importance, and where barriers in time and space become non-existent:

> A ranger is lifting fingerling trout from a pickup
> with his scoop. The rangers are weighing them for
> stocking. The man in black boots pours them out of his
> scoop into a tub set on a scale. The fish slip off the
> scoop shovel, five or six inches long, shiny, gleaming,
> full of life! How they twist and turn in the Wyoming
> sun, about to fall! Oh, they are immense reserves of
> pure energy, like snowbanks, like mountains, like
> millions of hands, hands moving on breasts... and when
> they do fall, they leave behind pure strokes in the air,
> and fall into the washtub of fish, like the white stones
> dropped by glaciers, or washed by chilly streams; or
> the furs wrapped around old shoulders in the back of
> caves, where the skins have been chewed by women with
> luminous faces, who glow because their child has come
> into the universe; and now lies on their naked breast,
> which gleams in the risen light like a fish.

When Bly sits down in his shack to meditate, the flow of inner
energy sometimes manifests itself for him as birds, whales or fish, as
described in "Shack Poem."[2] In the dream world of "Meeting the Man Who
Warns Me"[3] Bly talks about his own life. He looks around and sees manifestations of life energy in creatures moving; he looks back on his past
life and talks about inner experiences of solitude, using a language of
images.[4] In "Water Drawn Up Into the Head"[5] Bly talks about solitude at
night, a solitude in which he identifies with almost everything in
Nature and in the Universe, and experiences the flow of energy through
life:

---

1 The Morning Glory, p. 22. Cf. also below, p. 142, footnote 1.
2 Sleepers, p. 8. See also above, p. 58, where the poem is quoted.
3 Ibid., pp. 56-58.
4 For quotation and interpretation see below, p. 155.
5 Sleepers, pp. 64-67.

. . .

I sit alone at night,
I sit with eyes closed, thoughts shoot trough me.

. . .

I am the single splinter that shoots through the
          stratosphere leaving fire trails!
I walk upright, robes flapping at my heels,
I am fleeing along the ground like a frightened
          beast.

. . .

I am the steelhead trout that hurries to his
          mountain mother,
to live again in the stream where he was born,
gobbling up the new water.

. . .

I am an angel breaking into three parts over the
          Ural Mountains!

. . .

I am the evening light rising from the ocean plains
I am an eternal happiness fighting in the long reeds.[1]

Absorbed in his own poetry he feels close to a manifestation of naked
energy:

. . .

Sometimes when I read my own poems late at night,
I sense myself on a long road,
I feel the naked thing alone in the universe,
the hairy body padding in the fields at dusk....[2]

. . .

In the final stanza of the poem, life energy is envisioned as a panther'
joy and also as the togetherness of all sleepers, of those who have felt
the hidden energy of inwardness:

The panther rejoices in the gathering dark.
Hands rush toward each other through miles of space.
All the sleepers in the world join hands.[3]

Bly's poems seem to have captured what Jung regrets as lost in
modern society:

---

1 Sleepers, pp. 66-67.
2 Ibid., p. 66.
3 Ibid., p. 67.

As scientific understanding has grown, so our world
has become dehumanized. Man feels himself isolated in
the cosmos, because he is no longer involved in nature
and has lost his emotional "unconscious identity" with
natural phenomena. These have slowly lost their symbolic implications. Thunder is no longer the voice of
an angry god, nor is lightning his avenging missile.
No river contains a spirit, no tree is the life principle of man, no snake the embodyment of wisdom, no
mountain cave the home of a great demon. No voices now
speak to man from stones, plants, and animals, nor does
he speak to them believing they can hear. His contact
with nature has gone, and with it has gone the profound
emotional energy that this symbolic connection supplied.[1]

---

1 C. G. Jung, "Approaching the Unconscious," Man and His Symbols, p. 95.

III. THE VOYAGE OF THE UNCONSCIOUS

In this chapter I intend to study Bly's use of certain concepts and archetypes related to the human psyche. This involves references to myth ogy and pshychoanalysis. First I intend to deal with some words and con cepts connected with ordinary experiences of the psyche, such as dream, sleep, and meditation, and then to turn to archetypes that function in myths and psychoanalysis - as presented by C. G. Jung and his followers to describe the process that a person has to go through in order to beco acquainted with the unconscious parts of his psyche in the hope of ob-taining wholeness or inner maturity.

In the preceding chapter I have made occasional references[1] to Jung and the Jungian school. That Bly is influenced by Jungian psychoanalysis is evident. He has said so himself[2] and he mentions and discusses Jungia ideas in interviews and prose articles. In an interview[3] conducted in November, 1971, Robert Bly refers to Jung when speaking of an individual movement inward and his facing or not facing of the flow into the ego of unconscious material. He also explains how this movement might turn into depression which develops into a positive experience as the individual becomes actively aware of it or else battles with it. As we have seen above[4] these are ideas that very early entered Bly's poems, even, I woul say, before he studied Jungian psychoanalysis.

Anthony Libby writes about the influence on Bly of C. G. Jung and Erich Neumann, after having heard Bly himself talk about it at a poetry reading at Antioch College, Yellow Springs, Ohio, in the autumn of 1970. Apparently, what Bly said on that occasion was what he later put into hi essay "I Came Out of the Mother Naked."[6] Libby's article shows that Bly was well acquainted with the ideas of a masculine and a feminine conscio ness - with what Jung calls the animus and the anima of an individual's

---

1 See above, for example, pp. 38, 94, 99-100, 103-104, 106, 110, 112-11 and 116-117.
2 See above, p. 5.
3 Peter Martin, "Robert Bly: Poet on the Road Home," The Straight Creek Journal (Oct. 24, 1972), pp. 10-11 and 16.
4 See above, pp. 37, 42-43, 53, 54-55.
5 See Anthony Libby, "Robert Bly: Alive in Darkness," The Iowa Review, 3/3 (Summer, 1972), pp. 78-90.
6 Sleepers, pp. 29-50. See below, p. 185.

psyche. To be exact, he read Erich Neumann's The Great Mother during the
winter of 1968-69 (he says so himself in an interview conducted in March,
1969[1]) and he has started to read Jung occasionally as early as 1961.[2]
However, as will be seen from my analyses in Chapter IV these ideas occur
in Bly's poems still earlier than that.

In two articles from 1973 and 1974 Bly explicates central Jungian
ideas. In "Developing the Underneath"[3] he refers the reader to Jung's
lectures to English psychiatrists, published as Analytical Psychology:
Its Theory and Practice, and to Jung's book Psychological Types when
explaining the idea of four basic types: the thinking type, the feeling
type, the grasp-of-sensual-fact type, and the intuitive type. What is important for the individual is to develop not only his dominant function, which
makes him one of these types, but also, and especially, his inferior function. To do that, a person has to become acquainted with his, or her,
psyche, has to go into himself and then return and share his experience
with the community he lives in. How this is dealt with by some writers, is
put forward in the other article, "The Network and the Community."[4] The
process of becoming acquainted with the whole of one's psyche is often
called a rebirth experience - in Jung's terminology the individuation process. This experience is the subject of some of Bly's poems, something I
deal with in the second section of this chapter.

Sleep, Dream, and Meditation

Bly often employs words for "sleeping," "dreaming," and "waking up,"
and in many poems these mean just what they stand for in ordinary speech,
while in other poems these terms become vehicles for the idea of turning
inward and of returning from inwardness. Terms borrowed from the vocabulary of meditation also convey these experiences in some poems, both early
and recent ones. Also, the more complex the experience seems to be, the
more indirect is Bly's way of presenting it to the reader. So again we
shall be moving from simple poems to intricately woven ones, both in terms

1 Franz Albert Richter and Lew Hyde, "An Interview with Robert Bly,"
  The Lamp and the Spine, 3 (Winter, 1972) p. 57.
2 See above, p. 5.
3 Robert Bly, "Developing the Underneath," The American Poetry Review
  (Nov./Dec., 1973).
4 Robert Bly, "The Network and the Community, The American Poetry Review
  (Jan./Febr., 1974), pp. 19-21.

of structure and of theme.

In "Waking from Sleep,"[1] the body's awakening is described through
the image of life and activity returning to a harbor on a spring morning.
Consciousness in all its strength returns to the body and fills it with
new lust for life because "our master" is gone. "Our master" might refer
to any depressive and negative forces and feelings from which sleep has
freed one:

> Inside the veins there are navies setting forth,
> Tiny explosions at the water lines,
> And seagulls weaving in the wind of the salty
>   blood.
>
> It is the morning. The country has slept the
>   whole winter.
> Window seats were covered with fur skins, the
>   yard was full
> Of stiff dogs, and hands that clumsily held
>   heavy books.
>
> Now we wake, and rise from bed, and eat
>   breakfast! –
> Shouts rise from the harbor of the blood,
> Mist, and masts rising, the knock of wooden
>   tackle in the sunlight.
>
> Now we sing, and do tiny dances on the
>   kitchen floor.
> Our whole body is like a harbor at dawn;
> We know that our master has left us for the
>   day.

Similar feelings pervade the short poem "In a Train,"[2] which ends with th
happiness gained in refreshing sleep:

> There has been a light snow.
> Dark car tracks move in out of the darkness.
> I stare at the train window marked with soft
>   dust.
> I have awakened at Missoula, Montana, utterly
>   happy.

Often the actual awakening is described, a stage between unconsciousness
and consciousness, as in "Laziness and Silence,"[3] in which the poet is
lying in a bed near a lake and letting his thoughts wander. He gives himself up to creative dreaming:

---

1 Silence, p. 13.
2 Ibid., p. 47.
3 Ibid., p. 53.

I

On a Saturday afternoon in the football season,
I lie in a bed near the lake,
And dream of moles with golden wings.

While the depth of the water trembles on the
      ceiling,
Like the tail of an enraged bird,
I watch the dust floating above the bed,
      content.

I think of ships leaving lonely harbors,
Dolphins playing far at sea,
Fish with the faces of old men come in from
      a blizzard.

II

A dream of moles with golden wings
Is not so bad; it is like imagining
Waterfalls of stone deep in mountains,
Or a wing flying alone beneath the earth.

I know that far out in the Minnesota lake
Fish are nosing the mouths of cold springs,
Whose water causes ripples in the sleeping
      sand,
Like a spirit moving in a body.

It is Saturday afternoon. Crowds are
      gathered,
Warmed by the sun, and the pure air.
I thought of this strange mole this morning,
After sleeping all night by the lake.

His dreams, as described here, are anchored in reality: he states the time
and place and the fact that he is dreaming. The details of the dream,
however, exist on surreal conditions: a mole with golden wings is a creature created by the imagination, just like the waterfalls of stone and the
lonely wing flying, to which the "dream of moles with golden wings" is
compared. The poet seems to have privileged information about things far
out in the Minnesota lake or deep down in the mountains, and finally he
compares what happens in the lake to "a spirit moving in a body." We are
brought from a real scene via (mostly) water imagery into an imaginary
world in which we understand the movements of the spirit inside the body.
In the last two stanzas we are brought back to reality. This seems to
point toward Bly's later poems in which water carries the traditionally
symbolic meaning of the unconscious.

The situation is similar in "Afternoon Sleep"[1] in which the introductory stanza states the poet's feelings when he wakes up and remembers
a dream he has just had:

I
I was descending from the mountains of sleep.
Asleep I had gazed east over a sunny field,
And sat on the running board of an old
        Model A.
I awoke happy, for I had dreamt of my wife,
And the loneliness hiding in grass and weeds
That lies near a man over thirty, and
        suddenly enters.

Maybe the poet's ability to benefit from his dreams, to recall them and
talk about them, is one of the things that saves him from the depressing
loneliness that a man might experience when entering middle age. The rest
of the poem tells us about a Norwegian immigrant who had not had this inner
strength; he had grown tired, had given up his farm and his belongings and
left:

II
When Joe Sjolie grew tired, he sold his farm,
Even his bachelor rocker, and did not come
        back.
He left his dog behind in the cob shed.
The dog refused to take food from strangers.

III
I drove out to that farm when I awoke;
Alone on a hill, sheltered by trees.
The matted grass lay around the house.
When I climbed the porch, the door was open.
Inside were old abandoned books,
And instructions to Norwegian immigrants.

Note the word "field" in the first stanza, as it is one of the conspicuous
elements of the dream, and the word "grass," used twice in this poem. The
fact that in more recent poems a field[2] sometimes stands for the unconscious and grass[3] for inner growth seems to be compatible with the poet's
attitude toward loneliness and depression as expressed in this poem.

In the poem "Depression"[4] the pattern of falling asleep, dreaming,
and awakening again occurs:

---

1 Silence, p. 43. See also above, pp. 36 and 95.
2 Cf. above, pp. 38-39, and below, p. 129.
3 Cf. above, p. 106.
4 Silence, p. 37.

I felt my heart beat like an engine high in
          the air,
Like those scaffolding engines standing only
          on planks;
My body hung about me like an old grain
          elevator,
Useless, clogged, full of blackened wheat.
My body was sour, my life dishonest, and I
          fell asleep.

I dreamt that men came toward me, carrying
          thin wires;
I felt the wires pass in, like fire; they
          were old Tibetans,
Dressed in padded clothes, to keep out cold;
Then three work gloves, lying fingers to
          fingers,
In a circle, came toward me, and I awoke.

Now I want to go back among the dark roots;
Now I want to see the day pulling its long
          wing;
I want to see nothing more than two feet high;
I want to see no one, I want to say nothing,
I want to go down and rest in the black earth
          of silence.

This poem shows no trace of the bodily happiness that fills the poem
"Waking from Sleep."[1] Instead, it expresses the seeming uselessness of the
poet's body and the dishonesty of his life. In his nightmare the poet has
to undergo torture. What he has experienced, both awake and asleep, both
in his conscious and his unconscious mind, arouses in him a desire to
withdraw from life. The poem seems to end in a death wish, but I think it
is rather a wish for withdrawal from the rest of the world, for a retreat
into isolation and silence, into one's self. This interpretation would be
in accordance with two other poems that have similar themes, namely "The
Fire of Despair Has Been Our Saviour,"[2] ending "Not finding the road, we
are slowly pulled down," and "Night"[3] ending ". . . and soon to be
swallowed / Suddenly from beneath." In the discussion above[4] of "The Fire
of Despair Has Been Our Saviour" I pointed to a pattern of first a turning
outward, then a turning inward, and finally a submergence in physical or

---

1   Cf. above, p. 120.
2   Light, pp. 48-49.
3   Silence, p. 55.
4   Pp. 53-55.

mental darkness, a pattern that appears to underlie "Depression" also.
That a positive experience may result from this downward movement is
suggested in "Night" - a poem dominated by the word "sleep" - in which
plants, insects, and animals exist in an atmosphere of joy and rest, while
yielding to the forces pulling them downward.[1]

A similar withdrawal is expressed in the later part of the concluding
stanza of "Evolution from the Fish":[2]

> In the dark we blaze up, drawing pictures
> Of spiny fish, we throw off the white
>   stones!
> Serpents rise from the ocean floor with
>   spiral motions,
> A man goes inside a jewel, and sleeps. Do
> Not hold my hands down! Let me raise them!
> A fire is passing up through the soles of
>   my feet!

A dream state is described in these lines. Only in dreams are we able to
throw off the white stones, which in their polished whiteness may stand
for our civilized consciousness. That this is a dream state is made
clearer in an earlier version of the poem, in which Bly actually says,
"And ourselves, blazing up, drawing spiny fish / As we sleep, we throw off
the white stones!"[3] In dreams we are confronted with the contents of our
unconscious, pictured as an ocean floor with serpents rising. Bly describes how a man really enters his own unconscious and experiences its
fire.[4] In the early version this is seen as a return to the original
energy: "I am curving back into the mammoth pool!"[5]

Another experience, brought about by contemplation, sleep, and dream,
is communicated in "On the Rocks at Maui"[6] in which the poet goes into
himself while contemplating life around him on the sea shore:

---

1   The poem is quoted above on pp. 85-86.
2   Light, p. 59.
3   The Lion's Tail and Eyes, p. 45, and Choice: A Magazine of Poetry and
    Photography, Vol. 3 (1963), p. 109.
4   Cf above, p. 104.
5   Cf Anthony Libby, "Robert Bly Alive in Darkness," The Iowa Review,
    3/3 (Summer, 1972), p. 85.
6   The Morning Glory, p. 34.

> . . . I am alone inside myself, . . . I think
> my thoughts, I pray all day, . . . I withdraw
> into the desert and return, . . . I hurry
> through the womb-systems at night, I meet
> shining boulders, I fail in sleep, in my
> dream people whisper to me that I have lost
> their friendship, I sleep next to women, I
> wake.

In the poem that follows, called "Waterfall Coming over a Cliff,"[1] a
sleeper's experience and that of a meditator are paralleled in images that
describe the "floating" of a waterfall:

> . . . It is a deep plunge, loveless, float-
> ing; it falls by the cliff like tufts of
> sleep, the long sleep the truckdriver sinks
> into after having driven three days from the
> coast, or the clouds that pass across the
> heaven of a dog's eyes, when he dies in a
> room with human beings, or the glimpses the
> meditater has of something floating under the
> water, neither moving nor not moving, seeming
> to slow as it nears the bottom.

In Bly's more recent poems the concepts of dream and sleep come to
mean something near to contemplation or meditation, though this is not
always suggested by specific parallelism, as in the last two poems mentioned above. In Jumping Out of Bed poems of this type are very few. As I
have said above, the theme of the title poem is the spiritual awakening of
the inward-turning individual who has hitherto led a materialistic and
secular life,[2] which is symbolized by the Sadducean pillow. The Sadducees
are presented in the Bible as deniers of what they cannot see or touch –
for example, the resurrection and the existence of angels and spirits –
and as believers only in the written law.[3] Thus, the rebirth of a Sadducee
can stand for a change from outwardness to inwardness and can be seen as a
discovery of hidden values, as suggested by the imagery of the last two
lines of the poem.

The last poem in this book actually consists of several short poems,
and it carries the title "Six Winter Privacy Poems."[4] Only in the last one
is a word used that refers to sleep:

---

1 The Morning Glory, p. 35.
2 Jumping, p. 43. Cf. also above, p. 106-107, where the poem is quoted and
   analyzed.
3 See The Bible, Acts 23:8.
4 Jumping, pp. 45-46.

1

About four, a few flakes.
I empty the teapot out in the snow,
    feeling shoots of joy in the new cold.
By nightfall, wind,
the curtains on the south sway softly.

2

My shack has two rooms; I use one.
The lamplight falls on my chair and table,
and I fly into one of my own poems -
I can't tell you where -
as if I appeared where I am now,
in a wet field, snow falling.

3

More of the fathers are dying each day.
It is time for the sons.
Bits of darkness are gathering around
      the sons.[1]
The darkness appears as flakes of light.

4

"A Sitting Poem"
There is a solitude like black mud!
Sitting in the darkness singing
I can't tell if this joy
is from the body, or the soul, or a
      third place!

5

"Listening to Bach"
There is someone inside this music
who is not well described by the names
of Jesus, or Jehovah, or the Lord of Hosts!

6

When I woke, new snow had fallen.
I am alone, yet someone else is with me,
drinking coffee, looking out at the snow.

What is referred to in poem 6 is probably not an awakening from ordinary sleep but from spiritual privacy and contemplation. In poem 1 Bly enjoys being alone, enjoys - as in some of his quite early poems[2] - the privacy emphasized by the falling snow and the "new cold." By nightfall, however, the wind causes movement in the curtains, which in poem 2 becomes a call

---

1   This line has been changed by Robert Bly from "gathering around them" to "gathering around the sons."
2   Cf. "Driving to Town Late to Mail a Letter," _Silence_, p. 38. Cf. also above, p. 33.

to movement for the poet soul, a movement into his own poem. An interpretation of the movement in the curtains as a call for the poet to move into
his own imagination fits well into the context of Bly's interests in
Taoism. The shack would then become a kind of teahouse, by the Japanese
called "'the abode of the unsymmetrical.'"[1] According to Joseph Campbell
"the unsymmetrical suggests movement; the purposely unfinished leaves a
vacuum into which the imagination of the beholder can pour."[2] The room he
uses would be the tearoom, "'the abode of fancy'"[3] and again according to
Campbell the tearoom "is an ephemeral structure built to enclose a moment
of poetic intuition."[4]

Moving inside his imagination, the poet feels close to the regenerative powers. It is time for the father consciousness, the rational energy,
to give way and to let the sons take over. In Jung's terms, and also in
mythological terms, the sons are closer to their mothers than to their
fathers. Therefore, to say "It is time for the sons" may mean that it is
time for a movement toward mother consciousness, a movement into darkness
toward rebirth. The result is a new consciousness seen in the poem as
"flakes of light." At a poetry reading[5] at Antioch College, in the autumn
of 1970, Bly mentioned this poem and spoke about this new consciousness
as a restoring of the balance between the father and the mother,[6] which
would mean between rationalistic and intuitive thinking.

The connection between spatial form and female consciousness should
also be considered, as is done by Robert E. Ornstein, a psychologist who
has influenced Bly: "The employment of spatial form, the special province
of the right hemisphere, plays a large role in esoteric psychology. Often
a room or an entire structure will be built in order to affect that mode
of consciousness directly in a certain manner."[7] In poem 4 Bly describes
how he himself has had a regenerative experience in darkness and solitude.

---

1 Joseph Campbell, The Hero with a Thousand Faces, p. 168.
2 Ibid.
3 Ibid.
4 Ibid.
5 See above, p. 118.
6 See Libby, "Robert Bly Alive in Darkness," p. 89.
7 Robert E. Ornstein, The Psychology of Consciousness (San Franscisco,
   Calif., 1972), p. 163. Notice that according to Ornstein female consciousness is located in the right hemisphere of the brain. See also
   below, p. 173. That Robert Bly is familiar with Ornstein's book is
   evident from his reference to it in his article "The Network and the
   Community."

In poem 5 we understand that listening to Bach turns his thoughts away from the male Christian divinities. In poem 6 he is back to ordinary consciousness but his regenerative experience has added a newness to his existence, like a new friend who shares his simple everyday life.[1]

The Rebirth Experience

The pattern of "Six Winter Privacy Poems" is similar to the pattern o the four phases of rebirth, known from old myths[2] and from Jung's psychoanalytic ideas[3]: The quest hero a) hears "the call to adventure,"[4] b) descends into darkness, c) experiences rebirth, and d) returns with a gift or a prize.[5] These different phases of what is called the "night journey" are referred to in several poems all through Bly's poetry, but not fully explored until in the long title poem of Sleepers Joining Hands the whole quest is enacted in mythological and mystical terms.

"Six Winter Privacy Poems" is, in fact, also the introductory poem of Sleepers Joining Hands, which seems to support the idea that the underlying pattern of this poem is the same as that of the long composite poem that ends the book and has the same title as the whole book. Other poems in this book refer in passing to meditation and to the rebirth archetype, for instance "The Turtle."[6] The turtle coming out of the water is described in terms similar to those that Bly uses to present individuals who have been immersed in meditation, and who, through meditation, have experienced rebirth:[7]

> How shiny the turtle is, coming out
> of the water, climbing the rock, as if
> the body inside shone through!
> As if swift turtle wings swept out of darkness,
> crossed some barriers,
> and found new eyes.
>   . . .

---

1 Cf below, p. 166, footnote 2.
2 See Joseph Campbell, The Hero with a Thousand Faces, passim; David Adams Leeming, Mythology: The Voyage of the Hero (New York, N.Y., 1973), passim; and Maud Bodkin, Archetypal Patterns in Poetry (London, 1963), passim.
3 Cf. C. G. Jung, Four Archetypes: Mother, Rebirth, Spirit, Trickster (Princeton, N.J., 1959; Paperback ed., 1970), passim; and Man and His Symbols, passim.
4 See Campbell, p. 245.
5 See ibid.
6 Sleepers, p. 5. See also below, pp. 183-184, for a full quotation and a further interpretation.
7 See below, footnote 1, p. 153, and p. 159.

In "Water Under the Earth," a poem about the contents of the unconscious - water being one of its symbols - the poet's effort to enter his
unconscious through meditation is part of the theme:

> . . .
> And I am there, prowling like a limp-footed
>   bull outside the circle of the fire,
> praying, meditating,
> full of energy, like a white horse, saddled,
>   alone on the unused fields.[1]

The white horse as a symbol of life and energy is often encountered in the
writings of Jung and his followers;[2] the field as a symbol of the unconscious, or of a part of it, is also in accordance with Jungian terminology.[3]

Considering Bly's whole poetic output I find a possible reference to
the rebirth archetype in "The Man Whom the Sea Kept Awake"[4] but the
speaker in the poem is not aware of the implications of the "call to
adventure." He is asking questions, and cannot see beyond the surface of
the sea, and, therefore, does not heed the call; he is not ready for a
regenerative experience:

> I've heard the sea upon the troubled rocks
> Waste this past night, with dreams more
>   troubled still,
> And where the images that you and I
> Would smooth a sullen morning by? The fly,
> Some mottled bird, the new brood of the fox?
> O nothing will be born again, until
> The monkish body and the eye can see
> Down to the darkened sea's nobility
> That now but seems a dancer on a bed
> Glutting the clumsy storm-delighted dead.
>   (1st stanza)

---

1 Sleepers, p. 7.
2 See for example, C. G. Jung, "Approaching the Unconscious," Man and His
   Symbols, p. 98, or M.-L. von Franz, "The Process of Individuation," Man
   and His Symbols, p. 174.
3 See for example, C. G. Jung, Four Archetypes, p. 15, where the field is
   associated with the Mother archetype; or M.-L. von Franz, "Conclusion:
   Science and the Unconscious," Man and His Symbols, p. 308, where the
   unconscious is compared with the field concept in physics; and above,
   p. 122.
4 MA thesis, p. 16, and The Paris Review (Spring - Summer, 1957), p. 141.

Or, perhaps, at the end the poem the speaker understands the meaning of
the call and contemplates that:

> When sparrows fall, they say its count is
> taken.
> When one mouse shivers, the King upon his
> throne is shaken.
> Let us turn our face to terror before we lose
> The nine steps to the bottom of the sea.
> (End of 3rd and last stanza)

In another poem, written about the same time, the call from the sea
is heard again, and this time the call is answered, and "the hero" is
about to depart. The poem is "Departure," or "The Sorb is the Tree of
Thor, who Hung Nine Days Wounded."[1] Two images are important in this poem,
that of the tree and of the sea. The sea - in some poems called the
waters - stands for an untraveled passage, or, as in the myths, the
darkness of the world that the hero has to conquer; or, as in Jungian
psychoanalysis, the darkness of the psyche, the unconscious, that the
individual must acquaint himself with. In terms of the rebirth archetype
the sea is the region where the transformation takes place, where the tree
of life is also the death tree bringing salvation:

> "Thor died on sorb; the sorb is Thor's salvation!"[2]

Leeming, in a chapter called "Death and the Scapegoat," refers to Jung:
"Jung saw in the association of hero and tree the sacred burial of the
hero in the great mother - the tree being the world tree with its roots
the depths of man's subconscious mind. Not only is the tree the world
navel and the world heart, it springs as a phallic symbol from the world
womb. As it is the place of Adam and Eve's first sin, so it is the place
of the death out of which will grow new life."[3]

In disscussing the first stage of the night journey as it is brought
out in myths and religions Campbell says:

> The two worlds, the divine and the human, can be
> pictured only as distinct from each other - different
> as life and death, as day and night. The hero adven-
> tures out of the land we know into darkness; there he
> accomplishes his adventure, or again is simply lost to us,

---

1 The poem is quoted above on p. 92.
2 See above, pp. 92-93, for the interpretation of the tree.
3 Leeming, p. 218.

> imprisoned or in danger; and his return is described
> as a coming back out of that yonder zone. Neverthe-
> less - and here is a great key to the understanding
> of myth and symbol - the two kingdoms are actually
> one. The realm of the gods is a forgotten dimen-
> sion of the world we know. And the exploration of
> that dimension, either willingly or unwillingly, is
> the whole sense of the deed of the hero. [1]

Bly sees himself as a partially unsuccessful quest hero in an early poem
that was published as one "Poem"[2] out of "Five American Poems" in The Paris
Review in 1962. The same poem was included in The Light around the Body,
now under the title "Turning away from Lies."[3] He is unsuccessful in that
he has tried to penetrate into that other region and has accomplished
nothing. However, he has come to an understanding of the idea in the quotation above: "the two kingdoms are actually one." In the final stanza Bly
shows us the difference between the state of mind of individuals who have
experienced the night journey and of those who have not: the difference
between the saints' rejoicing and the thieves' crying. Again the sea - the
waters - becomes the symbol of that yonder zone that one has to move
through.

A sequence of five poems written at this time is dominated by the
idea that different attitudes of mind relate to varying amounts of inner
experience. "Poems on the Voyage"[4] is the title of this composite poem,
in which the phrase "not to care" becomes the carrier of the theme. In a
prose article, "The Three Brains,"[5] Bly connects this phrase to the
American neurologist Paul MacLean's idea about our three brains: the reptile brain which fights for survival; the mammal brain which is capable
of a sense of community, of love; the new brain which is the source of
abstract thought, of spiritual ideas. Bly thinks that energy not used by
one of these brains can be transferred to another, for example through the
practice of meditation:

---

1 Campbell, p. 217.
2 The Paris Review (Winter/Spring, 1962), p. 18.
3 Light, p. 43. See above, pp. 73-74, for quotation and a preliminary
   interpretation.
4 The Quarterly Review of Literature (Fall, 1962), pp. 144-148, and
   Contemporary Poetry: A Retrospective from the Quarterly Review of
   Literature (Ed. by T. Weiss and Renée Weiss) (Princeton, N.J., 1975),
   pp. 245-249.
5 Robert Bly, "The Three Brains," The Seventies, 1 (Spring, 1972),
   pp. 61-69.

> The reptile brain thinks constantly of survival,
> of food, of security: When Christ says, "The lilies
> do not work, and yet they have better clothes than
> you do," he is urging his students not to care so
> much for themselves. If he student wills "not-caring,"
> and that "not-caring" persists, the "not-caring"
> will eventually cause some transfer of energy away from
> the reptile brain . . . to the mammal, and then to the
> new brain.[1]

This seems to be the pattern of "Poems on the Voyage" but obviously it is also the pattern of the rebirth experience.

In the first stanza of the first poem, "not to care" means to give worrying about material things in life - to live like the lilies, to lie content like dogs in the sun. The images of gold leaves, the cross, water and blood suggest a turning inward, something that is difficult if the reptile brain is dominant. The Wild Man in the second stanza illustrates the difficulties. He is in a rage because his reptile brain cannot accept meditation: "In oriental meditation the body is sitting in the foetal position, and this further infuriates the reptile brain, since it is basically a mammalian position."[2] In the last stanza the reader is invited to join the poet in contemplation:

> I
> Let us live inside ourselves,
> Like dogs among the sunlight;
> Keep us indoors among
> The world of rose and stair,
> Of harbor and twilight,
> Gold leaves and the cross,
> The dark roots washing water,
> Blood, and horns that toss.
>
> If that Wild Man had cared -
> Stamping from his tents,
> Goat black at midnight,
> Black, ragged, and mad -
> Did he care or not care?
> I say he did not care.
> If he had cared, he would never
> Have fallen into a rage.

---

1 Robert Bly, "The Three Brains," The Seventies, 1 (Spring, 1972), p. 6
2 Ibid., p. 67.

> We can sit down and brood
> Upon these things.
> Let the waters spring up!
> The bird sings crossly.
> Wave crosses the wave
> In the pastures of the sea.
> The hand of the sun
> Is stretched out still!

A turning in the direction of unconscious parts of the psyche is
rendered in terms of water images, and the potential energy stored there
is seen as the outstretched hand of the sun.

In the second poem we are reminded of different ways of life: those
of the warriors, the workers in the fields, and the saints:

> II
>
> We wander through vast expanses
> Like the Conestoga
> In the cottonwoods,
> Returning home to joy,
> Seeing again the small grave,
> The two sticks, meaning
> War, the distant glimpse
> Of smoke on hills:
>
> When the saint's body was taken
> On a plain wagon,
> The odor from its body
> Was like a lilac bush
> In the French fields, the odor drifting
> Through fence posts and groves, so that
> The reapers paused: this shows
> How much he did not care.
>
> When the sun falls
> From clear heavens on pale walls,
> We too must shake off
> These fierce longings,
> Shake off the flies of noon
> And the briars,
> Imagine ourselves on a sea
> Or entering a cave.

Wee see signs that mean war: the two sticks and the smoke upon the hill
would be a call to armor. An affirmative answer to that call would show
that you care more for the community than for yourself, but it is still a
fight for survival. The saint's body being brought to the cemetery is a
reminder to the harvesters that an alternative way of life exists. The
last stanza of this poem, as of the first one, is an admonition to turn
inward. Images of the sea and the cave suggest a rebirth experience
attained through a withdrawal from life.

The sea as a symbol for the unknown region and the cave as the place
for withdrawal and meditation are common concepts in myths and religions.
In poem III St. Anthony is mentioned as an example of one who chose the
cave and thus showed that he did "not care" about the world:

III

Among the images
Loitering, in gaiety,
Picking a campanile of grass
Amid deafening bells
Of gold and of silver,
Or in riotous moonlight loitering
With the goats, living
Quietly, like an alchemist.

Caring for nothing,
As Anthony in his scorn
Beneath the thorn-bush
Among hellish noise
Of the destroyed dead,
Who could not bear
Howling as owls and jackals
That he did not care -

We step then
On the first step;
Now we send the newsboy
Saddened, away;
Sunlight now is more
Than laughter, leading
As it does, far ahead
To the doors of despair.

St. Anthony withdrew from the world and founded the first monastery.
Whatever temptations the devil conjured up before his inner eye, he did
"not care." In Bly's prose article[1] St. Anthony is seen as a person dominated by the mammal brain, but practicing meditation. If the mammal brain
does not get enough excitement and sexual joy it conjures up visions of
temptations. For us, as is suggested in the last stanza, the first step
on this road would be to cut ourselves off from the world, to "send the
newsboy, / Saddened away." Then we can follow the sunlight - what the
first poem calls the stretched-out "hand of the sun."

We are moving toward a regenerative experience. That Bly sees hope
in despair we have already seen in other poems, for example "The Fire of

---

1   The Seventies, 1 (Spring, 1972), p. 67.

Despair Has Been Our Saviour."[1] But to go through despair means to "grasp the thorn," to subdue the lion as St. Jerome did, who, according to legend, pulled a thorn out of a lion's paw and so made the lion his friend. Then one can live "a rare life":

IV

Then we grasp the thorn.
For the thorn is
The ravages of joy,
Bursting of tombs, des-
Tructions of chains,
The willow bending,
And the blowing air,
The bare sticks of delight.

Beside St. Jerome
The lion lies,
The roots of his joy.
Like a tree stump
At his feet, the rare beast
In cantankerous joy
Covers the bare earth
Like a snow-storm.

The life of the dark sheath
Is a rare life,
Beyond breakfast
And wife, beyond
Body and hills,
A strange satisfaction
Of a strange need
As if in the sea.

The subduing of the lion, which makes possible "a rare life," seems to be an image for the movement from the mammal brain into the new brain, which in turn means the adoption of a spiritual life attitude. M.-L. von Franz sees such a situation as "the typical experience of the hermit - the animals make friends with him and bring him the spiritual life."[2]

In the concluding poem various acceptable "not-caring" attitudes are described: the life of the meditator who contemplates the five wounds of Christ or the wheel of the sun, the joy of David who did not care about life around him but instead let himself become absorbed in the depths of

---

1 See above, pp. 53-55.
2 M.-L. von Franz, The Feminine in Fairytales (Zürich, 1972), p. 86. (Robert Bly is familiar with the works of M.-L. von Franz. He mentions her in Ekbert Faas, "An Interview with Robert Bly," and he says so in a letter of Nov. 30, 1976, to the present writer.)

music, and finally the self-denial of the lover of humanity and of the
accepter of death as a reunion with Nature:

V

To live in the dark
Ocean, swimming or floating!
Meditating on the lion
With five spikes,
Or on the blazing wheel;
Meditating on the lion's
Wheel, that rolls in the ocean,
Throwing up fountains!

When David danced for joy
We guess he did not care.
When David played
The Song of Degrees
On his lute, when he cried,
"My bones cry out
From the depths," then we know
He did not care.

For not to care is this:
To love the orphans
And the fatherless,
And let the body
Reenter the leaves.
It is to hug the grave
All night, and live
In the dancing of the bones.

"Not-caring" thus embraces stages ranging from an attitude that is
near to indifference to the ascetic attitude of the hermit and the meditator to a final attitude of universal love and a longing to go back to
the origins of life.

The lion in the last two poems has a fourfold function. It is part
of the legend of Saint Jerome, but it also becomes symbolic in a religious, a mythological, and a psychoanalytic sense. The "lion[1] with five
spikes" is in all probability a symbol of Christ with his five wounds.
But a five-times-wounded Christ is one who has completed his life cycle
on earth. Therefore, the symbol of the lion metamorphoses into "the
blazing wheel" and "the lion's wheel," which is a circular symbol of the
fulfillment of a cyclic process, the process in this case being either
Christ's redemption of man or the sun's regeneration of the earth, the

---

1 See Aniela Jaffé, "Symbolism in the Visual Arts," Man and His Symbols
   p. 238, where the lion is mentioned as one of the animal symbols of
   Christ.

later process symbolized by the sun wheel in mythology and in non-
Christian art. Finally, the lion and the wheel symbols extend the meaning
of the phrase "not to care" which in fact refers to the individuation
process of the individual. According to Jung every man has to become
acquainted with his own psyche, with his instincts, in order to gain
wholeness. He has to heal and tame the lion as Saint Jerome did. "Primitive man must tame the animal in himself and make it his helpful compan-
ion; civilized man must heal the animal in himself and make it his
friend."[1] The "Wild Man" in poem I, who fell into a rage, had not yet
tamed his animal instincts, did not <u>understand</u> inwardness - that is, withdrawal, meditation, universal love, acceptance of death and reunion with
nature; therefore he behaved like a "Goat black at midnight / Black,
ragged, and mad." Thus the symbol for the sun in this first poem has to
be a stretched-out hand, a possible way of life, not an accepted way of
life. This way of depicting the life-giving power of the sun can be seen,
for example, in Egyptian art.[2] Not until the individual has come to terms
with his own psyche can his Self be seen as a whole, or a circle:

> Dr. M.-L. von Franz has explained the circle
> (or sphere) as a symbol of the Self. It
> expresses the totality of the psyche in all
> its aspects, including the relationship bet-
> ween man and the whole of nature. Whether the
> symbol of the circle appears in primitive sun
> worship or modern religion, in myths or dreams,
> in the mandalas drawn by Tibetan monks, in the
> ground plans of cities, or in the spherical con-
> cepts of early astronomers, it always points to
> the single most vital aspect of life - its
> ultimate wholeness."[3]

Ultimate wholeness is described in the last poem of the sequence. It is to
be seen in Christ's redemption of man, in the sun's renewal of the earth -
"Throwing up fountains" of life; in the individual's absorption into
expressions of the Self - as when "David danced for joy" and his bones
cried "out from the depths;" and finally in universal love, reunion with

---

1 Aniela Jaffé, "Symbolism in the Visual Arts," <u>Man and His Symbols</u>,
   p. 239.
2 <u>Man and His Symbols</u>, p. 22, illustration.
3 Aniela Jaffé, "Symbolism in the Visual Arts," <u>Man and His Symbols</u>,
   p. 240.

nature and acceptance of death as a means of going back to life's origins.
Thus, the voyage becomes the voyage of the individual, the voyage of
Christianity, the voyage of Nature, and the voyage of all life.

In three poems in the part of Silence in the Snowy Fields that is
called "Eleven Poems of Solitude" in the American edition and "We Know the
Road" in the British edition, the so-called "night journey" is the theme,[1]
but different stages of it are stressed in each of the three poems.
"Return to Solitude"[2] deals with the moment before the hero departs, at
which he feels the urge to go. The grass is shown as the manifestation of
life energy in the world around us;[3] and the sea serves as the image for
the place we move into in solitude, at night, in moments of grief, or in
death; and the tree with new leaves symbolizes the strength that might be
gained by a regenerative experience:[4]

                    I
        It is a moonlit, windy night.
        The moon has pushed out the Milky Way.
        Clouds are hardly alive, and the grass leaping.
        It is the hour of return.

                    II
        We want to go back, to return to the sea,
        The sea of solitary corridors,
        And halls of wild nights,
        Explosions of grief,
        Diving into the sea of death,
        Like the stars of the wheeling Bear.

                    III
        What shall we find when we return?
        Friends changed, houses moved,
        Trees perhaps, with new leaves.

In "Surprised by Evening"[5] what is described is the actual entrance into
the unknown, first as an awareness of something just beyond our reach,
then as a perception of on-coming evening, and finally as an immersion in
rising water:

---

1 Justin interprets these three poems in somewhat similar terms
   (pp. 76-78).
2 Silence, p. 12.
3 See above, pp. 101-108.
4 See above, p. 96.
5 Silence, p. 15.

There is unknown dust that is near us,
Waves breaking on shores just over the hill,
Trees full of birds that we have never seen,
Nets drawn down with dark fish.

The evening arrives: we look up and it is
                there,
It has come through the nets of the stars,
Through the tissues of the grass,
Walking quietly over the asylums of the
                waters.

The day shall never end, we think:
We have hair that seems born for the daylight;
But, at last, the quiet waters of the night
                will rise,
And our skin shall see far off, as it does
                under water.

"Poem in Three Parts"[1] speaks of the joy of the person who has come back
from the night journey. The first stanza conveys the joy felt by the body
in the morning, and the energy of the body is compared to that of grass.
The second stanza tells of the joy of the soul that has come back from
dream adventures arising out of the unconscious during the night. The
final stanza imagines a spiritual night journey that implies an eternal
union with the cosmos:

                          I
Oh, on an early morning I think I shall live
                forever!
I am wrapped in my joyful flesh,
As the grass is wrapped in its clouds of green.

                          II
Rising from a bed, where I dreamt
Of long rides past castles and hot coals,
The sun lies happily on my knees;
I have suffered and survived the night
Bathed in dark water, like any blade of grass.

                          III
The strong leaves of the box-elder tree,
Plunging in the wind, call us to disappear
Into the wilds of the universe,
Where we shall sit at the foot of a plant,
And live forever, like the dust.

The sense of newness brought about by the rebirth experience is
similar to the renewal of poetry felt by the poet through his acquaintance

---

1 Silence, p. 21.

with the work of Wallace Stevens. "Thinking of Wallace Stevens on the
First Snowy Day in December"[1] exemplifies the freshness of "deep image
poetry," which results from the associative leaps made by poets who go to
their unconscious for their imagery. The poem itself consists of sudden
associative shifts with the new-fallen snow serving both as a starting-
point and a conclusion:

> This new snow seems to speak of virgins
> With frail clothes made of gold,
> Just as the old snow shall whisper
> Of concierges in France.
>
> The new dawn sings of beaches
> Dazzling as sugar and clean as the clouds
>   of Greece,
> Just as the exhausted dusk shall sing
> Of the waves on the western shore.
>
> This new strength whispers of the darkness
>   of death,
> Of the frail skiff lost in the giant cave,
> Just as in the boat nearing death you sang
> Of feathers and white snow.

The poem is best understood if read side by side with Bly's article
"Spanish Leaping,"[2] in which he asserts that rapid association in a poem
is not just a device or a technique but a form of content. He sees Wallace
Stevens's early poems as ones "in which it is clear that the poet himself
considered association to be a form of content."[3] Pointing out "the distance between what Stevens was given as fact and what he then imagined,"[4]
he states: "The farther a poem gets from its initial worldly circumstance
without breaking the thread, the more content it has."[5] The "worldly circumstance" in Bly's poem is the new snow that reminds him of frail-
clothed, glittering virgins. He conjures up the old snow as a contrast,
something heavier and in darker clothes. The French concierges are probably
associated with the French poets who stand at the entrance to a new kind
of poetry. In America the freshness of these French poets does not seem
to be recognized, according to Bly:

---

1 Silence, p. 16.
2 The Seventies, 1 (Spring, 1972), pp. 16-21.
3 Ibid., p. 16.
4 Ibid.
5 Ibid.

> . . . the French poets were the first, as a group, to
> adopt underground passages of association as the major
> interest. We hide all that by calling them symbolists,
> but poet after poet through several generations gave
> his entire work to exploring these paths of association -
> Gérard de Nerval, Lautrémont, Aloysious Bertrand,
> Baudelaire, Mallarmé, also Poulet, whom Wallace Stevens,
> in some Harmonium poems, resembles fantastically. Eliot
> too entered association through a French Poet."[1]

The next associative leap in the poem is to another newness: the "new
dawn" is far off to the east, is dazzling and clean and is comparable to
"the clouds of Greece" which is the cradle of culture. The "new dawn" is
contrasted with what is exhausted - what is on the poet's own western
shore - the sunset region, the symbol of the entrance into death. The
associative leap between the last two stanzas is a leap into the world of
archetypes. The darkness of death becomes the positive darkness of rebirth[2]; it covers that other region in which new strength is gained by
the quest hero in old myths, by the individual who comes to terms with
his unconscious, and by the deep image poet who turns inward for his
images. The cave is a traditional symbol for this dark region. Jung says
about "the process of transformation":

> I have chosen as an example a figure which plays a
> great role in Islamic mysticism namely Khidr, "the
> Verdant One." He appears in the Eighteenth Sura of
> the Koran, entitled "The Cave." This entire Sura is
> taken up with a rebirth mystery. The Cave is the place
> of rebirth, that secret cavity in which one is shut
> up in order to be incubated and renewed.[3]
>
> Khidr may well be a symbol of the self. His qualities
> signalize him as such: he is said to have been born
> in a cave, i.e. in darkness.[4]

The final associative leap in Bly's poem leads back to Wallace Stevens
who, approaching this darkness, creates frail and bright images of
feathers and white snow. The poem returns to where it started: the snow

---

1 The Seventies, 1 (Spring, 1972), p. 17.
2 Cf. above, p. 43, and pp. 53-54, the discussion about "containers of a
   positive darkness."
3 C. G. Jung, Four Archetypes, p. 69.
4 Ibid., p. 75.

opens and closes it, completes the circle - the symbol of wholeness.[1]
This also suggests a Taoist idea which would surely be familiar to Bly:
"To reach wholeness one must return!"[2]

Piccione[3] sees this poem as a comparison between the poetries of B
and Stevens: the differences would, then, be brought out in the images
new and old in the first and second stanzas, and the similarities in th
boat symbols in the last stanza. This seems to be a possible interpreta
tion, although, in light of what Bly says about Stevens in the prose
article referred to above - which, by the way, was published later than
Piccione's thesis - it is hard to believe that Bly would refer to
Stevens's poetry as "the old snow" and "the exhausted dusk." These imag
would rather refer to those American poets of the 40's and 50's who und
rated and, therefore, did not read or translate the Spanish poets who
"loved the new paths of association even more than the French."[4] It is
worth noting that Bly says that the French Surrealists were the only on
accepted by the American poets I just mentioned. I think that is why Bl
uses the image of the French concierges; they stand at the entrance to
new poetry, but they are employed by the old school for some kind of pr
tection.

The poem called "The Hermit"[5] presents a man who has gone through
darkness, reached wholeness, and brings calm and courage to others:

> Darkness is falling through darkness,
> Falling from ledge
> To ledge.
> There is a man whose body is perfectly whole.
> He stands, the storm behind him,
> And the grass blades are leaping in the wind.
> Darkness is gathered in folds
> About his feet.
> He is no one. When we see
> Him, we grow calm,
> And sail on into the tunnels of joyful death.

---

1 Cf. above, p. 115, the chain of associative leaps in "At a Fish Hatche
   in Story, Wyoming," which starts with facts about the trout, moves c
   snowbanks, mountains, breasts, white stones from glaciers, chilly
   streams, furs, caves, women, a child, and back to breasts and fish.
   See also above, pp. 24-25, about snow as transformer, and above,
   p. 137, about the wheel as the symbol of the fulfillment of a cyclic
   process.
2 The White Pony, p. 71. See also below, p. 164.
3 Piccione, Robert Bly and the Deep Image, pp. 71-72.
4 Robert Bly. "Spanish Leaping," The Seventies 1, p. 18.
5 Light, p. 55.

The last poem of The Light around the Body, "When the Dumb Speak,"[1]
relates a dream experience - in a way a transformative experience - that
makes the individual lose everything but finally results in wholeness.
Energy, which previously existed only as a potentiality, is plenished
with life:

> There is a joyful night in which we lose
> Everything, and drift
> Like a radish
> Rising and falling, and the ocean
> At last throws us into the ocean,
> And on the water we are sinking
> As if floating on darkness.
> The body raging
> And driving itself, disappearing in smoke,
> Walks in large cities late at night,
> Or reading the Bible in Christian Science
>   windows,
> Or reading a history of Bougainville.
> Then the images appear:
> Images of death,
> Images of the body shaken in the grave,
> And the graves filled with seawater;
> Fires in the sea,
> The ships smoldering like bodies,
> Images of wasted life,
> Life lost, imagination ruined,
> The house fallen,
> The gold sticks broken,
> Then shall the talkative be silent,
> And the dumb shall speak.

We notice again the traditional symbols associated with the rebirth archetype: ocean, water, darkness, the grave, and fire. What Bly adds to this
night journey is the juxtaposition of the traditional images of sinking
into darkness and into water with images of modern man walking "in large
cities late at night," reading the Bible through a window, or studying
the history of a distant island. The joining of the traditional images to
images of modern life refurbishes the older tropes: they come to suggest
the death of the body, the death of the imagination, the death of special
gifts. This is the moment in which slumbering potentialities are endowed
with life. Anna Balakian notices a similar phenomenon in a French Surrealist poem:

---

1 Light, p. 62.

Verbal expression linking the visions of the dream
state with conscious perceptions is also the core
of one of the most original of Paul Eluard's works,
Les Dessous d'une Vie ou la Pyramide Humaine, wherein
the poet envisions human experiences in the form of a
pyramid, the narrow peak of which is the limited range
of the lucid state, and the broad base the receptivity
of the full, solid subterranean strata of the subconscious, the dream where all his desires are born, where
receptivity is keener than the sense perceptions of his
waking hours. He can hear the language of the deaf and
dumb and with the "pure faculty of sight" can envisage
such images as "perpendicular green" upon which he picks
"raspberries white as milk."[1]

The idea that one must lose everything before being reborn also co
cludes the prose poem "A Small Bird's Nest Made of White Reed Fiber":"
It is something made and then forgotten, like our own lives that we wil
entirely forget in the grave, when we are floating, nearing the shore
where we will be reborn, ecstatic and black."[2] At the end of "I Came Ou
of the Mother Naked,"[3] a long piece of prose in Sleepers Joining Hands,
Bly comments indirectly on the rebirth theme in his own poems: "I see i
my own poems and the poems of so many other poets alive now fundamental
attempts to right our own spiritual balance, by encouraging those parts
in us that are linked with music, with solitude, water, and trees, the
parts that grow when we are far from the centers of ambition."[4] Joyce
Carol Oates in her review of Sleepers Joining Hands sees the extraordinary importance of these "fundamental attempts"[5] and considers this ess
"fascinating, since it puts into urgent and very timely images the more
generalized, diffuse arguments of Erich Neumann, and ties in the traged
of America's involvement in Indochina with Jung's warning about the ca-
tastrophe that awaits the world unless civilized man is willing to face
the maniacal depths of his own psyche."[6]

---

1 Anna Balakian, Surrealism: The Road to the Absolute, p. 128.
2 The Morning Glory, p. 9.
3 Sleepers, pp. 29-50. In this essay Bly develops and comments on Eric
   Neumann's ideas of mother consciousness as put forward in his book,
   The Great Mother (Princeton, N.J., 1963). See also below, p. 185.
4 Ibid., p. 50.
5 See quotation above.
6 Joyce Carol Oates, "Where They All Are Sleeping," Modern Poetry Stud
   (Winter, 1973), pp. 342-343.

However, the only poem that Bly has written in which the rebirth archetype is consciously used as a pattern seems to be the long poem "Sleepers Joining Hands,"[1] which takes up one fourth of the book of the same title. The titles of the four poems of which in its turn it consists suggest the four main phases in a quest hero's adventure, frequently dealt with in myths, or of the individual's individuation process described in Jungian psychoanalysis. In terms of the quest-myth, "The Shadow Goes Away" describes the "threshold crossing" and includes a "shadow presence" and a "brother battle;" "Meeting the Man who Warns Me" brings in the "helper;" "The Night Journey in the Cooking Pot" contains the actual deed, reward, and return of the hero; and, finally, "Water Drawn Up Into the Head" deals with the "elixir" that the hero brings back.[2] In terms of Jungian psychoanalysis, the titles in turn suggest "the realization of the shadow;" the "wise old man" or "superior insight;" the "transformation" process or actual change, "often symbolized by the action of crossing water;" and finally the result of the individuation process, the realization of the totality of the Self.[3] These four poems accordingly contain one dominant archetype each, all four of which are included in the main rebirth archetype: the shadow, the wise old man, the womb-shaped vessel, and the circle.

The persona[4] of Bly's quest poem hears the call to adventure, or feels the urge to turn inward, when he encounters "the woman chained to the shore."[5] In mythological terms this might be Daphne who in her flight from Apollo was changed into a laurel tree on the shore of her father's

---

1 Sleepers, pp. 51-67.
2 For these myth elements see Campbell, pp. 245 f.
3 For these psychoanalytical terms see M.-L. von Franz, "The Process of Individuation," Man and His Symbols, pp. 168, 196, and 198; and Aniela Jaffé, "Symbolism in the Visual Arts," Man and His Symbols, p. 240. See also C. G. Jung, Four Archetypes, pp. 151, and 81. Justin gives in his thesis (pp. 109-119) a short interpretation of "Sleepers Joining Hands" based on Jungian terms.
4 I use the word persona here since the "I" in this poem seems to be used in a more general sense than in Bly's earlier poems. However, it should not be understood in the Jungian sense of the term, that is, man wearing a mask in his role as a civilized human being. Rather, it stands for the hero on his quest, for individual man in search of his lost identity.
5 Sleepers, p. 53, the opening phrase of "The Shadow Goes Away," the first poem in the sequence "Sleepers Joining Hands." From now on I am going to give very few page references to the four poems in this sequence since I shall quote them in order as they stand.

river. She can also be seen as the maiden in distress of old myths.
Campbell says:

> The hegemony wrested from the enemy, the freedom
> won from the malice of the monster, the life energy
> released from the toils of the tyrant Holdfast - is
> symbolized as a woman. She is the maiden of the
> innumerable dragon slayings, the bride abducted from
> the jealous father, the virgin rescued from the un-
> holy lover. She is the "other portion" of the hero
> himself - for "each is both": if his stature is that
> of world monarch she is the world, and if he is a
> warrior she is fame. She is the image of his destiny
> which he is to release from the prison of enveloping
> circumstance. [1]

Thus, in psychoanalytical terms she is the part of a man's psyche that
has until now been locked up and unknown to him. The persona of the poem
does not want to share the fate of Daphne and Apollo. The alternative
for him is to let the water take him. He notices it coming, and he is
without protection:

>   . . .
>   I don't want to wake up in the weeds, and
>   find the light
>   gone out in the body, and the cells dark....
>   I see the cold ocean rise to take us
>   as I stand without feathers on the shore
>   and watch the blood-colored moon gobbling
>   up the sand....

The owl, representing Nature, also feels threatened by strange powers:

>   The owl senses someone in the hole of his
>   tree,
>   and lands with wings closing, claws out....

The persona gives in to the call and starts his quest, that is, enters his
unconscious:

>   I fall asleep, and dream I am working in the
>   fields....

The shadow - "that other side of ourselves," "the primitive, uncontrolled
and animal part of ourselves," that is both personal, and common to all

---

1   Campbell, p. 342.

mankind at the same time[1] - is the part of the unconscious that the persona encounters first. What follows is therefore an account of the persona's childhood, the time when the shadow was first pushed away into the
dark. It is partly given in the form of a "brother battle,"[2] and it is
rendered in terms of the Biblical story of Joseph and his treacherous
brothers. The shadow, the brother, is sent away and lives a life not
shared by the persona who himself is in high school "asleep in the Law,"
which might mean that he follows worldly rules - like the Sadducees[3] -
and not his own inner urge. He is, however, aware of this inner urge - it
manifests itself as temporary disappearances into another dimension of
place and time:

> Now I show the father the coat stained with
>   goat's blood....
> The shadow goes away,
> we are left alone in the father's house.
> I knew that.... I sent my brother away.
> I saw him turn and leave. It was a schoolyard.
> I gave him to the dark people passing.
> He learned to sleep alone on the high buttes.
> I heard he was near the Missouri, taken in by
>   traveling Sioux.
> They taught him to wear his hair long,
> to glide about naked, drinking water from his
>   hands,
> to tether horses, follow the faint trail
>   through bent grasses....
> Men bound my shadow. That was in high school.
> They tied it to a tree, I saw it being led
>   away.
> I dreamt that I sat in a big chair,
> and every other second I disappeared.
> This was during Stanley's visit to Africa.
>
> In highschool I was alone, asleep in the Law.

The biblical phrase to be "asleep in the Law" is explained by Jung:

> Obedience under the law on one hand, and the
> freedom of the "children of God," the reborn,
> on the other, is discussed at length in the
> Epistles of St. Paul. He distinguishes not
> only between two different classes of men,

---

1 See Frieda Fordham, An Introduction to Jung's Psychology, pp. 49-50.
2 See Campbell, pp. 245-246.
3 See above, p. 125.

> who are separated by a greater or lesser development
> of consciousness, but also between the higher and
> lower man in one and the same individual. The sarkikos
> (carnal man) remains eternally under the law; the
> pneumatikos (spiritual man) alone is capable of being
> reborn into freedom. [1]

The persona of the poem, however, does not remain "eternally under the law." When he begins to understand what he has done to his brother, to his shadow, he starts out to find him and so to find out about that other way of life. He gives in to his feelings; depression and impulses from the dark are signs that his unconscious is starting to awake. This inner experience is also rendered in the description of his encounter with the Indians, since earlier in the poem his brother had been described as living among Indians after having been given to "the dark people." As he approaches the Sioux he notices that his shadow - the "maiden" of fairy tales - is in great danger:

> I slipped off one night into the water,
>   swam to shore with no one watching,
> left my brother alone on the ship!
> On 66th Street I noticed he was gone.
> I sat down and wept.
> Hairs of depression come up through the palm
>   laid on the ground,
> little impulses shoot up in the dark,
> in the dark the sleeping marmoset opens his
>   eyes.
> There are nights in which everything is torn
> away, all piers gone....
> I walk through the trees, and come into the
>   ˙ Indian encampment.
> The Sioux are struggling up the mountain in
>   disordered lines,
> the field littered with robes, dogbones, thongs,
> the great cooking iron in which my shadow was
>   boiling!

Then the description of the persona's walk through the camp turns into one of his psyche:

> Walking through the camp, I notice an old chest
>   of drawers.
> I open a drawer and see small white horses
>   gallop away toward the back.
> I see the birds inside me,
> with massive shoulders, like humpbacked Puritan
>   ministers,

---

[1] Jung, Four Archetypes, p. 71, n.

> a headstrong beak ahead,
> and wings supple as the stingray's,
> ending in claws, lifting over the shadowy
>   ·peaks.

He starts to sort out the experiences of his own life and realizes his
dishonesty towards his own Self, symbolized by a gift from his mother, a
shirt, now stained:

> Looking down, I see dark marks on my shirt.
> My mother gave me that shirt, and hoped that
>   her son would be the one man in
>   the world
> who would have a happy marriage,
> but look at me now –
> I have been divorced five hundred times,
> six hundred times yesterday alone.

The marks on his shirt then take on larger dimensions: his treachery
toward his brother, his shadow, and his dishonesty toward his own Self
become that of the whites toward the Indians:

> I hear the sound of hoofs...coming....Now the men
> move in, smashing and burning. The huts
> of the Shadowy People are turned over, the wood
> utensils broken, straw mats set on fire,
> digging sticks jumped on, clay bowls
> smashed with dropped stones....

The numerousness of the attackers and the swiftness of their destruc-
tive actions, depicted in unusual imagery is contrasted with the absence
of spiritual guides and with the lonely flight of the persona over an
imaginary forest in which only one creature isolates himself with his
feminine partner. Probably this is to be seen as a parallel with the persona and his unconscious:

> Thousands of men come,
> like dwarf antelopes in long streaming herds,
> or hair flying behind the skidding racer....
>
> No ministers or teachers come out,
> I am flying over my bed alone....
> I am flying over the Josephine forests, where
>   only the rat builds his nest of
>   leaves,
> and keeps his mistress in the white dusk....

Then the persona views a sick universe where feminine and masculine forces
are split apart and perishing. He is offered money but refuses it. In the
darkening masculine world, he distinguishes the symbol of a feminine force

but the masculine part of him tries to protect itself with armor and
scales:

>The moon swims through the clogging veins,
>the sun leaps from its dying bed,
>divorced men and women drown in the paling,
>   reddening sea.
>
>The Marines turn to me. They offer me money.
>I turn and leave. The sun sinks toward the
>   darkening hills.
>My mother's bed looms up in the dark.
>The noose tightens,
>servants of the armor brain, terrified hired
>   men whom the sharks feed,
>scales everywhere, "glittering on their bodies
>   as they fall."

This dramatic encounter with the shadow ends in chaos, a chaos described
in images of our own world of moonlandings, energy waste, minority re-
volts, counter-culture, and war:

>The Sea of Tranquility scattered with dead
>   rocks,
>and black dust resembling diesel oil.
>The suppressed race returns: snakes and
>   transistors filling the beaches,
>pilots in armored cockpits finding their way
>   home through moonlit clouds.

These images show the horror of a society in which the individual is not
acquainted with the shadowy part of his own psyche. Thus, the woman
chained to the shore at the beginning of the poem has also turned out to
be our contemporary society. She is the one who is to be rescued.

At the beginning of the next poem, "Meeting the Man Who Warns Me,"[1]
we return to the persona of the poem, to the myth hero on his quest. He
seems to have crossed the threshold to that other land but is far away
from his goal:

>I wake and find myself in the woods, far from the castle.

He is on his way somewhere, but without knowledge of the world around him:

>The train hurtles through lonely Louisiana
>   at night.
>The sleeper turns to the wall, delicate
>aircraft dive toward earth.

---

1 Sleepers, p. 56.

He needs guidance. Campbell depicts the myth hero in this situation:
"Beyond the threshold, then, the hero journeys through a world of unfamiliar yet strangely intimate forces, some of which severely threaten
him (tests), some of which give magical aid (helpers)."[1]

In the case of the persona of this poem, the first intimate force he
encounters is in the shape of a woman. She urges him to be true but doubts
his ability to be so. In Jungian terms we have to do with the archetype
of the anima, the feminine part of a man's psyche. Jung says, "The
[figure] standing closest behind the shadow is the anima, who is endowed
with considerable powers of fascination and possession."[2] She is a manifestation of another part of the persona's own self, although he does not
recognize it as such. He experiences it as separate manifestations of
female energy:

> A woman whispers to me, urges me to speak
> truths.
> "I am afraid that you won't be honest with me."
> Half or more of the moon rolls on in shadow.
> Owls talk at night, loons wheel cries through
> lower waters,
> fragments of the mother lie open in all low
> places.

Bly speaks about the anima in his prose essay "I Came Out of the Mother
Naked" and points to the importance for the individual of reaching a
balance between his animus and anima, or, in Bly's terms, between father
consciousness and mother consciousness.[3] He also sees in contemporary
writing "a revaluation of the anima, the feminine soul, following centuries of depreciation of it."[4]

In the poem the reference to "lower waters" and "low places" shows
that the persona is getting to know his unconscious, but he is not yet
successful; the conscious part of his psyche holds him back. He starts
out but returns. However, his movements have brought him into contact with
water and wood, and this becomes symbolic of the actual "threshold
crossing." Jung mentions that the unconscious "is frequently expressed
through wood and water symbols."[5] The persona falls asleep and meets a

---

1   Campbell, p. 246.
2   Jung, Four Archetypes, p. 150.
3   See Sleepers, pp. 48-49.
4   Ibid., p. 49.
5   Jung, Four Archetypes, p. 100.

divine guide - a manifestation of the "wise old man" archetype. Jung sa
that the anima "hides in her turn the powerful archetype of the wise ol
man (sage, magician, king, etc.)."[1] By touching him the guide leads him
deeper into the new land:

> I have been alone two days, and still every-
> thing is cloudy.
> The body surrounds me on all sides.
> I walk out and return.
> Rain dripping from pine boughs, boards soaked
> on porches,
> gray water awakens, fish slide away underneath.
> I fall asleep. I meet a man from a milder
> planet.
> I say to him: "I know Christ is from your
> planet!"
> He lifts his eyes to me with a fierce light.
> He reaches out and touches me on the tip of
> my cock,
> and I fall asleep.

This experience seems to be similar to what Marie-Louise von Franz describes:

> If an individual has wrestled seriously enough and
> long enough with the anima (or animus) problem so that
> he, or she, is no longer partially identified with
> it, the unconscious again changes its dominant char-
> acter and appears in a new symbolic form, representing
> the Self, the innermost nucleus of the psyche. . . .
> In the case of a man, it manifests itself as a mascu-
> line initiator and guardian (an Indian guru), a wise
> old man, a spirit of nature, and so forth.[2]

What follows in the poem is an exposition of the contents of the u
conscious. Since the persona is a man, he moves away from his male consciousness. Therefore, his first perception is that of male authorities
dying, of passivity and weakness displayed by men:

> I dream that the fathers are dying.
> Jehovah is dying, Jesus' father is dying,
> the hired man is asleep inside the oat straw.
> Samson is lying on the ground with his
> hollow hair.

---

1 Jung, Four Archetypes, p. 150.
2 M.-L. von Franz, "The Process of Individuation," Man and His Symbols
   p. 196.

After the fading of consciousness brings this negative experience, the
persona registers the existence of an energy that manifests itself in
various ways: electricity, divination, water power. He sees the effect
that this power has on an individual:

> Who is this that visits us from beneath the
> earth?
> I see the dead like great conductors
> carrying electricity under the ground,
> the Eskimos suddenly looking into the womb
> of the seal....
> Water shoots into the air from manhole covers,
> the walker sees it astonished and falls;
> before his body hits the street
> he is already far down the damp steps of the
> Tigris,
> seeing the light given off under the door
> by shining hair.

The images embodying this experience indicate that through this energy
the individual is sent deeper into his unconscious. The "damp steps of
the Tigris" is a water image which suggests Oriental meditation or a return to the original energy. The light given off by the "shining hair"
probably has the same meaning as "the light around the body," which is
the light around holy men or around a place where such men are meditating.[1] But the fact that a door is partly hiding the light, and the
light is given off by hair[2] - a symbol of togetherness and love and not
of solitary meditation - seems to indicate that the individual en-
countering this power is still only approaching the center of his unique
experience. Light becomes the dominant image of the next stanza, which
begins with a white darkness,[3] of which the shadow is a part - the shadow
is now accepted by the persona. The light is another manifestation of the
energy seen in the preceding stanza. The persona moves toward it but
meets an old man who questions him:

---

1 Cf. what Bly says in "The Three Brains," The Seventies, 1, p. 64: "As
   the reptile brain power is symbolized by cold, and the mammal brain by
   warmth, the mark of the new brain is light. The gold light always
   around Buddha's head in statues is an attempt to suggest that he is
   living in his new brain. Some Tibetan meditators of the 13th century
   were able to read books in the dark by the light given off from their
   own bodies."
2 Cf. ibid., pp. 61-69, and the poem "Hair," Sleepers, pp. 10-12.
3 Cf. above, p. 141: "the positive darkness of rebirth."

Something white calls to us:
it is the darkness we saw outside the cradle.
My shadow is underneath me,
floating in the dark, in his small boat bobbing
                among reeds.
A fireball floats in the corner of the Eskimo's
                house -
It is a light that comes nearer when called!
A light the spirits turn their heads for,
suddenly shining over land and sea!
I taste the heaviness of the dream,
the northern lights curve up toward the roof
                of my mouth.
The energy is inside us....
I start toward it, and I meet an old man.
He looms up in the road, his white hair
                standing up:
"Who is this who is ascending the red river?
Who is this who is leaving the dark plants?"
I don't want to leave, and walk back and forth,
looking toward the old landing.

Bly's description of the light encountered on this journey is very close
to what surrealists in general wanted to communicate. Marcel Raymond says
"The specific characteristic of the surrealists is this, that they
aspired to be kings of a nocturnal kingdom, illumined by a strange aurora
borealis, by phosphorescences and phantasms emanating from unfathomed
regions."[1] The persona has reached another crucial point on his journey.
To reach the light of the "unfathomed region," he has to cross a river,
but he hesitates. The old man who "looms up in the road" is again a manifestation of the archetype of the wise old man. This time he helps the
persona to self-knowledge, to overcome what holds him back; he urges the
persona to come to terms with those past experiences which he has pushed
down into his unconscious:

I dream that I cannot see half of my life.
I look back, it is like the blind spot in a car.
So much just beyond the reach of our eyes,
what tramples the grasses while the horses are
                asleep,
the hoof marks all around the cave mouth...
what slips in under the door at night, and
                lies exhausted on the floor in the
                morning.

---

1   Marcel Raymond, From Baudelaire to Surrealism, p. 268.

What cannot be remembered and cannot be
            forgotten,
the chaff blowing about my father's feet.
And the old man cries out: "I am here.
Either talk to me about your life, or turn
            back."

The persona's response is to take in the landscape around him, to
notice creatures moving in close relationship to the earth. These creatures – cattle, a lizard, frogs, horses – are in certain religions, myths,
and other symbolic contexts considered bearers of life energy: the cow is
a holy animal in India, the frog and the lizard are disguised princes in
fairy tales, the horse is a symbol of life in Jung's interpretation of
dream language. The persona experiences this psychic landscape and listens
to his guide talking:

I look from bridges at cattle grazing,
the lizard moving stiffly over the November
            road,
the night frogs who give out the croak of
            the planet turning,
the great knees of horses loyal to the earth
            risen in their will.
"I am the dark spirit that lives in the dark.
Each of my children is under a leaf he chose
            from all the leaves in the universe.
When I was alone, for three years, alone,
I passed under the earth through the night-
            water,
I was for three days inside a warm-blooded
            fish.
'Purity of heart is to will one thing.'
I saw the road...." "Go on! Go on!"
"A whale bore me back home, we flew through
            the air....
Then I was a boy who had never seen the sea!
It was like a King coming to his own shores.

It seems to me that when listening to the wise old man, to "the dark
spirit that lives in the dark," the persona realizes that he is listening
to his own self and is coming to terms with still another part of his
psyche. Therefore, it seems that in the end it is the persona himself who
is speaking. He himself – Bly himself– has been alone for three years; he
has come to realize the meaning of the night journey he has started out
on. The initiation rites are just being performed:

I feel the naked touch of the knife,
I feel the wound,
this joy I love is like wounds at sea...."

Having realized that the shadow, the anima, and the wise old man are
actually parts of his own psyche, the persona is ready to go through the
actual transformation process, to reenter a womb and be reborn – to
undertake "The Night Journey in the Cooking Pot."[1] The cooking pot in t
poem just mentioned has a function similar to that of "the cave," explained above on page 141. Jung's discussion of the mother archetype is
pertinent: "It can be attached to a rock, a cave, a tree, a spring, a
deep well, or to various vessels . . . Hollow objects such as ovens and
cooking vessels are associated with the mother archetype, and, of cours
the uterus, yoni, and anything of a like shape."[2] The corresponding ep
sode in the quest myth would be the actual ordeal for which the hero is
rewarded. Campbell says:

> When he arrives at the nadir of the mythological round,
> he undergoes a supreme ordeal and gains his reward. The
> triumph may be represented as the hero's sexual union
> with the goddess-mother of the world (sacred marriage),
> his recognition by the father-creator (father-atonement),
> his own divinization (apotheosis), or again – if the
> powers have remained unfriendly to him – his theft of
> the boon he came to gain (bride-theft, fire-theft);
> intrinsically it is an expansion of consciousness and
> therewith of being (illumination, transfiguration,
> freedom).[3]

"The Night Journey in the Cooking Pot" is composed of several sec-
tions which could each be seen as a separate poem, with the rebirth
experience as a common theme. The introductory section contains seven
lines which embody seven variations on the basic theme:

> I was born during the night sea-journey.
> I love the whale with his warm organ pipes
>   in the mouse-killing waters,
> I love the men who drift, asleep, for three
>   nights in octopus waters,
> the furry men gathering wood, piling the
>   chunks by walls,
> I love the snow, I need privacy as I move,
> I am all alone, floating in the cooking pot
> on the sea, through the night I am alone.

---

1 Sleepers, pp. 59-63.
2 Jung, Four Archetypes, p. 15. See also ibid., p. 69: "Anyone who get
   into that cave, that is to say into the cave that everyone has in hi
   self, or into the darkness that lies behind consciousness, will find
   himself involved in an – at first – unconscious process of transform
   tion."
3 Campbell, p. 246.

In the next section we see the persona as a shaman in the shape of a
bird.[1] Leeming sees the shaman in the context of the rebirth archetype:

> When the hero withdraws into the wilderness or to
> the mountain or cave (the last of these is reminiscent
> of the womb-cave of the birth myth), he literally
> withdraws into himself to emerge later with the
> divinity he has found there; he emerges as a shaman,
> who has had direct experience of the unknown in him-
> self. As is the case with all of the major rites
> of passage, this is a losing of the self to find the
> self, and it involves physical and mental suffering;
> the god within is not so easily born.[2]

The voice of the persona in the following section seems - as it often
does in Bly's poems - to be identical with Bly's own voice. He retells
his own transformation experience at the time when he was living in
seclusion in New York.[3] This description of his first acquaintance with
inwardness turns into a chain of images suggesting its wide range:

> I felt the wings brushing the floors of the
>   dark,
> trailing longer wings,
> the wing marks left in the delicate sand of
>   the corridors,
> the face shining far inside the mountain.
> There is a certainty that makes the fingers
>   love each other,
> and makes the body give up sleep.
> The animals open their mouths, and come, glad,
> in a ring.
> The snow begins falling.
> A winter of privacy is before us,
> winter privacy,
> the vast halls inside the heads of animals
> lie before us, the slow
> breaking of day, warm blood moving, moving,
> and immense pine trees.

* * *

We see how, moving through the darkness, he reaches the stage at which he
understands the light from the faces of people living in seclusion. Also
the body benefits from the experience of inwardness. The fullness of life

---

1 See above, pp. 112-113.
2 Leeming, p. 119.
3 For quotation see above, p. 56.

that seems to be gained is symbolized by animals coming in a ring, which
is, of course, the circle, the traditional symbol of wholeness. After
these general images Bly employs the more personal image of snow to communicate to the reader his own custom of winter withdrawal - its scope
like the vastness inside animals' heads. The flow of energy, with which
he is brought into contact, is symbolized by dawn, blood, and trees.

The feeling of privacy in this section extends into the imagery he
chooses for a particular rebirth experience in the section that follows:

> For the first time in months I love the dark.
> A joy pierces into me, it arrives like a
>   runner,
> a radio signal from inside a tree trunk,
> a smile spreads over the face, the eyes fall.
>
> Someone is asleep in the back of my house.
> I feel the blood galloping in the body,
> the baby whirling in the womb.
> Dark bodies pass by far out at the horizon,
> trailing lights like flying saucers,
> the shadows go by long after the bodies have
>   passed.
> Nuns with faces smoothed by prayer
> peer out from holes in the earth.

The movement into darkness conveys joy, togetherness, and a feeling of
new life. Other creatures, also existing in the dark areas, appear and
disappear; they are holders of visual or spiritual light. The following
stanza develops the imagery of light-emitting creatures:

> The mouse goes down the tunnel where the
>   mice-infants light the whole room!
> I start down, after him,
> I see owls with blue flames coming from the
>   tops of their heads,
> watching from firs on each side of the road,
> and snow just beginning to fall.

The images of the persona sitting in the dark, the nuns peering out from
holes in the earth, and the mice-infants lighting up the room at the end
of the tunnel, are used in preparation for a more traditional and more
final chain of images for the loss of self by which the self is found:

> They broke from the house, walked in the
>   trees, and were lost,
> slept in the earth, brooded like wells in
>   the deep ground,
> sleeping in anguish like grain, whole,
>   blind in the old grave.

> Who is it that visits us from beneath the snow?
> Something shining far down in the ice?
> Deep in the mountain the sleeper is glad.
> Men with large shoulders covered with furs,
> eyes closed, inexplicable.
> Holy ones with eyes closed,
> the cracking sound in the ice under our feet,
> the frozen lake marked with caribou feet...

To undertake the night journey is to become lost in the woods, to go as
deep down into the ground as a well, or to let oneself be buried and
sleep in the ground like a grain of corn. To walk in the trees and be lost
would carry the same meaning here as it does in fairytales according to
M.-L. von Franz: "The forest would be the place of unconventional inner
life, in the deepest sense of the word,"[1] or, "the forest is the place
where things begin to turn and grow again; it is a healing regression."[2]
The well and the grave are other locations for the regenerative experience, as are the places "beneath the snow" or "far down in the ice." A
person who returns from one of these places is touched by the light, is
"shining" and "glad," The experience is related to that of the Seven
Sleepers who woke to new life after having been asleep in a cave for 372
years.[3] The legend tells us that their faces were "like roses in bloom,"[4]
that "their faces shone like the sun."[5] Bly is probably referring to this
legend or a similar one. He stresses thereby the traditional nature of
the experience but also deepens its mysticism. Modern man touches upon
the same experience as legendary men in the same way that his feet touch
the ice "marked with caribou feet," the caribou representing the antiquity of the North American continent.

At this point the central section of "The Night Journey in the Cooking Pot" moves from the general rebirth experience to a private one. It
deals with the reward, the boon, gained by the hero of the quest myth, or
with the climax of the rebirth experience, or with the part of the individuation process wherein the individual accepts the totality of his Self
and gains wholeness. The section begins with imagery that presents the
tree and the individual as parallel. A description of the persona's own

---

1   M.-L. von Franz, The Feminine in Fairytales, p. 85.
2   Ibid.
3   Leeming, pp. 113-117.
4   Ibid., p. 116.
5   Ibid.

experience ends with a similar comparison, stressing the idea of wholeness:

> Leaves slip down, falling through their own
>   branches.
> The tree becomes naked and joyful.
> Leaves fall in the tomby wood.
> Some men need so little, and even that I
>   need very little.
> Suddenly I love the dancers, leaping
> in the dark, jumping
> into the air, and the singers and dancers
>   and leapers!
> I start to sing, and rove around the floor,
> singing like "a young Lioun"
>
> I want to rise far into the piney tops
>
> I am not going farther from you,
> I am coming nearer,
> green rain carries me nearer you,
> I weave drunkenly about the page,
> I love you,
> I never knew that I loved you
> until I was swallowed by the invisible,
> my black shoes evaporating, rising about my
>   head....
>
> For we are like the branch bent in the water...
> Taken out, it is whole, it was always whole....

With minor variations this section was published as a single poem
1972.[1] Called "Fall Solitude" it has an introductory stanza not include
in "Sleepers Joining Hands," which in more direct terms mentions the an
tiquity conveyed by the references to the holy men and the caribou rein
deers:[2]

> I sit here, I have sat here all day.
> I can feel my own breath enter and leave.
> What is very old comes toward me flying slowly.
> Alone for hours my hands become friendly to me.
> Night gathers outdoors, the night inside slips
>   over the sill, and goes to meet it.

This early version does not have the impact that the section acquires a
a part of the whole rebirth cycle. It does not have the same wide range
of meaning, since it does not include the concluding image signifying
wholeness.

---

1 See The Lamp and the Spine, No. 3 (Winter, 1972), p. 67.
2 See above, p. 159.

The next section also appears to be a closed entity but again it
pertains to the quest myth and the rebirth theme. One has the impression
that the persona faces difficulties. He is involved in a fight with his
own body, he is misunderstood, but the fish in the water - a symbol of
life in the unconscious - suggests a direction. The birth of Christ becomes the symbol of newness. But the new way of life is not so easily
established. Its enemy, in the shape of King Herod, is powerful:

> I see the road ahead,
> and my body cries out, and leaps into the air,
> and throws itself on the floor, knocking over
>   the chairs.
> I think I am the body,
> the body rushes in and ties me up,
> and then goes through the house....
>
> I am on the road, the next instant in the ditch,
>   face down on the earth,
> wasting energy talking to idiots.
> Clumsy wings flop around the room,
> I know what I must do,
> I am ashamed looking at the fish in the water.
>
> The barn doors are open. His first breath
>   touches the manger hay
> and the King a hundred miles away
> stands up. He calls his ministers.
> "Find him.
> There cannot be two rulers in one body."
> He sends his wise men out along the arteries,
> along the winding tunnels, into the mountains,
> to kill the child in the old moonlit villages
>   of the brain.

In realizing the totality of his psyche the persona gains a new awareness,
a new consciousness, but this is not to be done without overcoming ob-
stacles. In the quest myth this part is called "the threshold struggle"[1]
or the "crossing of the return threshold."[2] Marie-Louise von Franz speaks
of this part of the individuation process as both a burden and a blessing:

> If you listen to your unconscious and obey it, you must
> expect constant interference with your conscious plans.
> Your will is crossed by other intentions - intentions
> that you must submit to, or at any rate must seriously

---

1 Campbell, p. 245.
2 Ibid., pp. 217-225.

> consider. This is partly why the obligation attached to
> the process of individuation is often felt to be a
> burden rather than an immediate blessing.[1]

Looked upon in these terms the King symbolizes the old consciousness, th
part of the psyche known to the persona before the rebirth experience
begins, and the child symbolizes the new consciousness, the wholeness of
the Self. This interpretation is in accordance with Marie-Louise von
Franz's interpretation of the meaning of the Christ child in the legend
of St. Christopher:

> This miraculous child is a symbol of the Self that
> literally "depresses" the ordinary human being, even
> though it is the only thing that can redeem him. In
> many works of art the Christ child is depicted as,
> or with, the sphere of the world, a motif that clearly
> denotes the Self, for a child and a sphere are both
> universal symbols of totality.[2]

However, the King probably also represents collective consciousness as
opposed to the individual spiritual experience.[3] As Jung sees it, "The
self is the hero, threatened already at birth by envious collective
forces; the jewel that is coveted by all and arouses jealous strife; and
finally the god who is dismembered by the old, evil power of darkness."[4]

The last section of "The Night Journey in the Cooking Pot" continue
the image of the killing of the child, and then in various images shows
the related struggle that the persona, returning from his unique experience, faces in ordinary life:

> The mind waters run out on the rug.
> Pull the mind in,
> pull the arm in,
> it will be taken off by a telephone post.
>
> Suddenly I am those who run large railroads
>   at dusk,
> who stand around the fallen beast howling,
> who cannot get free,

---

1 M.-L. von Franz, "The Process of Individuation," Man and His Symbols,
   p. 218.
2 Ibid., p. 219.
3 Cf. M.-L. von Franz, The Feminine in Fairytales, pp. 80, 89, and 118,
   and also below, p. 195, about Hamilton and the President.
4 Jung, Four Archetypes, p. 80.

> the man the lion bounding catches in the
>   African grass.
> I stop, a hand turns over in my stomach,
> this is not the perfect freedom of the
>   saints.

Back in ordinary life and ordinary consciousness, the persona finds himself involved in various tasks; for example, he is in charge of communica-
tion systems in the border zone between light and dark. Everything he
does, however, is connected with a loss of freedom and that is not the
way he wanted to communicate his experience to others. In interpreting the
quest myth Campbell says: "There must always remain, however, from the
standpoint of normal waking consciousness, a certain baffling inconsist-
ency between the wisdom brought forth from the deep, and the prudence
usually found to be effective in the light world."[1] The hero returning
with the elixir, as well as the individual who has completed the individuation process, wants to share his experience with others, but "the boon
brought from the transcendent deep becomes quickly rationalized into non-
entity."[2] The persona in Bly's poem seems to ask the same question as the
myth hero in Campbell's interpretation: "How communicate to people who
insist on the exclusive evidence of their senses the message of the all-
generating void?"[3] The final acceptance of the facts of the return are
presented - as in Campbell's interpretation of the myth[4] - in terms of
death, here coming as a friend:

> I decide that death is friendly.
> Finally death seeps up through the tiniest
>   capillaries of my toes.
> I fall into my own hands,
>   fences break down under horses,
> cities starve, whole towns of singing women
>   carrying to the burial fields
>   the look I saw on my father's face,
> I sit down again, I hit my own body,
> I shout at myself, I see what I have betrayed.
> What I have written is not good enough.
> Who does it help?
> I am ashamed sitting on the edge of my bed.

The persona realizes that his experience has isolated him. To the world
he is dead, and being back in the world is like entering death. He has

---

1 Campbell, p. 217. Cf. also above, p. 59.
2 Campbell, p. 218.
3 Ibid.
4 See Campbell, p. 259.

fallen into his own hands. Even his father is estranged from him. What he
has accomplished seems to have no saving effect upon the world. However,
the persona is aware of his situation. Campbell understands the dilemma
of the returned quester and sees two possibilities for him: either he
withdraws again into the land unfamiliar to the general world or he
accepts the task of "representing eternity in time, and perceiving in
time eternity."[1]

Bly starts the next poem - "Water Drawn Up Into the Head"[2] - by jux-
taposing a prose statement about a man who went on a quest and returned,
with a question to his readers, asking if they understand the persona's
blissful existence in the "other awareness" - if they understand the joy
of inwardness:

>   Now do you understand the men who laugh all
>   night in their sleep?
>   Here is some prose:
>
>   O n c e   t h e r e   w a s   a   m a n   w h o
>   w e n t   t o   a   f a r   c o u n t r y   t o
>   g e t   h i s   i n h e r i t a n c e   a n d
>   t h e n   r e t u r n e d.
>
>   There are places for our feet to go.

The persona of Bly's poem has been to far places, but now he is back to
tell his story. The return is important; the circle has to be completed.

Before the persona turns his quest into poetry he wants to lay bare
all the facts of the situation. He comes face to face with his readers,
and the one who considers himself "the holder" (the holder of the truth?)
feels joy:

>   When we come face to face with you,
>   the holder laughs and is glad!
>   He laughs like the mad condor in his stickly
>   nest!

In the next stanza the scene is similar to that of the first lines
of "The Shadow Goes Away," and, thus, again a circle is completed: a
female figure is held prisoner, and the persona finds himself on the
shores of the ocean, in a state of passivity:

---

1   Campbell, p. 218.
2   Sleepers, pp. 64-67.

> The feminine creature at the edge of town,
> men with rifles all around.
> I am passive, listening to the lapping waves,
> I am divine, drinking the air,
> consciousness fading or sweeping out over the
>   husky soybean fields like a
>   revolving beacon all night,
> horses at the end of their tethering ropes,
> the wing of affection passes over,
> flying bulls glimpsed passing the moon disc.

The men with guns around the female figure symbolize the rational mind,
the father consciousness, that is afraid of the intuitive mind, the
mother consciousness. Thus, the "maiden in distress" in this poem becomes
a symbol of contemporary society[1] where the problem of differences in
views is solved by violence. She also becomes a symbol of the persona's
goal[2] in life at his return; his goal is her release, a broadening of the
understanding of a mother-oriented awareness.

Thus, we find the persona back in the same rational world, but he
himself has changed. His consciousness illuminates his surroundings like
a revolving light; it moves in a circle like a horse at the end of a
tethering rope. Back in a state of normal awareness, consciousness cannot
concentrate on everything - the whole circle - at the same time. The persona's attention must, therefore, be compared to something that flies
over the scene, glimpsing in passing. He becomes aware of a manifestation
of male energy momentarily seen against the circle of the moon, a manifestation of female energy.[3] According to Jung, consciousness works like
a searchlight: "When interest turns elsewhere, it leaves in shadow the
things with which one was previously concerned, just as a searchlight
lights upon a new area by leaving another in darkness. This is unavoid-
able, for consciousness can keep only a few images in full clarity at one
time, and even this clarity fluctuates."[4]

Next the persona makes clear what is within our range of knowledge
and what is not. The conclusion is that since there is nothing we can

---

1   Cf. above, p. 150.
2   Cf. above, p. 146, the end of the Campbell quotation.
3   Cf. C. G. Jung, "Approaching the Unconscious," Man and His Symbols,
    p. 97; and Jolande Jacobi, "Symbols in an Individual Analysis,"
    Man and His Symbols, p. 277, where it is mentioned that the moon in
    ancient cultures was often seen as a feminine principle.
4   C. G. Jung, "Approaching the Unconscious," Man and His Symbols, p. 34.

name as God, all we can do is to enter – as he did – the energy that we
can see and feel manifest in life within and without ourselves:

> We know the world with all its visible stars,
> earth, water, air, and fire,
> but when alone we see that great tomb is not God.
> There are spirits,
>   who wheel with sparks at night in a room,
> but everyone knows they are not God.
> We know of Christ, who raised the dead,
>   and started time.
> He is not God, and is not called God.
>
> When the waterholes go, and the fish
>   flop about
> in the caked mud, they can moisten each other
>   faintly.
>   That is good, but best
> is to let them lose themselves in a river.
> So rather than saying that Christ is God or
>   he is not,
> it is better to forget all that
> and lose yourself in the curved energy.
> I entered that energy one day,
> that is why I have lived alone in old places,
> that is why I have knelt in churches, weeping,
> that is why I have become a stranger to my
>   father.
> We have no name for you, so we say:
> he makes grass grow upon the mountains,
> and gives food to the dark cattle of the sea,
> he feeds the young ravens that call on him. [1]

* * *

The effect that this energy has had on him is then disclosed by the
persona, who turns inward and brings forth his whole Self. He is now at
one with the other parts of his psyche – the shadow, the anima, the old
man, the King. This is the effect of the suffering he has passed through
the loss of everything – as if he were a tree in autumn – that has resulted in the gaining of joy:

> I have sat here alone for two hours....
> I have sat here alone for two years!
> There is another being living inside me.
> He is looking out of my eyes.
> I hear him
> in the wind through the bare trees. [2]

---

1 Cf. above, p. 107.
2 Cf. above, p. 128, and Jung, Four Archetypes, p. 55: "the parable of
   the two Friends," and p. 65: "This 'other being' is the other person
   in ourselves – that larger and greater personality maturing within us
   whom we have already met as the inner friend of the soul."

I met the King coming through the traffic.
He said, I shall give to you more pain than
            wounds at sea.

That is why I am so glad in fall.
I walk out, throw my arms up, and am glad.
The thick leaves fall,
falling past their own trunk,
and the tree goes naked,
leaving only the other one.

Having summed up his rebirth experience in these short lines, the
persona communicates the extraordinary joy that is his. In "An Extra
Joyful Chorus for Those Who Have Read This Far" the particulars of the
quest, the details of the night journey, the private experiences of the
individuation process, are given in imagery inspired by old sagas, fairy
tales, natural history, anthropology, mythology, psychology, human rela-
tions, by all areas of human knowledge. The formal pattern though, is
that of a riddle of the type that the old bards and minstrels used to
recite in the courts:

An Extra Joyful Chorus for Those
Who Have Read This Far

I sit alone late at night.
I sit with eyes closed, thoughts shoot through me.
I am not floating, but fighting.
In the marshes the mysterious mother calls to
            her moor-bound chicks.
I love the Mother.
I am an enemy of the Mother, give me my sword.
I leap into her mouth full of seaweed.

I am the single splinter that shoots through the
            stratosphere leaving fire trails!
I walk upright, robes flapping at my heels,
I am fleeing along the ground like a
            frightened beast.
I am the ball of fire the woodman cuts out of
            the wolf's stomach,
I am the sun that floats over the Witch's house,
I am the horse sitting in the chestnut tree
            singing,
I am the man locked inside the oakwomb,
waiting for lightning, only let out on stormy
            nights.
I am the steelhead trout that hurries to his
            mountain mother,
to live again in the stream where he was born,
gobbling up the new water.

Sometimes when I read my own poems late at night,
I sense myself on a long road,
I feel the naked thing alone in the universe,
the hairy body padding in the fields at dusk....

I have floated in the eternity of the cod
            heaven,
I have felt the silver of infinite numbers
            brush my side -
I am the crocodile unrolling and slashing
            through the mudded water,
I am the baboon crying out as her baby falls
            from the tree,
I am the light that makes the flax blossom at
            midnight!
I am an angel breaking into three parts over the
            Ural Mountains!
I am no one at all.
                              * * *
I am a thorn enduring in the dark sky,
I am the one whom I have never met,
I am a swift fish shooting through the troubled
            waters,
I am the last inheritor crying out in deserted
            houses
I am the salmon hidden in the pool on the
            temple floor
I am what remains of the beloved
I am an insect with black enamel knees hugging
            the curve of insanity
I am the evening light rising from the ocean
            plains
I am an eternal happiness fighting in the long
            reeds.

Again a complete circle is formed: the word "fighting" is found both in
the first and the last of the lines starting "I am." His fight with the
Mother in the marshes - with forces within his own psyche, that is - has
turned into an eternal happiness, felt by the returning hero, who now
fights against forces in the world without.

Finally, having communicated his experience to the world, he feels
united with all those who recognize it as their own:

            Our faces shine with the darkness reflected
                        from the Tigris,
            cells made by the honeybees that go on growing
                        after death,
            a room darkened with curtains made of human
                        hair.

                              .

> The panther rejoices in the gathering dark.
> Hands rush toward each other through miles of
>   space.
> All the sleepers in the world join hands.

Above[1] I have called this chorus a Whitmanesque catalogue. Several
critics have seen an influence by Whitman both in content and in form.
Howard Nelson[2] speaks of Bly's "central enterprise" as akin to Whitman's
concern with helping "the growth - the deepening and unfolding and transcendence - of the self." Quoting two lines[3] from Whitman's "The
Sleepers," he points to that poem as a possible direct source of inspiration for Bly in the writing of the chorus, especially the ending. The
comparison seems quite convincing.

A comparison of the chorus with old riddles, as they are presented
for example in Robert Graves's The White Goddess,[4] which Bly has studied,[5]
brings out many similarities in formal arrangement, as well as in basic
ideas and even in individual lines. These riddles contain a number of
lines beginning "I am . . ." and "I have been . . ."[6] which probably inspired Bly's similar use of lines beginning "I am . . ." and "I
have . . .". Some basic ideas that appear in the chorus - and also in the
whole composite poem - are expressed in the riddles, too. In the examples
in the footnote below, there is the notion that one may appear in a multi-
tude of different shapes. Also the idea that one may travel everywhere is
spelled out in the riddles:

---

1 See Chapter II, p. 58.
2 Howard Nelson, "Welcoming Shadows: Robert Bly's Recent Poetry," The
   Hollins Critic, Vol. XII: 2 (April, 1975), pp. 1-15.
3 The two lines from Whitman run:
       The sleepers are very beautiful as they lie unclothed,
       They flow hand in hand over the whole earth, from east
                to west. . . (from "Leaves of Grass").
4 London, 1961.
5 In a letter of Nov. 30, 1976, to the present writer Bly confirms this.
6 Example I: I have been a drop in the air.
             I have been a shining star.
             I have been a word in a book.
             I have been a book originally. (Robert Graves, The White
                                             Goddess, p. 30.)

   Example II: I am water, I am a wren,
              I am a workman, I am a star,
              I am a serpent;
              I am a cell, I am a chink,
              I am a depository of song,
              I am a learned person, etc. (Robert Graves, The White
                                            Goddess, p. 100.)

> I have travelled, I have made a circuit,
> I have slept in a hundred islands;
> I have dwelt in a hundred cities.[1]

When the idea of rebirth turns up in the riddles in terms of entrance into a womb, it sounds strangely familiar to a reader who is also acquainted with Bly's poem:

> And it is not known whether my body is flesh
>   or fish.
> Then I was for nine months
> In the womb of the hag Caridwen;
> I was originally little Gwion,
> And at length I am Taliesin.[2]

The final joy expressed at the end of the chorus forms a parallel to the ending of one of the riddles:

> With a golden jewel set in gold
> I am enriched;
> And I am indulging in pleasure
> Out of the oppressive toil of the goldsmith.[3]

Similarities in single lines could be exemplified by

> I am a salmon in a pool[4]

and

> I am the salmon hidden in the pool on the
>   temple floor[5].

Another interesting similarity between single lines should be mentioned, although it occurs not in the final chorus but earlier in the poem. The identical spelling of the word "Lioun" in the lines

> He raged like a young Lioun[6]

and

> singing like 'a young Lioun'[7]

appears not to be a coincidence but rather to support my hypothesis of a

---

1 Robert Graves, _The White Goddess_, p. 35.
2 Ibid., p. 82.
3 Ibid., p. 36.
4 Ibid., pp. 13 and 206.
5 _Sleepers_, p. 67.
6 Robert Graves, _The White Goddess_, p. 86.
7 _Sleepers_, p. 61.

conscious application, on Bly's part, of the pattern of the riddles as it
is presented in Graves's book. This conclusion, of course, in its turn
suggests that Bly's poem is actually a riddle which could be deciphered
in detail as Graves attempts to do with the riddles. The limited scope of
this thesis, however, does not allow me to attempt such a deciphering.

As a conclusion to my interpretation of "Sleepers Joining Hands", I
want to focus again on ideas related to the rebirth archetype, seen as a
return to the "original darkness", or the "original state", suggested at
the end of the chorus by the phrase "the darkness reflected from the
Tigris."[1] The original state is described by Campbell,[2] also. In applying
the pattern of the quest myth to Buddhism, he equates the goal of a certain type of modern psychotherapy with that of Buddhism and Hinduism,
which aim at illumination and freedom, gained through a yoga experience –
gained, that is, through an expansion of consciousness – a process that
finally enables the individual to behold "himself in all beings and all
beings in himself,"[3] which would mean a return to the original state with
infinite possibilities. This experience seems to me a parallel to that
described in the joyful chorus that concludes "Sleepers Joining Hands."

Thus, the expansion of consciousness, symbolized by the rebirth
archetype and illustrated by details from various myths, religions,
psychoanalytic ideas, and private readings and experiences, develops in
Bly's poetry into an experience shared by individuals who know of no
limitations in time and space. The power that cuts through such limitations is the common denominator of many of the poems relating to the
"voyage of the unconscious"; it reveals itself as a movement toward
female energy, toward mother consciousness. Since this movement, however,
is evident also in other poems by Bly, I will devote a special section of
the next chapter to his use of the myth of the Mother.

---

1 The Garden of Eden is sometimes said to have been located on the
   banks of the Tigris.
2 See Campbell, p. 166.
3 Ibid.

IV. THE LADY OF THE HOUSE

What has been treated in the preceding chapters can also be defined as different modes of consciousness. Within every chapter, as well as in moving from each chapter to the next, I have proceeded from visual perception and wide-awake, rational consciousness to an extended awareness that includes the experiences of the intuitive mind and of the unconscious part of an individual's psyche. These two modes of consciousness have sometimes been referred to above as "male and female consciousness" or "father and mother consciousness," terms often employed by Jung and his followers.[1]

Marie-Louise von Franz in her book The Feminine in Fairytales, which is a collection of lectures that she gave at the C. G. Jung Institute in 1958-59, mentions the difference between the masculine and the feminine psyches in their respective ways of turning inward toward the unconscious. She refers to the masculine principle as a hero on an active quest "into the Beyond", in contrast to the feminine principle that withdraws into passive isolation.[2] - "There are problems which cannot be solved by following them into consciousness, but only by following one's own feeling, and that is very often essential in a woman's process of individuation".[3]

Gaston Bachelard in The Poetics of Reverie[4] in a similar way bases his ideas on a division of the psyche into masculine and feminine dispositions. The introductory paragraph of the first chapter presents "a need to make everything feminine which is enveloping and soft above and beyond the too simply masculine designations for our states of mind."[5] Further on he differentiates between the activity of the masculine and the passivity of the feminine although he uses a different terminology: "To love things for their use is a function of the masculine. . . . But to love them intimately, for themselves, with the slownesses of the feminine, that is what leads us into the labyrinth of the intimate Nature of things."[6] Bachelard presents his arguments in the Jungian terms of "animus" and "anima" quests and illustrates them with references to poets and novelists.

Robert E. Ornstein, research psychologist at the Langley Porter Neuropsychiatric Institute, San Francisco, and professor at the University of

---

1 See for example Fathers & Mothers (ed. Patricia Berry) (Zürich, 1973), passim.
2 See M.-L. von Franz, The Feminine in Fairytales, p. 94.
3 Ibid., p. 139.
4 Boston, Mass., 1971. The title of the original: La Poétique de la Rêverie (Presses Universitaires de France, 1960).
5 Bachelard, p. 29.
6 Ibid., pp. 31-32.

California Medical Center, San Francisco, deals in his book The Psychology
of Consciousness with two kinds of consciousness that have separate locations, one in each of the hemispheres of the brain. He refers to these
two kinds of consciousness in several different sets of terms: for example
rational and intuitive, causal and acausal, lineal and nonlineal, light
and dark, active and receptive, or male and female.[1]

Bly mentions these ideas in an interview: "Mother-consciousness involves passion, tenderness, love of nature, love of animals, ecstacy...
music, and then the father-consciousness . . . some of the characteristics
are logical thought, rational thought, movement in straight lines, disci-
pline, Calvinism, dislike of tenderness."[2] Two years later Bly writes in
his essay "I Came Out of the Mother Naked ": "We have then inside us two
worlds of consciousness; one world associated with the dark, and one world
with the light. Surely this double consciousness is precisely what the
yin-yang circle of the Chinese describes. The dark half corresponds to the
consciousness developed in the matriarchies, the white to the consciousness
developed in the patriarchies that followed . . . . The yin-yang circle
is the hope of a balanced consciousness. What they called 'yin,' I will
call here mother-consciousness or feminine consciousness; yang, father or
masculine consciousness."[3]

In this chapter I will study male and female elements in Robert Bly's
poems with the intention of tentatively establishing a relation between
these elements and the two kinds of consciousness mentioned above. As my
discussion proceeds, however, it will develop into an explication of the
feminine principle of the psyche and what Bly calls the myth of the
mother, as seen in Bly's poetry and prose. We shall again follow a line
of movement from the outer toward the inner world, and we may notice how
the ideas of a male and a female consciousness are discernable before Bly
seems to have seriously studied either Jung's ideas or the results of
Ornstein's experiments.

A poet's muse is by tradition feminine. Maud Bodkin sees the power

---

1 See Ornstein, pp. X, 66, 67, and 68.
2 Jay Bail and Geoffrey Cook, "With Robert Bly: An Interview," The San
   Francisco Book Review, No. 19 (April, 1971), no pagination.
3 Sleepers, pp. 31-32.

that inspires a poet's song as a maid who sings to him or as the Muse
who visits him.[1] For Robert Graves "the function of poetry is religious
invocation of the Muse; its use is the experience of mixed exaltation
and horror that her presence excites."[2] Bly wants to prepare the way for
his muse in an early poem called "The Possibility of New Poetry,"[3] in
which she appears as a "strong-haunched woman." After enumerating the
subjects of a "new poetry" he entreats intelligence to cover the advertising men with clear water[4] and the factories with space,[5] which means
that he wants the flow of an inner strength to touch, or envelop the outer
world. Then "the strong-haunched woman," associated with the moon, which
is often a symbol of the feminine,[6] may come to the poet, and "all the
Shell stations" will be "folded in a faint light," which would mean that
the factual world would be transformed.

In his socially-engaged poems Bly again and again turns against the
business world. In "Merchants have Multiplied"[7] this world is seen as
populated by merchants, advertising men, executives, and insurance men,
all holders of jobs usually thought of as masculine. Although Bly does
not explicitly set up a contrast between a masculine and a feminine world
he conveys the disastrous grasshopper-like effect of modern society on
Nature. The business world, characterised by loneliness and death[8] almost
kills the world of natural life, which in this poem is mainly symbolized
by the grass,[9] which in some other poems embodies innocence, new life,
and female energy:

> Merchants have multiplied more than the stars
>   of heaven,
> And the advertising men awake in the suburbs
>   at dawn,
> Like grasshoppers in the bushes in the cool of
>   the day;

---

1 See Maud Bodkin, Archetypal Patterns in Poetry, p. 153.
2 Robert Graves, The White Goddess, p. 14.
3 Poetry, XCVI (April, 1960), p. 31. See also below, p. 201, for quotati
   of the poem. The first line is slightly different in the early version
   It begins: "Singing of . . ." instead of "We are writing of . . ."
4 See the preceding chapter for a common symbolic meaning of water.
5 See Ornstein, pp. 65-67 and p. 163, about space being considered feminine.
6 See above, p. 165, note 3.
7 Chelsea, 8 (Oct., 1960), p. 64, later in a different version, publishe
   in Light, p. 3.
8 Cf. above, pp. 27-28 and 64-65.
9 Cf. above, pp. 103-104 and pp. 105-106.

They walk the cold streets like lions, or
                ·butterflies,
And the grass is trampled down where they have
                been,
And they come by the thousands, and cover the
                hills;
Some fly over the ocean all night in the storm
Carrying whole ships down with them as they alight;
The cemeteries are full of those coming out of
                Detroit:

In the high air, executives walk in the snow that
                leads to death,
And the insurance men live in mansions on the side
                of the great mountains.
And talk at night to coffins and funeral wreaths,
And sway like hollow reeds in the dawn wind;
They arrive at Hartford at dusk like small moles
Or tiny hares flying from a fire behind them,
And the dusk in Hartford is full of their sighs;
Their trains come through the air like a dark music,
And hang on the leaves of trees like the sound of
                grasshoppers in winter.

The earliest poem in which Bly openly uses male and female terms,
seems to be "A Man Writes to a Part of Himself,"[1] a poem that is symbolic
on several levels. It is based on contrasts: city life vs. country life,
company vs. loneliness, activity vs. withdrawal, husband vs. wife. If it
had not been for the title one might assume that Bly wants to bring out
the loneliness that results from the hectic life of the modern world,
both for the active, traveling husband and for the wife who is left behind.
But although Bly probably had not yet studied Jung seriously, it is obvious that he is discussing two worlds experienced by one individual,
perceived as being male and female worlds. Bly first conveys the female
world through traditional images which are frequently also associated
with the inner world: the cave and the valley, places for passive withdrawal; and water, the symbol of the unconscious. Then the male world
is seen as a barren world of city streets, lacking warmth:

        What cave are you in, hiding, rained on?
        Like a wife, starving, without care,
        Water dripping from your head, bent
        Over ground corn...

---

1 Silence, p. 36.

You raise your face into the rain
That drives over the valley –
Forgive me, your husband,
On the streets of a distant city, laughing,
With many appointments,
Though at night going also
To a bare room, a room of poverty,
To sleep among a bare pitcher and basin
In a room with no heat –

Which of us two then is the worse off?
And how did this separation come about?

The two questions that end the poem suggest that Bly is trying to come to terms with two different force fields which he perceives as existing both in his psyche and in the physical world around him. Bachelard uses similar images of husband and wife in his chapter on the animus and the anima: "Fundamentally, considered in ordinary life, the anima would hardly be anything more than the worthy bourgeois wife linked to this bourgeois animus. . . ."[1] Ornstein discusses another set of individuals, the scientist, or logician, and the artist, or dreamer, as representing two "major modes of consciousness which exist across cultures and which simultaneously coexist within each person."[2] Thus it seems that Bly in his employment of male and female terms conveys not only opposite cultural spheres but also the opposites of the rational and the intuitive mind and of the conscious and the unconscious parts of an individual's psyche.

Husband and wife are presented as complementary in two more quite early poems. In "Watching Fall Dust inside Sheds"[3] Bly depicts the husband as turning toward the sunshine, which would mean the active male world of daylight. The sun is usually conceived of as male, and in fact is of the masculine gender in most languages. The husband wants his wife to join him and share in his return from an inner experience, a rebirth that is suggested in the first stanza by the image of the birth of a prince. In this poem the male and female, the outer and the inner worlds, seem to be in harmony. In "Looking Backward"[4] Bly gives surrealistic glimpses of the time when the American continent was settled, when the Indians were defeated and, finally, freedom was gained, at least theoretically. The wife in this poem is seen as the one who wants the security

---

1 Bachelard, p. 67.
2 Ornstein, p. 50.
3 The Beloit Poetry Journal, 14:1, (Fall, 1963), p. 42. See also above, p. 93.
4 The Paris Review (Winter/Spring, 1964), p. 107. See also above, p. 75.

of land ownership in a male world of defeat, dishonesty, and loss.

In several poems of social engagement Bly criticizes modern America
as a society governed by male consciousness. In"The Great Society"[1] den-
tists exemplify affluence, and evangelists stand for uselessness and
waste. This society holds no joy: the movies offer murder as entertain-
ment and inside the status symbols are the coffins of the poor. Those who
are in charge of this society are troubled, or insane, or planning war.
The outdoors is forgotten, except by the "dark children" who are playing
on the distant beach:

> Dentists continue to water their lawns even in the
>   rain;
> Hands developed with terrible labor by apes
> Hang from the sleeves of evangelists;
> There are murdered kings in the light-bulbs outside
>   movie theaters;
> The coffins of the poor are hibernating in piles of
>   new tires.
>
> The janitor sits troubled by the boiler,
> And the hotel keeper shuffles the cards of insanity.
> The President dreams of invading Cuba.
> Bushes are growing over the outdoor grills,
> Vines over the yachts and the leather seats.
>
> The city broods over ash cans and darkening mortar.
> On the far shore, at Coney Island, dark children
> Play on the chilling beach: a sprig of black seaweed,
> Shells, a skyful of birds,
> While the mayor sits with his head in his hands.

"A Dream of Suffocation"[2] deals with the same theme. Accountants, who
symbolize business and male consciousness, dominate the world like machines.
They spread a rationalism - here symbolized by Hegel's name - that kills
natural life - symbolized by a family of badgers in its den.[3] The den is a
kind of cave or womb used as a symbol to represent the world of female
consciousness, which in the next stanza is depicted as a chorus girl who
passively watches a barren street with an artificial show window.[4] Besides
representing feminine passivity and withdrawal,[5] the girl, being a chorus

---

1 Light, p. 17. See also above, p. 100.
2 Ibid., p. 8. The poem is quoted above, pp. 89-90.
3 Cf. Mersmann, p. 144.
4 Cf. above, p. 89.
5 Cf. M.-L. von Franz, The Feminine in Fairytales, pp. 82-83, where, in reference to a girl in a fairytale, she mentions "the type of woman who
   has to live a completely passive life and, in the positive sense of the
   word, only a feminine life, . . ."

girl, possibly illustrates that such a disposition of mind might be combined with certain artistic ability,[1] although not individually developed.
The final stanza of the poem seems to show the strength of the dreaming
unconscious in the nightly dreams, which rise from a society in the image
of a honeycomb. This unconscious experience conveys the futility of
machines and war materials, setting them against the strength of a rain-
drop.

But more frequently the inner world, the world of dreamers and
artists, is shown not to be the stronger. In the American edition of
The Ligth around the Body "The Busy Man Speaks,"[2] which was written as
early as 1958, is included in the section called "The Two Worlds,"
which takes its motto from Jacob Boehme: "For according to the outward
man, we are in this world, and according to the inward man, we are in
the inward world.... Since then we are generated out of both worlds, we
speak in two languages, and we must be understood also by two languages."
This motto seems to show the two worlds in balance, which is not the case
in the poem mentioned above, where the busy man, who is also the business
man, rejects the female, inner world of withdrawal and sorrow, but also
of love, affection, and nature. He chooses the male outer world of cheerfulness, but also of strictness, hardness, and dryness. The two worlds
are presented as domains of the mother and the father respectively:

> Not to the mother of solitude will I give myself
> Away, not to the mother of love, nor to the mother
>   of conversation,
> Nor to the mother of art, nor the mother
> Of tears, nor the mother of the ocean;
> Not to the mother of sorrow, nor the mother
> Of the downcast face, nor the mother of the suffering
>   of death;
> Not to the mother of the night full of crickets,
> Nor the mother of the open fields, nor the mother of
>   Christ.
>
> But I will give myself to the father of righteousness,
>   the father
> Of cheerfulness, who is also the father of rocks,
> Who is also the father of perfect gestures;
> From the Chase National Bank
> An arm of flame has come, and I am drawn
> To the desert, to the parched places, to the land-
>   scape of zeros;

---

1 Cf. above, p. 176, quotation from Ornstein.
2 Light, p. 4. Cf. also above, p. 115.
3 Ibid., p. 1.

And I shall give myself away to the father of right-
    eousness,
The stones of cheerfulness, the steel of money, the
    father of rocks.

In the British edition of The Light around the Body this poem is included
in a later section called "In Praise of Grief" which has another motto
from Jacob Boehme: "O dear children, look in what a dungeon we are lying,
in what lodging we are, for we have been captured by the spirit of the
outward world; it is our life, for it nourishes and brings us up, it rules
in our marrow and bones, in our flesh and blood, it has made our flesh
earthly, and now death has us."[1] The message of the poem is more compatible with this second motto, which in its turn increases the impact of
the poem on the reader, especially as it is the first poem in this section. The theme of this poem - a man's refusal to belong to the feminine
world - is similar to Jungian ideas. James Hillman says that assertive
masculinity must react against feminine attachments,[2] and he quotes Jung's
Collective Works (5, §540): "Again and again the hero must renew the
struggle, and always under the symbol of deliverance form the mother."[3]
Bachelard has noticed the same hostile relationship: "After the fall, . . .
Adam became the depository for the 'severe force'; Eve 'the guardian of
tender softness.' Such values are hostile as long as they are separated."[4]
Since Bly could have read neither Hillman's essay nor Bachelard's book
before he wrote this poem, and since he "didn't seriously read Jung until
around 1970,"[5] or Neumann at all until 1969,[6] the poem seems to be an independent expression of these ideas (a conclusion reached by Libby also)[7].
It seems to me, however, that Bly employs the idea of separate male and
female worlds not so much to illustrate the different kinds of consciousness, as to criticize modern society. Mersmann arrives at a similar conclusion in his comments on "A Man Writes to a Part of Himself" and other
related poems: "When Bly in later poems condemns the outward world, it is
never the physical and social 'man' that he condemns, but rather the implicit assertions of modern life that this is the only man there is. Though
the modern world gives itself to the 'husband,' the outward man, he too

---

1 Light (British ed.), p. 29.
2 See James Hillman, "The Great Mother, Her Son, Her Hero, and Puer,"
    Fathers & Mothers, p. 105.
3 Ibid.
4 Bachelard, p. 85.
5 See above, p. 5.
6 See above, p. 119.
7 See Anthony Libby, "Robert Bly Alive in Darkness," p. 86.

is nevertheless starved, . . ."[1]

The psychical and emotional starvation of patriarchal man expresses itself not only through his words but also through his actions. In "Romans Angry about the Inner World"[2] men torture and murder a representative of the world of the mother, a world that is unknown to them but that astonishes and disturbs them. Time in this poem is, as Mersmann points out, o no importance: "The American enterprise and the Roman enterprise are the same. . . . The young girl the 'Angry Romans' torture could as well be a early martyr, a modern occultist, or a transtemporal symbol. . . . it is once again noteworthy that the poet, who might have chosen a St. Stephen picks a female as his advocate of the inner life, . . ." [3] This pattern of ideas is old and belongs to all patriarchal societies. Marie-Louise v Franz discerns it in fairytales: "Our laws are based on Roman law and patriarchal mentality, so that we always think of punishment as having t do with the masculine world, and of women as representing the principle of charity and the making of exceptions."[4]

The two worlds - the outer and the inner, or the male and female - are shown as the worlds of business and religion that exclude each other although they exist side by side, in "Turning away from Lies,"[5]

> . . .
> No one in business can be a Christian
> The two worlds are both in this world
> . . .

Those who understand the inner world will finally react against the world of materialistic values, as Bly shows in "Written in Dejection nea Rome,"[6] but they will react by isolating themselves, not by trying to sa those "captured by the spirit of the outward world."[7] Some will take refuge on rafts on the ocean, which - with the ocean again functioning as a symbol of the unconscious - could be interpreted as an experiencing of inner energy, a deepening of the inner life. Some will go inside tree trunks, which suggests a turning toward utter selfishness, as Bly himsel has confirmed in an interview.[8] This desertion by the inward men would

---

1 Mersmann, <u>Out of the Vietnam Vortex</u>, p. 135.
2 <u>Light</u>, p. 9. See above, pp. 24-25, for quotation and a primary interpretation.
3 Mersmann, p. 144.
4 M.-L. von Franz, <u>The Feminine in Fairytales</u>, p. 33.
5 <u>Light</u>, p. 43. Cf. also above, p. 131.
6 Ibid., p. 15. See also above, pp. 74-75, where this poem is quoted.
7 Ibid., p. 39. (Quotation from Jacob Boehme).
8 See above, pp. 74-75.

mean spiritual starvation for the outward men, the "bankers" of this poem.

However, other poems suggest a union of the two worlds, hitherto described as hostile to, and isolated from each other. "Moving Inward at Last" depicts an idealistic union in a language of masculine and feminine symbols.[1] The feasibility of such a union has also been expressed by a representative of the Jungian school: "For the masculine as for the feminine, wholeness is attainable only when in a union of opposites, the day and the night, the upper and the lower, the patriarchal consciousness and the matriarchal, come to their own kind of productivity and mutually supplement and fructify one another."[2] Mersmann sees the idea of this poem as borrowed from Zen Buddhism,[3] an interpretation that would go well with a Jungian interpretation, since both doctrines emphasize the idea of wholeness gained as the result of a balanced psyche.[4] It seems, however, also likely that the idea has grown out of Bly's reading of Robert Graves's The White Goddess, in which finds of primitive burial caves, built of and topped with big slabs of stone, are described. These caves contain, besides skeletons, such things as antlers, bones, the remains of oak coffins, or oak branches.[5] Graves also describes the sacrifice of bulls and the importance in ritual of bull's blood, which is "a poison deadly to anyone but a Sibyl or a priest of Mother Earth."[6] The meaning that presents itself is still the same as in Mersmann's interpretation: the sacrifice of the bull, or the masculine consciousness, makes possible new life inside the cave, the feminine consciousness. Finally, the primitive burial rites mentioned in the poem also include what Graves calls "the idea of a voyage by water to the next world."[7] The next world is not mentioned directly, but in the context of the poem seems to be there beyond the dark water, and thus is a symbol of the unconscious.

In "A Journey with Women"[8] the union of the two spheres is conveyed in surrealistic imagery that suggests a sexual relationship. But in the last line of the second stanza the traditional masculine and feminine

---

1 For quotation and a primary interpretaiton see above, p. 66.
2 Erich Neumann, "On the Moon and Matriarchal Consciousness," Fathers & Mothers, p. 60.
3 See Mersmann, p. 155.
4 See Christmas Humphreys, Zen Buddhism (London, 1976; 1st ed., 1949) passim, for the influence of Zen Buddhism on Jung.
5 See Graves, pp. 102 and 111.
6 Ibid., p. 105.
7 Ibid., p. 110.
8 Light, p. 56.

images of rock and sea generalize the meaning toward something more than
imaginative love-making:[1]

1

Floating in turtle blood, going backward and
          forward,
We wake up like a mad sea-urchin
On the bloody fields near the secret pass -
There the dead sleep in jars...

2

Or we go at night slowly into the tunnels of the
          tortoise's claws,
Carrying chunks of the moon
To light the tunnels,
Listening for the sound of rocks falling into
          the sea...

3

Waking, we find ourselves in the tortoise's beak,
As he carries us high
Over New Jersey - going swiftly
Through the darkness between the constellations...

4

At dawn we are still transparent, pulling
In the starlight;
We are still falling like a room
Full of moonlight through the air...

The strength of both feminine and masculine energy is shown in the
symbols of the grass - often feminine in Bly's poetry[2] - and the sword -
a traditional masculine symbol - at the end of "Looking at New-Fallen
Snow from a Train."[3] Both the grass and the sword reveal powerful inner
energies of their own:

Each blade of grass is a voice.
The sword by his side breaks into flame.

Together they are manifestations of the sleeping man's psyche, of a life
hidden under the mask of cold consciousness - this is expressed earlier
in the poem in the description of life hidden under the cold snow.

In his earlier poems - as we have seen - Bly is more inclined to
express criticism of the outer world than an explicit predilection for the
inner world. The mottoes[4] of <u>Jumping Out of Bed</u>, however, reveal a change,

---

1 Mersmann has a similar interpretaiton. See his book, p. 153.
2 See above, pp. 105-106.
3 Light, pp. 45-46. Cf. also above, p. 31 and p. 107.
4 <u>Jumping</u>, p. 5.

a turning toward the Mother:

> All around me men are working;
> but I am stubborn, and take no part.
> The difference is this:
> I prize the breasts of the Mother.
>   -Tao Te Ching

> I came out of the Mother naked,
> and I will be naked when I return.
> The Mother gave, and the Mother takes away,
> I love the Mother.
>   -Old Testament, restored

In this book the world of the Mother - the feminine or the inner world -
is described as old and hidden. The turtle that comes out of the water and
climbs the rock brings, in its shininess, a message of some underwater
treasure:

> How shiny the turtle is, coming out
> of the water, climbing the rock, as if
> Buddha's body were to shine!
> As if swift turtle wings swept out of darkness,
> crossed some barriers,
> and found new eyes.
> An old man falters with his stick,
> later, walkers find holes in black earth.
> The snail climbs up the wet trunk glistening
> like an angel-flight trailing long black banners.
> No one finds the huge turtle eggs
> lying inland on the floor of the old sea.[1]

The symbolism of the inner and outer worlds is quite clear. The turtle, a
new element in Bly's poetry, is one of the four creatures of the Mother.[2]
The shiny turtle that first comes from the water, then from the darkness,
embodies a secret that man has not yet come upon. The holes in the earth
reveal a man's faltering walk through life. Even the snail's passage seems
more glorious than the old man's. The secret of what is hidden belongs to
a bygone age, buried and forgotten, like the turtle eggs. Suggesting something unborn, and thus still near to the Mother, these eggs symbolize a
time of female dominance, a time when land was covered by water, "the old
sea." "Mother consciousness was in the world first", says Bly in a prose
essay, "and embodied itself century after century in its favorite images:
the night, the sea, animals with curving horns and cleft hooves, the moon,
bundles of grain. Four favorite creatures of the Mother were the turtle,
the owl, the dove, and the oyster - all womb-shaped, night, or ancient

---

1 "Turtle Climbing from a Rock", Jumping, p. 7. See also above, p. 128,
   where the same poem in a slightly different version is discussed.
2 See Sleepers, p. 32, and below.

round sea creatures."[1] The womb-shaped oyster is utilized in "On a Moon-lit Road in the North Woods," in which it stands for a prenatal stage inside the womb, for original energy, and for mother consciousness.[2]

In "A Windy December Night"[3] the feminine world is rendered through a terminology of myths and fairytales and through images of night, the moon, the womb, the owl, and water:

> There is a connection between the feminine and
> this windy December night.
> "Do not be frightened, children!"
> But the birds have eaten the womb-shaped, owl-
> shaped seeds we dropped in the moonlight.
> When the salmon dives, it comes up carrying
> a sack of wedding rings!
> This love is like the sun held inside a tiny solar
> system,
> like the moon kept in a pouch.
> "Come in, do not be frightened, children!"
> Some of us will die,
> others will lenghen out years on islands,
> but this night blows against hubcaps.
> Men will die for this night.

A striking new element in this poem is the darker, the more shadowy part of the feminine principle. The December night is not only dark (darkness is positive in Bly's poetry) but it is also windy. The trail-markers, the seeds - whose close symbolic connection with the Mother is indicated by the words "womb," "owl," and "moonlight" - have disappeared, as in the fairytale of Hansel and Gretel. The evil counterforce, which thus mani-fests itself, speaks out in the second line in the voice of the witch in the fairytale, who at first pretends to be a good motherly woman and then drops her disguise and appears as the death principle. This seems to me t be the embodiment of the theme of this poem: the hidden, evil side of the feminine principle. Images of something hidden inside a protective sack o space that is reminscent of the womb, dominate the poem: A sack of rings brought out of the water, the sun is made indiscernible by the brightness of a solar system, the moon is hidden in a pouch, and men withdraw to an island.[4] This false hidden side of the feminine principle is the killer o life, unless disclosed.

---

1 "I Came Out of my Mother Naked," Sleepers, p. 32.
2 See above, pp. 56-57.
3 Jumping, p. 27.
4 This probably refers to Odysseus, held prisoner on the island of Ogygi by the sea nymph Calypso.

The disclosure of this murderous human force is the theme of the long
poem "The Teeth Mother Naked at Last," first published as a separate book
in 1970, and later included in Sleepers Joining Hands, in which it is
followed by the explanatory prose essay "I Came Out of the Mother Naked."[1]
In this essay Bly summarizes ideas concerning matriarchal societies put
forward by the Swiss scholar Bachofen in his book Mother Right, published
in 1861, as well as ideas more recently expressed by Erich Neumann in his
book The Great Mother, first published in 1955. The main part of the essay
is devoted to Neumann's theory about the Great Mother understood as a union
of four force fields.[2] These force fields can be illustrated by a cross, of
which the vertical line stands for the physical life-death line and the
horizontal line for the mental or spiritual life-death line. The two ends
of the vertical line are ruled by the Good Mother and the Death Mother
respectively, and the two ends of the horizontal line are ruled by the
Ecstatic Mother and the Stone Mother respectively. The Good Mother gives
birth and nourishes what is born. There exist ancient sculptures of her
in which she seems to be in her thirties, sitting with a child in her lap.
She is said to like men, although she treats them as children. Good is
part of her name because she cares for life. The Death Mother tries to
annihilate everything the Good Mother has given birth to. She is the evil
witch of fairytales. The Ecstatic Mother intensifies the growth of mental
and spiritual life toward ecstasy. She is traditionally imagined as dancing
and as being in her teens or twenties. The Greek name for her is the Muse.
The Ecstatic Mother is seen as the "abundant" mother on the spiritual plane.
Her opposite, the Stone Mother, is seen as making efforts to extinguish the
mental life begun by the Ecstatic Mother, and to kill ecstasy and spiritual growth. The results of her efforts may be numbness, paralysis, cata-
tonia, or a psyche torn to pieces. In some cultures she is called the
Teeth Mother and stands for the end of psychic life, the dismembering of
the psyche. The Teeth Mother is dangerous to women as well as to men. In
concluding Bly asserts that what he really wants to do in this essay is to
praise the feminine soul: "We know that the despising of the feminine soul
has been the cause of some of our greatest errors and disasters."[3]

---

1 Sleepers, pp. 29-50.
2 This basic idea is, naturally, an essential part of all interpretations
   of the "Teeth Mother"-poem; thus, also of those given by Justin, Wosk,
   and Sage.
3 Sleepers, p. 49.

In the preceding section Bly warns scholars not to examine his poems
for evidence of these ideas "for," he says, "most of my poems were written
without benefit of them."[1] It is quite clear, however, that an acquaintance
with these ideas is needed for the reader who wants to grasp the meaning of
"The Teeth Mother Naked at Last." The fact that the above mentioned prose
essay was published in close connection with that poem indicates the same.
That these ideas, to a certain extent, have entered some of his other poems
will be shown in this chapter. He has, of course, absorbed related ideas
from such writers as Robert Graves[2] and Marie-Louise von Franz.[3] The long
antiwar poem, "The Teeth Mother Naked at Last" therefore, will be discussed
against the background of these ideas, which are common ground for members
of the Jungian school. James Hillman, for example, states: "Jung makes a
clear distinction between the role of the mother archetype as regressive
and devouring, on the one hand, and as the creative matrix, on the other."[4]

The first part of the poem shows the cruelty and the meaninglessness
of the Vietnam War by contrasting the powerful death machines to the humble
"huts with dirt floors" and to the fear aroused in innocent creatures:
"The chickens feel the new fear deep in the pits of their beaks."[5] Innocent people are killed by "the deathbee": Supersabres / like knots of neur-
otic energy sweep / around and return."[6] Teachers, a staff sergeant, and
children become the victims. The human force behind the inhuman deeds of
the War is personalized in Alexander Hamilton, who was one of the signers
of the Declaration of Independence, and as Secretary of the Treasury, was
one of the strong men in the first American administration. By encouraging
manufacturing and by founding a national bank, he laid the foundation for
the present economic system of the country, and for the linkage of business
and government. The Vietnam War is seen by Bly as the ironic result of the
economic development of the United States:

>   This is Hamilton's triumph.
>   This is the advantage of a centralized bank.[7]

---

1   Sleepers, p. 49.
2   See above, p. 169, about Bly's reading of Graves.
3   See above, p. 135, about Bly's reading of M.-L. von Franz.
4   Fathers & Mothers, Hillman, p. 115.
5   Teeth Mother, p. 5. Cf. also the early poem "Fall," dealt with above,
    pp. 41-42.
6   Ibid.
7   Ibid.

> . . .
> Hamilton saw all this in detail:
> "E v e r y   b a n a n a   t r e e   s l a s h e d,
> e v e r y   c o o k i n g   u t e n s i l   s m a s h e d,
> e v e r y   m a t t r e s s   c u t."[1]

This takes place simultaneously with changes in the intensity of life
energy in Nature:

> This happens when the seasons change,
> This happens when the leaves begin to drop from
>   the trees too early[2]

To interpret this in terms of the Mother archetype might seem far-fetched
but is possible. A rational consciousness, capable of structuring effective
machines, of founding banks, is the instrument of the Death Mother. Orders
are given to kill what the Good Mother has given life to:

> "K i l l   t h e m: I   d o n' t   w a n t   t o   s e e
> a n y t h i n g   m o v i n g."[3]

What is needed to nourish and sustain life is also destroyed:

> Now the Marine knives sweep around like sharp-
>   edged jets;
>   how easily they slash open the rice bags,
> the mattresses....[4]

The last line of this section,

> Old women watch the soldiers[5]

somehow emphasizes the central role of women in the battle of life and
death, although in this case theirs is a non-active role. The old women
passively register the disastrous events, as a fish does when winter comes
(an image used only a few lines earlier):

> That happens when the ice begins to show its teeth
>   in the ponds
> that happens when the heavy layers of lake water
>   press down on the fish's head and send
>   him deeper, where his tail swirls slowly,
>   and his brain passes him pictures of heavy
>   reeds, of vegetation fallen on vegeta-
>   tion....[6]

---

1 Teeth Mother, p. 8.
2 Ibid., p. 7.
3 Ibid., p. 7.
4 Ibid., p. 8.
5 Ibid.
6 Ibid., pp. 7-8.

Marine knives are mentioned among the instruments of death. The secon
section of the poem shows the terrible effect of Roman knives and conjures
up the screams of their victims. Knives, or swords, are traditional symbol
James Hillman[1] places them first in a Christian and in a mythological con
text, and then in a psychological one. In the Christian tradition the swo
is instrumental in killing what is evil,[2] and it is often seen as a symbo
for the word of God,[3] the logos. In Greek mythology the knife itself is e
Hillman prefers, however, to see the knife, or the sword, in connection
with consciousness, and he makes the connection concrete in the phrase "t
logos sword of discrimination." "Discrimination is the essential, the swo
only a secondary instrument. Consciousness requires discrimination, for a
Jung said, there is no consciousness without perception of differences."[4]
In Bly's poem the function of the Roman knives gradually changes into tha
of the logos sword:

> Excellent Roman knives slip along the ribs.
> A stronger man starts to jerk up the strips of
>   flesh.
>
> . . .
>
> The whines of jets
> pierce like a long needle.
> As soon as the President finishes his press con-
>   ference,
>   black wings carry off the words,
> bits of flesh still clinging to them.[5]

The cause of the killing is not to be found in the knives and the death-
machines; it is to be traced back to the human consciousness behind the
instigation of war, to the consciousness of a whole country that seems
to be moving toward mental impoverishment and spiritual death:

>   * * *
> The ministers lie, the professors lie, the television
>   lies, the priests lie....
> These lies mean that the country wants to die.
> Lie after lie starts out into the prairie grass,
> like enormous trains of Conestoga wagons.

---

1 Fathers & Mothers, Hillman, p. 106.
2 See, for example, Jeremiah 21:9: "He that abideth in this city shall d
   by the sword, . . ." or Romans 13:4: "But if thou do that which is evi
   be afraid; for he beareth not the sword in vain: for he is the ministe
   of God, a revenger to execute wrath upon him that doeth evil.
3 See, for example, Revelation 2:16: "Repent, or else I will come unto
   thee quickly, and will fight against them with the sword of my mouth."
4 Fathers & Mothers, Hillman, p. 106.
5 Teeth Mother, pp. 9-10.

And a long desire for death flows out, guiding
the enormous caravan from beneath,
stringing together the vague and foolish words.

It is a desire to eat death,
to gobble it down,
to rush on it like a cobra with mouth open,

It's a desire to take death inside,
to feel it burning inside, pushing out velvety
              hairs,
like a clothes brush in the intestines
This is the thrill that leads the President on to
              lie

. . .

This is only the deep longing for death.[1]

Mersmann interprets these lines as influenced by Freudian ideas:

> Because we have been captured by "death," the death-
> in-life of the outward man cut off from his vital cen-
> ter, Bly believes we long for real death, an annihila-
> tion of the alienated self. Undoubtedly influenced by
> Freud, Bly finds in our hatred and desire to kill others
> a double proof of our own self-hatred and death wish.
> According to Freud's theory of projection, we attribute
> to our enemy the hatred for us that we feel towards our-
> selves. We thus need to destroy the enemy because we are
> paranoically sure he is trying to kill us. And by a
> second law of sublimation and transference, we satisfy
> our desire for self-destruction by violence against
> our enemy.[2]

In the poem this longing for death then moves toward the Mother's force
fields; it turns into a longing to go back to the origins and finally to
turn to dust:

It is the longing for someone to come and take
              us by the hand to where they all are
              sleeping:
where the Egyptian Pharoahs are asleep, and your
              own mother,
and all those disappeared children, who used to
              go around with you in a swing at grade
              school....

Do not be angry at the President — he is longing
              to take in his hand
the locks of death hair —
to meet his own children sleeping, or unborn....
He is drifting sideways toward the dusty places[3]

---

1 Teeth Mother, pp. 10-12.
2 Mersmann, p. 129.
3 Teeth Mother, p. 12.

Considering the fact that American society is characterized by male domination to a high degree, but that the domestic society of the home is characterized by female domination, it appears right to explain the country's
national consciousness in terms of a relationship with the Mother. - "The
'negative mother' is visible in the voices of the women with their children
the faces of ugly mouths and flat eyes, the resentment and hatred. It is
a wonder anyone survives at all through the early years when mother-love
comes with its double, mother-hate."[1]

Section III shows the horrors of the War in contrast to the affluent
American society. A rich country makes war easily because the senses of
its inhabitants have become dulled in an environment of expensive hospi-
tals, successful businesses, air-conditioned houses, neatly packaged deli-
catessen, and efficient machinery. Residents in this society have not experienced the personal grief that accompanies war:

             . . .

        It is because we have so few women sobbing in back
                        rooms,
        because we have so few children's heads torn apart
                        by high-velocity bullets,
        because we have so few tears falling on our own
                        hands
        that the Super Sabre turns and screams down
                        toward the earth

        It's because tax-payers move to the suburbs that we
                        transfer populations.
        The Marines use cigarette lighters to light the
                        thatched roofs of huts
        because so many Americans own their own homes.[2]

Section IV indicates how a "high standard of living" may result in an op-
pressed inner life:

        I see a car rolling toward a rock wall.
        The treads in the face begin to crack.
        We all feel like tires being run down roads under
                        heavy cars.[3]

Mersmann comments on the "rightness" of these images: "One can no more
rationally explain how it feels to be a tire than one can explain the
oppression the Vietnam War has brought to the human spirit, yet both are
immediately known. . ."[4]

---

1 Fathers & Mothers, Hillman, p. 98.
2 Teeth Mother, p. 15.
3 Ibid., p. 16.
4 Mersmann, p. 128.

Teenagers escape from this society through drugs and suicide and the
general picture of life is dark and despairing:

> The teenager imagines herself floating through the
>   Seven Spheres.
> Oven doors are found
> open.
> Soot collects over the doorframe, has children,
>   takes courses,
> goes mad, and dies.[1]

It seems probable that the open oven doors symbolize the Death Mother – in
this case her instrument would be a gas stove with the gas turned on –
and not the Good Mother, although Bly refers to her in his essay in connection with the oven, which "is her womb inside the house; in matriarchies,
only women are allowed to use it."[2] The inner life of modern man seems to
be ruled by the death principle, the "angry women dressed in black," which
seems to be a possible way of imagining the Stone Mother or Teeth Mother:

> There is a black silo inside our bodies, revolving
>   fast.
> Bits of black paint are flaking off,
> where the motorcycles roar, around and around,
> rising higher on the silo walls,
> the bodies bent toward the horizon,
> driven by angry women dressed in black.[3]

The spiritual climate is such that books – often products of the Ecstatic
Mother – leave, escape in the dark. The Bible, which offers justifications
for a patriarchal society, is forced to stay, but New Testaments manage to
get away in the disguise of women. But even victorious male consciousness
– in the shape of Plato, who to Bly represents abstract thinking – is un-
comfortable; he wants to go backwards in time, to "undo what he has done"[4]
and to return to the original state of formlessness, not to rise toward
a heaven of ideal forms:

* * *

> I know that books are tired of us.
> I _know_ they are chaining the Bible to chairs.
> Books don't want to remain in the same room with
>   us anymore.
>
> New Testaments are escaping!... Dressed as women ...
>   they go off after dark.

---

1   _Teeth Mother_, p. 16.
2   _Sleepers_, p. 34.
3   _Teeth Mother_, p. 16.
4   Mersmann, p. 147.

> And Plato! Plato.... Plato wants to go backwards....
> He wants to hurry back up the river of time, so he
>   can end as some blob of seaflesh rotting
>   on an Australian beach.[1]

Followers of Jung have mentioned a return to formlessness as a return to
the mother and as a necessary phase in the individuation process of a man.
Vitale discusses this in the terms of alchemy: "According to alchemists
it is necessary that the hardened element be dissolved, dismembered, and
buried in the primeval formless matter in order to be able to rise again
as a new man."[2] Hillman, pointing to Jungian ideas, sees this longing to
go back to the formless state as a phenomenon belonging to the later part
of a man's life: "For young consciousness 'entry into the mother' is a
fatal incest; for old consciousness it is the way of renewal and even
that which he calls the way of individuation."[3]

In section V Bly gives false invented reasons for the war, thus
emphasizing its utter meaninglessness. The excuses given are involved
with power and money:

> Why are they dying? I have written this so many
>   times.
> They are dying because the President has opened
>   a Bible again.
> They are dying because gold deposits have been
>   found among the Shoshoni Indians.
>
> . . .
>
> The Marines think that unless they die the rivers
>   will not move.
> They are dying so that mountain shadows can fall
>   north[4] in the afternoon,
> so that the beetle can move along the ground near
>   the fallen twigs.[5]

In section VI Bly tries to involve his readers personally. If we
could see the anguish of the victims of the war – if they were our own
children – then we would succumb to our own psychical reactions:

---

1 Teeth Mother, p. 17.
2 Augusto Vitale, "The Archetype of Saturn or Transformation of the Father
   Fathers & Mothers, p. 26. Cf. also above. p. 77.
3 Fathers & Mothers, Hillman, p. 115.
4 "North" has been changed to "east" in the slightly revised version published in Sleepers.
5 Teeth Mother, p. 18.

. . .
the pupils of your eyes would go wild –

. . .

you would ram your head against the wall of your
                bedroom
like a bull penned too long in his moody pen –

If one of those children came toward me with both
                hands
in the air, fire rising along both elbows,
I would suddenly go back to my animal brain,
I would drop on all fours, screaming,
my vocal chords would turn blue, yours would too,
it would be two days before I could play with my
                own children again. [1]

The personal involvement in this part of the poem is replaced by
passive withdrawal in section VII, the conclusion of the poem. The instinctive reaction of the animal brain when confronted with ghastly events
is replaced by a more calculated reaction. Modern man notices only what
he wants to notice. Unpleasant results of his experiments can be kept
in the dark. Over-use of natural resources, the deformity of children
caused by war or by medical side-effects can be concealed by religious
pretence; one can seek shelter in the shadow of Augustine's doctrine
about absolute predestination. Instead, we can talk about what is not
frightening:

I want to sleep awhile in the rays of the sun
                slanting over the snow.
Don't wake me.
Don't tell me how much grief there is in the
                leaf with its natural oils.
Don't tell me how many children have been born
                with stumpy feet
all those years we lived in Augustine's shadow.

Tell me about the dust that falls from the yellow
                daffodil shaken in the restless winds.
Tell me about the particles of Babylonian thought
                that still pass through the earthworm
                every day.
Don't tell me about "the frightening laborers who
do not read books."[2]

---

1   Teeth Mother, pp. 19-20.
2   Ibid., p. 21.

But that modern man is mentally and emotionally passive, that he ignores
the irrational parts of his psyche, invites disaster. The whole Nation
wavers as in a shipwreck. Forces from outside attack. Europe, which originally colonized the land, turns against it. The country is possessed
by evil and rushes toward its own death like a mad beast decked with
borrowed plumes, or like a herd of swine possessed by devils:[1]

> Now the whole nation starts to whirl,
> the end of the Republic breaks off,
> Europe comes to take revenge,
> the mad beast covered with European hair rushes
>   through the mesa bushes in Mendocino
>   County,
> pigs rush toward the cliff,[2]

The evil behind all these insane activities wishes to extirpate itself.
The force behind the war is laid bare, and shown in a feminine shape
beside its more positive counterpart. The water is divided into two
oceans. In one of these, luminous globes float up containing representative
of the Ecstatic Mother[3] - "hairy and ecstatic rock musicians."[4] In the
other ocean "the teeth-mother, naked at last,"[5] comes to the surface.
For a moment these two feminine principles of the unconscious, are seen
in balance, but history tells us that they alternately dominate humans.
Ecstasy might take us "up / the light beams / to the stars...."[6], but we
will only be made to return to a world of persecution and killing. The poe
that opens with the Good Mother and Death Mother in battle closes by show
the Ecstatic Mother and the Teeth Mother alternately in power:

---

1 See The Bible, Matthew 8:28-32, where is told how Jesus commanded evil
   spirits to leave two possessed men and take up their abode in a herd o
   swine, which then threw themselves down from a cliff into the sea.
2 Teeth Mother, pp. 21-22.
3 See Sleepers, pp. 42-43, where Bly comments on a movement in the Unite
   States toward the Mother: "Half the population still show their nearness to these Mothers [that is the Good Mother and the Ecstatic Mother]
   by their beads and long hair and ecstasy, by loving rock music, swayin
   back and forth half the afternoon." In his review of Robert Graves's
   Difficult Questions, Easy Answers he mentions a tradition of ecstati
   experience beginning with "the early ecstatic Vedic poems, whose spiritual intensity was so high" and ending with "our present low state of
   rock music." [See The New York Times Book Review (March 17, 1974), p.
4 Teeth Mother, p. 22.
5 Ibid.
6 Ibid.

> Let us drive cars
> up
> the light beams
> to the stars....
>
> And return to earth crouched inside the drop of
>   sweat
> that falls again and again
> from the chin of the Protestant tied in the fire.[1]

Fairytales and myths are evidence of the antiquity and the archetypal
quality of the idea that the dark side of the feminine principle causes
disaster and suffering. The evil fairy in the well-known tale "Briar Rose"
is seen by Marie-Louise von Franz as the ignored goddess coming to take
revenge,[2] or in more general terms "she is the dark side of the feminine
principle forgotten in our civilization, and also the dark, imperfect side
of mother nature."[3] In interpreting Grimm's fairytale called "The Six
Swans," Marie-Louise von Franz describes a situation ruled by the evil
stepmother that seems to parallel Bly's description of the American nation
dominated by the Teeth Mother: "In a collective conscious situation, this
would be where the feminine principle has disappeared in its positive form
and has turned evil. . . . Consciousness is too masculine and too rational,
so that the underworld reacts in this negative form."[4] In another of Grimm's
fairytales, "The Seven Ravens," the father himself is the instrument of evil
in pronouncing a curse on his sons, but according to Marie-Louise von Franz
what causes this is "not the father's conscious, but his uncontrolled
affect, i.e. his negative anima. . . . The father, if not a king, represents the habitual attitude, which has a dark background, the uncontrolled
affects which bring about destruction."[5] In Bly's poem Hamilton and the
President might be the counterparts of the father and the King. Many fairytales contain an incident entailing exposure of the evil principle, that is,
the Teeth Mother is seen naked. Often this occurs when someone goes into a
chamber to which entrance is forbidden. In some stories the one who enters
does not afterwards admit to opening the door, and in others he or she

---

1 Teeth Mother, p. 22.
2 See The Feminine in Fairytales, p. 35.
3 Ibid., p. 38.
4 Ibid., p. 120.
5 Ibid., pp. 120-121.

reveals the secret.[1] The conclusion of the Teeth Mother poem, in which the
two feminine principles rise out of the "waters" of the human unconscious
after having been neglected in a society ruled by male rational conscious
ness, also contains archetypal material that can be found in fairytales.
an Eskimo tale Sedna, who is disappointed in her husband, is saved from
marital life by her father, but is then thrown into the sea and crippled
by him. As a result of these damaging connections with the male principle
Sedna lives under the sea as the hidden goddess of nature, and from there
rules over life and death.[2]

In ancient myths from various cultures the different aspects of the
female principle are embodied - as is well known- in goddesses ruling
different fields of activity. In The White Goddess Robert Graves gives a
poetic and sometimes subjectively colored survey of the worship of a fema
divinity, alternately seen as several goddesses or as one with several
faces. Graves first mentions "a triad of Goddesses who presided over all
acts of generation whatsoever: physical, spiritual, or intellectual,"[3]
but then he discusses them as different aspects of an "all-powerful
Threefold Goddess."[4] "Her names and titles are innumerable. In ghost
stories she often figures as 'The White Lady' and in ancient religions,
from the British Isles to Caucasus, as the 'White Goddess.'"[5] He emphasizes her importance for the poet: "The test of a poet's vision, one
might say, is the accuracy of his portrayal of the White Goddess and of
the island over which she rules. . . . a true poem is necessarily an invocation of the White Goddess, or Muse, the Mother of All Living, the
ancient power of fright and lust - the female spider or the queen-bee
whose embrace is death."[6] The aspects that Graves attributes to this
Goddess seem to be roughly the same as those of the four-fold Mother post
ulated by Erich Neumann. Graves refers to Belili, the Sumerian White
Goddess, as "a goddess of trees as well as a Moon-goddess, Love-goddess
and Underworld-goddess."[7] In a later chapter each of her separate goddess
roles becomes a triple role, and she is thus given manifold control of

---

1   See Marie-Louise von Franz, Shadow and Evil in Fairytales (Zürich, 197
    The text of this book was comprised of two lecture series given in 195
    and 1964.
2   See Marie-Louise von Franz, The Feminine in Fairytales, pp. 176-177.
3   Graves, pp. 11-12.
4   Ibid., p. 24.
5   Ibid.
6   Ibid.
7   Graves, p. 58.

human life. As Moon-goddess only, for example, she appears as a triple
goddess in the records of Suidas the Byzantine: ". . . the New Moon is
the white goddess of birth and growth; the Full Moon, the red goddess of
love and battle; the Old Moon, the black goddess of death and divination."[2]
Thus, the nature of the White Goddess is difficult to grasp. Poets through
all times have dedicated themselves and their poetry to her. Graves quotes
or mentions Skelton, Keats, and other poets to show the relevance of the
theme of the White Goddess in later times: "Skelton in his 'Garland of
Laurell' thus describes the Triple Goddess in her three characters as
Goddess of the Sky, Earth and Underworld."[2] For Keats the White Goddess
was "La Belle Dame Sans Merci" and represented "Love, Death by Consump-
tion, . . . and Poetry."[3] "But," says Graves, discussing the various shapes
and roles of the Triple Goddess, "it must never be forgotten that [she]
. . . was a personification of primitive woman - woman the creatress and
destructress. As the New Moon or Spring she was girl; as the Full Moon or
Summer she was woman; as the Old Moon or Winter she was hag."[4]

To reveal the secret of the hag, or to show the Teeth Mother naked,
does not suffice for Bly. A remedy against the evil must be found. The
poem "Water Under the Earth"[5] points to the positive forces of the unconscious and to its reserve of energy:

> . . .
> So much is still inside me, like cows eating in
>   a collapsed strawpile
> all winter to get out.
> Everything we need now is buried,
> it's far back into the mountain,
> it's under the water guarded by women.
> . . .

Again the secret is in the hands of women, but it is hidden far to the
back of the masculine society. The poet is approaching the secret, but
there is much in his way - things belonging to the traditional past hold
him back, and he is not yet familiar with the force fields of the Mother:

---

1   Graves, p. 70.
2   Ibid., p. 386.
3   Ibid., p. 431.
4   Ibid., p. 386.
5   Sleepers, pp. 6-7.

. . .
> I am only half-risen,
> I see how carefully I have covered my tracks as
>   I wrote,
> how well I brushed over the past with my tail.
> I enter rooms full of photographs of the dead.
> My hair stands up
> as a badger crosses my path in the moonlight.[1]

He has to take into account the entire contents of his unconscious:

> I see faces looking at me in the shallow waters
> where I have thrown them down.
> Mother and father pushed into the dark.

But he is approaching the place where the secret is hidden, where the original energy can be discerned:

> That shows how close I am to the dust that fills
>   the cracks on the ocean floor,
> how much I love to fly alone in the rain,
> how much I love to see the jellyfish pulsing at
>   the cold borders of the universe.

What seems to hinder him is his relationship to fellowman:

> I have piled up people like dead flies between the
>   storm window and the kitchen pane.
> So much is not spoken!
> I stand at the edges of the light, howling to come in.

That seems, judging by this poem, to be as near to the secret as an individual can come. But this nearness gives him moments in which he feels the energy he is searching for, and ecstasy and understanding:

> Then, I follow the wind through open holes in the
>   blood -
> So much ecstasy....
> long evenings when the leopard leaps up to the
>   stars,
> and in an instant we understand all the rocks in
>   the world.
> And I am there, prowling like a limp-footed bull
>   outside the circle of the fire,
> praying, meditating,
> full of energy, like a white horse, saddled, alone
>   on the unused fields.

He has been close to the Ecstatic Mother; he knows now that

> There is a consciousness hovering under the mind's
>   feet,
> advanced civilizations under the footsole,
> climbing at times up on a shoelace!

---

1 In an earlier poem we have seen the badger as a creature close to the Mother. See above, p. 177. See also above, pp. 89-90.

He has experienced one of these rare moments in which the secret can be
divined. He is like a willow tree that has sensed water under the ground.
He is an ordinary man with a rational consciousness but still he is in
touch with irrational sources of energy in his unconscious:

> It is a willow that knows of water under the earth,
> I am a father who dips as he passes over underground
>   rivers,
> who can feel his childern through all distance and
>   time!

In this poem Bly describes his personal solution. In the poem "Hair"[1]
the same basic idea is applied to a collective situation. Society is seen
as a whirlpool splashing drops of black water: so many individuals are lost,
destroyed by drink or drugs, gamble with death, or suffer nervous break-
downs. They are discarded, sent into a living death, like hair that is cut
off in barbershops or like worn showlaces that are thrown away:

> . . .
>
> All that hair that fell to the floors of barber-
>   shops over thirty years
> lives on after death,
> and those shoelaces, shiny and twisted, that we
>   tossed to the side,
> gather in the palace of death;
> the roarer comes,
> the newly dead kneel, and a tip of the lace sends
>   them on into fire!
>
> . . .
>
> All those things borne down by the world
> corpses pulled down by years of death,
> veins clogged with flakes of sludge,
> mouths from which bats escape at death,
> businessmen reborn as black whales sailing under
>   the Arctic ice...
> . . .

The passages of the poem which describe human frustration are interfolia-
ted with passages presenting hair as the saviour - it can feel sorrow, be
merciful, create calm, and lead "the sleeper" to ecstasy, to the hidden
treasure that reflects "the glory of God":

> . . .
>
> But the hair weeps,
> because hair does not long for immense states,
> hair does not hate the poor,
> hair is merciful,
> like the arch of night under which the juvenile
>   singer lolls back drunk....

---

1 Sleepers, pp. 10-12.

. . .

But hair is overflowing with excitable children,
it is a hammock on which the sleeper lies,
dizzy with the heat and the earth's motion,
ecstatic waters, Ordovician hair,
hair that carries the holy, shouting, to the
          other shore.

In a bureau drawer there are tiny golden pins
          full of the glory of God -
their faces shine with power
like the cheekbones of saints radiant in their
          beds
or their great toes that light the whole room!

Hair is mammalian according to Bly in his essay "The Three Brains;" it
represents the positive forces of love and community.[1] Bly imagines hair
cathedrals underground - beyond our conscious life - in which priests in
furry robes preach about natural forces stronger than human heroes. Fina
hair is presented as a female attribute that makes possible an acceptance
of death:[2]

          . . .

Under the ground the earth has hair cathedrals
the priest comes down the aisle wearing cater-
          pillar fur.
In his sermons the toad defeats the knight

The dying man waves his son away.
He wants his daughter-in-law to come near
so that her hair will fall over his face.

There are other ways of dying, excruciating, bitter, and dark:

The senator's plane falls in an orchard in
          Massachusetts.
And there are bitter places, knots
that leave dark pits in the sawdust,
          . . .

But there are also almost unnoticable means of quiet escape for those
who know hair's ancient sheltering and saving force:

the nick on the hornblade through which the mammoth
          escapes....

Thus again we see the outer human condition as one of sadness, contraste

---

1 See _The Seventies_, 1, p. 62. See also above, pp. 58-59.
2 The hair of women as a saving force for men was mentioned above in the
   interpretation of "Walking in the Ditch Grass," pp. 105-106.

with an inner condition of love and mercy. The sadness in Bly's poems frequently springs from a situation in which one group or force suppresses
another; the whites, the Indians; the more educated, the less educated;
society, nature; the male principle, the female principle. This sadness
is the theme of the last stanza of "Calling to the Badger,"[1] a poem of
which the first stanza was published in 1960 as a separate poem called
"The Possibility of New Poetry."[2] This poem, as was mentioned early in
the present chapter, shows the poet and his muse together in another world.
Such a meeting makes it possible for the poet to describe the human condition:

> We are writing of Niagara, and the Huron squaws,
> the chaise longue, periwinkles in a rage like
>   snow,
> Dillinger like a dark wind.
> Intelligence, cover the advertising men with clear
>   water,
> and the factories with merciless space,
> so the strong-haunched woman
> by the blazing stove of the sun, the moon,
> may come home to me, sitting on the naked wood
> in another world, and all the Shell stations
> folded in a faint light.
>
> You feel a sadness,
> a sadness that rises form the death of the Indians,
> from the death of Logan, alone in the house,
> and the Cherokees forced to eat the tail of the
>   Great Bear.
> We are driven to Florida like Geronimo -[3]
> and the young men are still calling to the badger
> and the otter, alone on the mountains of South Dacota.

Thus, in the final analysis, the male and female elements stand for civilization versus nature, and, on another level, the world of reality versus the
world of poetry. Whatever society does to human beings there will be some
who still call to the badger and the otter, still move toward Nature,
toward the Mother. Bly has shown himself to be one of those both in his
life and his poetry. In Robert Graves's words, he has heeded and he passes
on the "warning to man that he must keep in harmony with the family of
living creatures among which he was born, by obedience to the wishes of
the lady of the house."[4]

---

1   Sleepers, p. 16.
2   See above, p. 174.
3   Logan and Geronimo were Indian chiefs.
4   Graves, p. 14.

CONCLUSIONS: PATTERNS IN THE POETRY OF ROBERT BLY

The basic pattern of movement in Bly's poetry has revealed itself in different kinds of poems. The movements through the Midwestern landscape have resulted in descriptive poems, showing us the land - the countryside and city - sometimes as it actually appears to the senses, but more often as Bly himself imaginatively perceives it through personifications and animations.

Movements in time have brought history into the poems and thus have often created a basis for political poetry. These movements in time are in some poems irrational and baffling, even surrealistic, as in the last two lines of "The Traveller."[1] The irrationality of Bly's surrealism is however, more often a symbol of the "surreal" world we have created for ourselves, as in "Those Being Eaten by America,"[2] and thus it is part of the technique of poems of social criticism. Or, as in "The Fire of Despair Has Been Our Saviour,"[3] the "surreal" world may be related to an inner world. This last poem ends with a movement downward, an image that occurs in many of Bly's poems. This downward movement is often equated with an inward one, a movement into darkness. This pattern, therefore, becomes a vehicle for the creation of poems of mystical vision, like the one called "Moving Inward at Last."[4]

Once the persona is inside the psyche the movement is renewed and becomes that of the shaman or the mythic hero. Strange symbolic objects, beings, and circumstances are revealed and constitute a framework for poems of mystical experience like "The Teeth Mother Naked at Last"[5] and "Sleepers Joining Hands."[6]

The movement inside a Bly poem, or through a sequence of his poems or through the whole body of his poems, becomes a movement away from the objective world toward the center of creative subjectivity. This movement exists on the level of personal engagement and development, on a structural level within the poems, and on a thematic level.

We can see how, on the personal level, the poet's perspective widens. His world is at first the countryside of Minnesota, with its

---

1 See above, pp. 21-22.
2 See above, pp. 37 and 51-52.
3 See above, pp. 37, 53, and 54-55.
4 See above, pp. 66 and 181.
5 See above, pp. 185-195.
6 See above, pp. 145-169.

small towns, and the Midwestern landscape in general, with its barns,
fields, and roads. These fields and roads become the United States, and
the poet's interest is engaged by political and social problems. Many of
his poems result from his personal conscience turning into the conscience of the whole nation. Frustrated by the smallness of his audience
and by a negative response - or a lack of response - to his kind of
poetry from people in positions of authority, Bly moves from an outer
engagement to an inner one. In the spring of 1973 he says in public, in
answer to a question about his future engagement in political poetry: "We
tried and lost. From now on it is going to be grief." To Bly, that means
a turning inward. Through grief a person becomes acquainted with his
inner dimensions, both negative and positive. That is the message that
Bly wants to bring to the readers of his mystical poems. "A person who
has not felt deep sorrow does not know his own self. There might still
be hope for the individual, for America. There has been so much grief
during these last decades; something positive must come out of that," Bly
said in a private conversation in 1975. In an early poem called "Melancholia"[1] this idea is contained in the last stanza:

> There is a wound on the trunk,
> Where the branch was torn off.
> A wind comes out of it,
> Rising, swelling,
> Swirling over everything alive.

On the structural level we find a development from haiku-like poems
and other quite short poems in Silence in the Snowy Fields and The Light
around the Body via the prose poem in The Morning Glory to the complex
associative patterns of long poems like "The Teeth Mother Naked at Last"
and "Sleepers Joining Hands." However, the basis for all these different
kinds of poems - except for some very early ones included in Bly's MA
thesis and published in magazines - seems to be the same: that is, the
image and the phrase. In the early poems included in his books the descriptive phrase is the major element, as I have shown in Chapter I. As
Bly's poems become more laden with meaning, the descriptive elements
become subjectively colored and reflect the poet's moods on particular
occasions and his attitudes toward general problems and, thus, gradually
turn into metaphors and symbols. These recur as seemingly surrealistic

---

1   See above, p. 91.

elements in his political poems and poems of social engagement, as I h
shown in Chapter II primarily, and in his mystical poems, as I have
shown in Chapters III and IV. On deeper consideration one realizes, h
ever, that hardly any of Bly's poems are surrealistic in the full sen
of the word. There is unity in the way the images are juxtaposed or
ordered into chains. There is logic in the ostensibly illogical arran
ment of words, phrases and lines - something I have endeavored to sho
when tracing themes in Bly's poetry.

There also seems to be an undercurrent of logic in the way that
curring words, concepts, archetypes, and myths occur in Bly's poetry
then fade away, or in the way they lie scattered, or buried like seed
in early poems, to come out in full bloom in his later poems. The descriptive elements of early poems, for example, recur in later poems
support themes mainly based on archetypes and myths, just as these ar
types and myths may be glimpsed in some of the early poems.

In tracing these various elements in Bly's poetry I have attempt
to consider them as carriers of themes. The snow, the fields, and the
barns are important elements in Bly's descriptions of the Midwestern
landscape. (The snow covers what is discarded and killed, and function
a preserver and a bringer of darkness and of death. Negative elements
such as alienation, regression, and insanity, are part of the darknes
In Bly's poetry, however, there is also to be noticed a pattern of op
sites. Out of the darkness brought by the snow grows a positive chang
the inward-turning individual feels in contact with the timelessness
Nature and with his own inner world.)

⟶ The fields are a major part of the outer landscape, and when pla
in juxtaposition with the inner landscape they serve to reflect the p
mood. They function as symbols of both the outer and the inner world;
turn into stages for the poet's own performances, for the madness and
disintegration of the world, and for the poet's inner experiences.⟵

The barns - very conspicuous in the agricultural Midwestern land
scape - grow into symbols of light and security; they are treated as
jects of love but also as containers of darkness and, as such, bringe
of new life. The newborn child, found in the barn, is not a saviour i
religious sense. It represents, instead, a new consciousness, one tha
is aware of the complexity of our world and has discovered inner resources of a similar complexity.

More is needed to balance the outward world than the short glimpses of the inner world given in passing in Bly's early poems. Nor can one achieve balance through a preoccupation with all the evil in the world – the evil so well described in Bly's political and social poems. It is, rather, all of this combined with a self-knowledge gained through the silence of sorrow and through contemplation experienced in seclusion; it is a submersion in the unconscious and a gaining of strength that enables the individual to face the outer world.

Whether description, or social engagement, or mystical experience will dominate a poem is mainly decided by Bly's technique of varying the degree to which he effaces borders in place and time, the intensity with which he represents Life Energy through animation of the elements and creatures of Nature, and finally the extent to which he employs archetypes and myths and adapts them to his own personal experiences.

Without systematically comparing Bly's poems to either the products of Romanticism, Symbolism, Imagism, or Surrealism, I shall try to draw some conclusions about the similarities between his poetry and that which issued from these movements.

Romanticism: What Bly has in common with the Romantics is, as Cleanth Brooks points out,[1] his way of using ordinary objects in his surroundings as starting-points for descriptive poems, and his way of then using these descriptions to reflect his moods and feelings. Furthermore, Bly's emphasis in his later poems on imagination, intuition, and vision is related to Romanticism, as is his use of fairytales and myths.

Symbolism: Bly seems at first to be the opposite of a Symbolist. He does not wish to create or approach an ideal world; he wants to go back to original, formless matter with its infinite possibilities. This is as far from the abstract ideal as one can get. What he has in common with the Symbolist is, however, the desire to penetrate to a world beyond our concrete reality. In Bly's case this means a movement downward into the original darkness and a movement inward toward the individual unconscious, not a movement upward toward a heaven of abstract ideal forms. Bly's movement inward seems to coincide with one aspect of Symbolism, the

---

1 See above, p. 9.

attempt to penetrate to a world of ideas and emotions within the poet, "not by describing them directly, nor by defining them through overt comparisons with concrete images, but by suggesting what these ideas and emotions are, by recreating them in the mind of the reader through the use of unexplained symbols."[1] But in this case, also, Bly takes a stand opposite to that of the Symbolists. He asserts that he produces his images out of the flow of the unconscious, and the Symbolists claim reality as their starting-point. In Bly's early poems his point of departure is closer to that of the Symbolists, but then, of course, many of these poems never become symbolic but remain descriptive. Bly's more recent poems have developed in a direction, opposite to that of the Symbolists, that is, out of an inner flow of images to symbolize an inner state of conditions.

Imagism: Bly does not appear to be closely related to the Imagists. Only in the short haiku-like poems of Silence in the Snowy Fields, and Old Man Rubbing His Eyes, does he use images intentionally created so as to let the image generate the whole poem and not suggest anything beyond it. "The Loon"[2] could perhaps serve as an example. It seems probable to me that Bly and the Imagist poets simply consulted the same models: like the Imagist poets Bly has shown an interest in Oriental poetry.

Surrealism: The movement with which Bly seems to have most in common is Surrealism. His way of handling place and time, of breaking down barriers and borders, classifies him as a Surrealist. Compatible with the surreal world thus created is his interest in the dream state and in the activities of the unconscious. Some of Bly's poems seem at first the result of automatic writing - what André Breton calls "a monologue spoken as rapidly as possible without any intervention on the part of the critical faculties"[3] - and thus Surrealistic. However, on a closer analysis one finds the undercurrent of logic. I would say that every poem of Bly has a planned pattern which carries a carefully considered theme, and I have tried to show this in dealing with seemingly Surrealistic poems such as "Suddenly Turning Away,"[4] "Wanting to Experience All Things,"[5]

---

1 Charles Chadwick, Symbolism (London, 1971), pp. 2-3.
2 See above, p. 109.
3 André Breton, Manifestoes of Surrealism (Ann Arbor Paperback, The University of Michigan Press, 1972), p. 23.
4 See above, p. 28.
5 See above, pp. 55-56.

"Walking in the Ditch Grass,"[1] and "Sleepers Joining Hands."[2] These poems - typical of a large part of Bly's poetry - appear on the surface to be structured out of disparate images but on examination each reveals an image pattern. I believe that this holds true not only for single poems but also for whole sequences of poems, such as "Poems on the Voyage"[3] and "The Teeth Mother Naked At Last,"[4] and for whole books, such as Silence in the Snowy Fields. My conclusion is therefore that Bly employs Surrealistic devices but makes them the tools of an intuitive, yet orderly, mind that creates unifying patterns.

In my thesis I have occasionally suggested a relationsship between Bly's poetry and that of earlier American poets. I have found this relationship to be mostly of a thematic kind.

Bly's descriptive regional poems, for example, show a distinctive personal character as well as a resemblance to poems by Robert Frost and Carl Sandburg. An anonymous reviewer of Old Man Rubbing His Eyes says, "Bly is unusual in handling material familiar in American poets from Frost to Wendell Berry - farmyard scenes, seasonal cycles in the countryside, snow-walking reveries - with an Oriental sense of the inner meaning rising out of a simple observation."[5]

In the way that Bly is personally engaged in beliefs that he puts forward in his writings, he is close to Thoreau. The latter's conviction that in order to write about Nature one must have experienced the silence and solitude of it, is shared by Bly, who has found his own Walden in Madison, Minnesota, where he lives close to the earth and is of the earth. Howard Nelson says about Silence in the Snowy Fields, "As an expression of a deep marriage between the inner and outer worlds in one man's life and place it is in the line of Walden."[6] Bly's self-chosen solitude also creates a distance between him and society, which supplies him with an unusual clearsightedness and strength in his political writings and in his

---

1 See above, pp. 105-106.
2 See above, pp. 145-169.
3 See above, pp. 131-138.
4 See above, pp. 185-195.
5 Publishers' Weekly (Febr. 3, 1975).
6 Howard Nelson, "Welcoming Shadows: Robert Bly's Recent Poetry," The Hollins Critic, XII:2 (April, 1975), p. 3.

acts of protest. In commenting on a passage in "Sleepers Joining Han
one critic says, ". . . Bly resembles Thoreau, another spokesman for
tude who desperately wanted to be inside the body of the redskin, the
poet-naturalist, the transcendentalist waiting to give birth to the n
man."[1] Bly himself said in his acceptance speech at "the National Boo
Awards" presentation in 1968: "No one needs to be ashamed of the acts
civil disobedience committed in the tradition of Thoreau."[2] Furthermo
as a writer of political poems Bly looks upon himself as carrying on
tradition begun by Whitman: "Whitman was the first true political poe
had in North America."[3]

Bly has several themes in common with Whitman. The idea of a ret
to the "original energy" is present in Whitman's poems also. In an in
view Bly says, "American poetry is attempting for the first time since
Whitman to follow the path backwards toward the womb and try to make
spiritual progress by going backwards into silence and into gentlenes
and into nature."[4] Bly's emphasis upon individual self-development ha
also been compared to Whitman's: "Bly's criticism and political poems
often have Lawrence's curtness and fervor, but the central enterprise
the poetry is more akin to Whitman, who was essentially concerned with
helping (rather than analyzing) the growth - the deepening and unfold
and transcendence - of the self."[5] The universal love experience that
the close of "Sleepers Joining Hands," results from the "growth and tr
scendence of the self" is seen by Peter Stitt as a parallel to the "tr
scendent union of Americans"[6] that serves as the theme of several of
Whitman's poems.[7]

Bly's interest in poetic theory, especially his ideas about "deep
image" poetry, seems to be reminiscent of Emerson's idea's of poetic

---

1   Charles Molesworth, "Thrashing in the Depths: The Poetry of Robert
    Bly," The Rocky Mountain Review of Language and Literature, 29:3 an
    (Autumn, 1975), p. 116.
2   Robert Bly, "A Poet On Vietnam: Murder as a Prudent Policy," Commor
    weal, 88:1 (March 22, 1968), 17.
3   Robert Bly, "On Political Poetry," The Nation (April 24, 1967), p.
4   "A Conversation with Robert Bly," The Harvard Advocate (Febr., 1970
    p. 8.
5   Howard Nelson, "Welcoming Shadows: Robert Bly's Recent Poetry," p.
6   Peter Stitt, "James Wright and Robert Bly," The Minnesota Review
    (Jan. 29, 1974), p. 92.
7   See also above, p. 169.

creativity: "The poet has a new thought; he has a whole new experience to unfold; he will tell us how it was with him, and all men will be richer in his fortune."[1] On the point that the source of poetry is inside the poet himself, Bly is in agreement not only with Emerson but also with Whitman: "The poetic quality is not marshalled in rhyme or uniformity or abstract addresses to things nor in melancholy complaints or good precepts, but is the life of these and much else and is in the soul."[2]

In his use of the image as the primary conveyor of his message, Bly takes his place in a long line of American writers, both poets and prose writers, beginning with such Puritans as Edward Taylor and Jonathan Edwards and continued by prose writers, for example, Nathaniel Hawthorne, and Herman Melville, and leading up to the modern poets from Whitman to Pound, and William Carlos Williams - to mention a few - and to the modernists of today. The modern poets - of which Bly is an interesting representative - have used imagery, among other methods, to bring out religious, political, and moral messages, but also to illustrate the immense possibilities of poetry itself when it is allowed to grow from within without the constraints of preconceived form.

> The thought and form are equal in the order of time, but in the order of genesis the thought is prior to form.[3]

> The greatest poet has less a marked style and is more the channel of thoughts and things without increase or diminution, and is the free channel of himself.[4]

---

1 Ralph Waldo Emerson, "The Poet," The Complete Essays and Other Writings of Ralph Waldo Emerson (New York, N.Y., 1940), p. 323.
2 Walt Whitman, "Preface to 1855 Edition of 'Leaves of Grass,'" Leaves of Grass and Selected Prose, p. 458.
3 Emerson, "The Poet," p. 323.
4 Whitman, "Preface . . .," p. 461.

BIBLIOGRAPHY

I   Works Quoted or Referred to

A   Primary Sources

a)   Books of Poetry

Bly, Robert. Jumping out of Bed. Barre, Mass., 1973.

———   The Light around the Body. New York, N. Y., 1967. British edition, London, 1968.

———   The Morning Glory. Santa Cruz, Calif., 1969. Revised and enlarged editions, Santa Cruz, Calif., 1970, and New York, N. Y., 1975.

———   Old Man Rubbing His Eyes. Greensboro, N. C., 1975.

———   Point Reyes Poems. Half Moon Bay, Calif., 1974.

———   Silence in the Snowy Fields. Middletown, Conn., 1962. British edition, London, 1967.

———   Sleepers Joining Hands. New York, N. Y., 1973.

———   Steps toward Poverty and Death. MA thesis, The Univ. of Iowa, 1956.

———   The Teeth Mother Naked at Last. San Francisco, Calif., 1970.

Wright, James; Duffy, William; and Bly, Robert. The Lion's Tail and Eyes. Madison, Minn., 1962.

Bly, Robert, ed.. Neruda and Vallejo: Selected Poems. Boston, 1971.

Bly, Robert, ed.. Forty Poems Touching on Recent American History. Boston, Mass., 1970.

Bly, Robert and Ray, David, eds. A Poetry Reading against the Vietnam War. Madison, Minn., 1966.

Bly, Robert, ed.. The Sea and the Honeycomb, A Book of Tiny Poems. Boston, Mass., 1971.

b)   Poems Published in Periodicals

Bly, Robert. "At the Ranch." Epoch, 13:1 (Fall, 1963), 42.

———   "Choral Stanza." The Paris Review (Summer, 1953), 79.

———   "Come with Me." Poetry, CIV:6 (Sept., 1964), 365.

———   "Cricket Calling from a Hiding Place." Kayak, 1 (Autumn, 1964), 31.

———   "Cricket on a Doorstep in September." Kayak, 1 (Autumn, 1964), 3

———   "Driving North from San Francisco." Poetry, CIV:6 (Sept., 1964), 366-367.

———   "Dusk in the Sixties." Epoch, 13:1 (Fall, 1963), 42.

———   "Evolution from the Fish." Choice: A Magazine of Poetry and Photography, 3 (1963), 109.

Bly, Robert. "Fall Solitude." The Lamp and the Spine, 3 (Winter, 1972), 67.

_____ "The Fire of Despair Has Been Our Saviour." The Paris Review (Spring, 1958), 123.

_____ "Looking Backward." The Paris Review (Winter/Spring, 1964), 107.

_____ "The Man Whom the Sea Kept Awake." The Paris Review (Spring/ Summer, 1957), 141.

_____ "Merchants Have Multiplied." Chelsea, 8 (Oct., 1960), 64.

_____ "On a Cliff." Poetry, CIV:6 (Sept., 1964), 367.

_____ "Poem." The Paris Review (Winter/Spring, 1962), 18.

_____ "Poem in Praise of Solitude." Poetry, CIV:6 (Sept., 1964), 368.

_____ "Poems on the Voyage." Contemporary Poetry: A Retrospective from the Quarterly Review of Literature. Edited by T. Weiss and Renée Weiss. Princeton, N. J. , 1975., 245-249.

_____ "Poems on the Voyage." The Quarterly Review of Literature (Fall, 1962), 144-148.

_____ "The Possibility of New Poetry." Poetry, XCVI (April, 1960), 31.

_____ "The President about to Address the Whole Nation in the Eighth Year of the Vietnam War." The Tennessee Poetry Journal, 4:1 (Fall, 1970), 5.

_____ "Pulling the Boat up among Lake Reeds." Kayak, 28 (1972), 54.

_____ "Running over the River." Kayak, 5 (1966), 33.

_____ "The Sorb is the Tree of Thor, Who Hung Nine Days Wounded." The Paris Review, (Autumn/Winter, 1958/1959), 26.

_____ "Supper." Epoch, 13:1 (Fall, 1963), 42.

_____ "This World is a Confusion of Three Worlds." Poetry, XCVI (April, 1960), 31.

_____ "The Traveller." Audience, 8:3 (Winter, 1962), 70.

_____ "Two Choral Stanzas," II. The Paris Review (Spring, 1953), 27.

_____ "Watching Fall Dust Inside Sheds." The Beloit Poetry Journal, 14:1 (Fall, 1963), 42.

_____ "Watching Television." Choice: A Magazine of Poetry and Photography, 3 (1963), 111.

_____ "Wind." The Paris Review (Winter/Spring, 1962), 19.

_____ "With a Naked Girl, up to See the Spring Dawn." Kayak, 2 (1965), 30.

c) Prose Articles Published in Periodicals

Bly, Robert. "American Poetry: On the Way to the Hermetic." Books Abroad, 46:1 (Winter, 1972), 17-24.

_____ "The Dead World and the Live World." The Sixties, 8 (Spring, 1966), 2-7.

_____ "Developing the Underneath." The American Poetry Review (Nov./Dec., 1973).

Bly, Robert. "Difficult Questions, Easy Answers." The New York Times Book
        Review (March 17, 1974), 6.

_____   "The First Ten Issues of Kayak." Kayak, 12 (1967), 45-49.

_____   "Five Decades of Modern American Poetry." The Fifties, 1 (1958)
        36-39.

_____   "Looking for Dragon Smoke." The Seventies, 1 (1972), 3-8.

_____   "The Network and the Community." The American Poetry Review
        (Jan./Febr., 1974), 19-21.

_____   "On Political Poetry." The Nation (April 24, 1967), 522-524.

_____   "A Poet on Vietnam: Murder as a Prudent Policy." (The acceptan
        speech of Robert Bly on winning the National Book Award for
        Poetry.) The Commonweal, 88:1 (March 22, 1968), 17.

_____   "Spanish Leaping." The Seventies, 1 (1972), 16-21.

_____   "The Three Brains." The Seventies, 1 (1972), 61-69.

Crunk (Bly, Robert). "The Work of Gary Snyder." The Sixties, 6 (1962), 25

Bly, Robert. "A Wrong Turning in American Poetry." Choice: A Magazine of
        Poetry and Photography, 3 (1963), 33-47.

B   Secondary Sources

a)   Writings on Robert Bly's Poetry

Atlas, James; Greer, Curt; Kingston, Roger; and Rizza, Peggy. "A Conver-
        sation with Robert Bly." The Harvard Advocate (Febr., 1970), 4

Bail, Jay and Cook, Geoffrey. "With Robert Bly: An Interview." The San
        Francisco Book Review, 19 (April, 1971).

Brooks, Cleanth. "Poetry since 'The Waste Land.'" The Southern Review, I:3
        (1965), 487-500. Also in Brooks, Cleanth. A Shaping Joy: Studie
        in the Writer's Craft. London, 1971, 52-65.

Crossley-Holland, Kevin. "On the Natural World." Books & Bookmen, 12
        (May, 1967), 24.

Faas, Ekbert. "An Interview with Robert Bly." (Quoted from off-print
        lacking indication of source.)

Hall, Donald, ed.. Contemporary American Poetry. Harmondsworth, Middlesex
        1962. Second edition (revised and expanded), Harmondsworth,
        Middlesex, 1972.

Heyen, William. "Inward to the World: The Poetry of Robert Bly." The Far
        Point, 3, 42-50.

Hughes, D. J.. "The Demands of Poetry." The Nation (Jan. 5, 1963), 16-18.

Janssens, G. A. M.. "The Present State of American Poetry: Robert Bly and
        James Wright." English Studies, 51 (1970), 112-137.

Justin, Jeffrey A.. Unknown Land Poetry: Walt Whitman, Robert Bly, and
        Gary Snyder. Ph. D. thesis, The Univ. of Michigan, 1973.

Lacey, Paul. The Inner War. Philadelphia, Penn., 1972.

Libby, Anthony. "Robert Bly Alive in Darkness." The Iowa Review, 3:3
        (Summer, 1972), 78-89.

Logan, John. "Poetry Shelf." The Critic, XXI (Dec., 1962 - Jan., 1963),
        84-85.

Martin, Peter. "Robert Bly: Poet on the Road Home." The Straight Creek
        Journal, 1:36 (Oct. 24, 1972), 10, 11, and 16.

Mersmann, James F.. Out of the Vietnam Vortex. Lawrence, Kansas, 1974.

Mills,Jr., Ralph J.. "Four Voices in Recent American Poetry." The Christian Scholar (Winter, 1963), 324-345.

Molesworth, Charles. "Thrashing in the Depths: The Poetry of Robert Bly." The Rocky Mountain Review of Language and Literature, 29:3 and 4 (Autumn, 1975), 95-117.

Moran, Ronald and Lensing, George. "The Emotive Imagination: A New Departure in American Poetry." The Southern Review, III:1 (1967), 51-67.

Mueller, Lisel. "Five Poets." Shenandoah, XIX (Spring, 1968), 65-72.

Nelson, Howard. "Welcoming Shadows: Robert Bly's Recent Poetry." The Hollins Critic, XII:2 (April, 1975), 1-15.

Nordell, Roderick. "From the Bookshelf: A Poet in Minnesota." The Christian Science Monitor, LV (Jan. 23, 1963), 9.

Oates, Joyce Carol. "Where They All Are Sleeping." Modern Poetry Studies (Winter, 1973), 341-344.

Otto, Kathy and Lofsness, Cynthia. "An Interview with Robert Bly." The Tennessee Poetry Journal, 2:2 (Winter, 1969), 29-48.

Piccione, Anthony. Robert Bly and the Deep Image. Ph. D. thesis, Ohio Univ., 1969.

Review of Old Man Rubbing His Eyes. Publishers' Weekly (Febr. 3, 1975).

Richter, Franz Allbert and Hyde, Lew. "An Interview with Robert Bly." The Lamp and the Spine, 3 (Winter, 1972), 50-65.

Sage, Frances, K.. Robert Bly: His Poetry and Literary Criticism. Ph. D. thesis, The Univ. of Texas, 1974.

Simmons, Charles. "Poets in Search of a Public." The Saturday Review (March 30, 1963), 46-48.

Simpson, Louis. North of Jamaica. New York, N. Y., 1972.

_____ "Poetry Chronicle." The Hudson Review (Spring, 1963), 130-140.

Stepanchev, Stephen. American Poetry Since 1945. New York, N. Y., 1965.

Stitt, Peter. "James Wright and Robert Bly." The Minnesota Review (Jan. 29, 1974), 89-94.

Wosk, Julie H.. Prophecies for America: Social Criticism in the Recent Poetry of Bly, Levertov, Corso, and Ginsberg. Ph. D. thesis, The Univ. of Wisconsin, 1974.

Zweig, Paul. "A Sadness for America." The Nation (March 25, 1968), 418-420.

b) Other Works

Bachelard, Gaston. The Poetics of Reverie. Boston, Mass., 1971.

Balakian, Anna. The Literary Origins of Surrealism. 2nd edition. New York, N. Y., 1965. (1st ed., 1947.)

_____ Surrealism: The Road to the Absolute. Revised edition. The Univ. of Michigan Press, 1972.

Becket, Samuel. Waiting for Godot. New York, N. Y., 1954.

The Bible. Authorized King James Version.

Bodkin, Maud. Archetypal Patterns in Poetry. London, 1963.

Breton, André. Manifestoes of Surrealism. Paperback edition, The Univ. of Michigan Press, 1972.

Bullock, Michael, ed.. Poems of Solitude. Belard, Schuman.

Campbell, Joseph. The Hero with a Thousand Faces. Princeton, N. J., 1972.

Chadwick, Charles. Symbolism. London, 1971.

Eliot, T. S.. Four Quartets. New York, N. Y., 1943.

Emerson, Ralph Waldo. "The Poet." The Complete Essays and Other Writings of Ralph Waldo Emerson. Edited by Brooks Atkinson. New York, N. Y., 1940.

Encyclopedia of Painting. New York, N. Y., 1970.

Fordham, Frieda. An Introduction to Jung's Psychology. Hammondsworth, Middlesex, 1953.

von Franz, Marie-Louise. "Conclusion: Science and the Unconscious." Man and His Symbols. Edited by C. G. Jung and M.-L. von Franz, New York, N. Y., 1964.

_____ The Feminine in Fairytales. Zürich, 1972.

_____ "The Process of Individuation." Man and His Symbols. Edited by C. G. Jung and M.-L. von Franz. New York, N. Y., 1964.

_____ Shadow and Evil in Fairytales. Zürich, 1974.

Frost, Robert. The Complete Poems. London, 1951.

Frye, Northrop. Anatomy of Chriticism. Princeton, N. J., 1971.

Graves, Robert. The White Goddess. Amended and enlarged edition. London 196

Hassan, Ihab. The Dismemberment of Orpheus. New York, N. Y., 1971.

"Havamal." Eddadigte. Edited by Jón Helgason. Köpenhamn, 1951.

Hawthorne, Nathaniel. "Young Goodman Brown." Selected Tales and Sketches. New York, N. Y., 1950, 108-122.

Henderson, Joseph L.. "Ancient Myths and Modern Man." Man and His Symbols. Edited by C. G. Jung and M.-L. von Franz. New York, N. Y., 1964.

Hillman, James. "The Great Mother, Her Son, Her Hero, and Puer." Fathers & Mothers. Edited by Patricia Berry. Zürich, 1973.

Humphreys, Christmas. Zen Buddhism. Mandala edition. London, 1976. (1st edition, 1949.)

Jacobi, Jolande. "Symbols in an Individual Analysis." Man and His Symbols. Edited by C. G. Jung and M.-L. von Franz. New York, N. Y., 1964.

Jaffé, Aniela. "Symbolism in the Visual Arts." Man and His Symbols. Edited by C. G. Jung and M.-L. von Franz. New York, N. Y., 1964.

Jung, C. G.. "Approaching the Unconscious." Man and His Symbols. Edited by C. G. Jung and M.-L. von Franz. New York, N. Y., 1964.

_____ Four Archetypes: Mother, Rebirth, Spirit, Trickster. Princeton, N. J., 1970.

Jung, C. G. and Kereny, C.. Introduction to a Science of Mythology. London, 1951.

Leeming, David Adams. Mythology: The Voyage of the Hero. New York, N. Y., 1973.

Neumann, Erich. The Great Mother. Princeton, N. J., 1963.

⎯⎯⎯⎯⎯ "On the Moon and Matriarchal Consciousness." Fathers & Mothers. Edited by Patricia Berry. Zürich, 1973.

Ornstein, Robert E.. The Psychology of Consciousness. San Francisco, Calif., 1972.

Raymond, Marcel. From Baudelaire to Surrealism. London, 1970.

Sandburg, Carl. Complete Poems. New York, N. Y., 1950.

Tu Fu, China's Greatest Poet. Edited by William Hung. Cambridge, Mass., 1952.

Vitale, Augusto. "The Archetype of Saturn or Transformation of the Father." Fathers & Mothers. Edited by Patricia Berry. Zürich, 1973.

The White Pony: An Anthology of Chinese Poetry. Edited by Robert Payne. New York, N. Y., 1947.

Whitman, Walt. "Preface to 1855 Edition 'Leaves of Grass.'" "Leaves of Grass" and Selected Prose. Edited by Sculley Bradley. New York, N. Y., 1949.

Yeats, W. B.. The Collected Poems. New York, N. Y., 1949.

II   Works Consulted

A   Single Poems Published in Periodicals and Booklets, as Broadsheets and Postcards

Bly, Robert. "About to Drink Wine." Kayak, 2 (1965), 31.

⎯⎯⎯⎯⎯ "Affection (for John and Muriel Ridland)." The Lamp and the Spine, 3 (Winter, 1972), 68.

⎯⎯⎯⎯⎯ "April." Choice: A Magazine of Poetry and Photography, 3 (1963), 110.

⎯⎯⎯⎯⎯ "Archaic Torso of Apollo" (after Rainer Maria Rilke). Choice: A Magazine of Poetry and Photography, 1 (Spring, 1961), 13.

⎯⎯⎯⎯⎯ "At Night." Field, 10 (Spring, 1974), 36.

⎯⎯⎯⎯⎯ "The Beauty of Women." Poetry, CIV:6 (Sept., 1964), 366.

⎯⎯⎯⎯⎯ "Being Born." Field, 10 (Spring, 1974), 36.

⎯⎯⎯⎯⎯ "Buffalo." Broadsheet.

⎯⎯⎯⎯⎯ "Christmas Eve Service at Midnight at St Michael's." Rushden, Northamptonshire, 1972.

⎯⎯⎯⎯⎯ "The Current Administration." Kayak, 5 (1966), 31.

⎯⎯⎯⎯⎯ "Death." Agenda, 4:3-4 (Summer, 1966), 4.

⎯⎯⎯⎯⎯ "Driving in Snow." The Midwest Quarterly, XII:2 (Jan., 1971), 144.

⎯⎯⎯⎯⎯ "Ducks." Marshall, Minn., 1972.

⎯⎯⎯⎯⎯ "Fall." Poetry, CIV:6 (Sept., 1964), 366.

⎯⎯⎯⎯⎯ "Fear of the Boar with Tusks." Choice: A Magazine of Poetry and Photography, 3 (1963), 108.

Bly, Robert. "The Fir." Morris, Minn., 1975.

_____ "Frost." The Iowa Review, 2:1 (Winter, 1971), 22.

_____ "Going Down." Agenda, 4:3-4 (Summer, 1966), 4.

_____ "Grass From Two Years" "Let's Leave" (Kabir translation). Denver, Colorado, 1975.

_____ "Hamilton's Dream." Choice: A Magazine of Poetry and Photography 3 (1963), 107.

_____ "Hearing Gary Snyder Read." Uniform Broadsheet Series 2:3 (April 20, 1971).

_____ "The Hockey Poem." Duluth, Minn., 1974.

_____ "In a Boat on Big Stone Lake." Postcard. Santa Barbara. Calif., 1968.

_____ "In the North Atlantic." Kayak, 5 (1966), 33.

_____ "Leaving Ithaca (For Ruth and Dave)." Choice: A Magazine of Poetry and Photography, 3 (1963), 109.

_____ "Lies." The Nation (March 25, 1968), 417.

_____ "Meditation on Olai and Pete Bly." The Paris Review (Summer/Fall 1964), 96.

_____ "The Moon." Kayak, 1 (Autumn, 1964), 30.

_____ "Nearing the Middle West." The Paris Review (Winter/Spring, 1962), 20.

_____ "November Fog." The Tennessee Poetry Journal, 2:2 (Winter, 1969) 13.

_____ "Nonsense Poem." The Twin Cities Express, I:1 (1973), 37.

_____ "On Listening to Stevenson and Kennedy Lie about the First Cuban Invasion." Coastlines, 19 (1962), 61.

_____ "Poem for the Drunkard President." The Paris Review (Winter/Spring, 1964), 106.

_____ From "Poems for J. P. Morgan." Choice: A Magazine of Poetry and Photography, 1 (Spring, 1961), 13.

_____ "Revolution." Kayak, 5 (1966), 32.

_____ "Salute to All the Countries which Helped Franco." The Paris Review (Spring/Summer, 1959), 73.

_____ "Scene with Respectable Men." The Tennessee Poetry Journal, 2:2 (Winter, 1969), 11.

_____ "The Sleeper in the Mountain." The Tennessee Poetry Journal, 2:2 (Winter, 1969), 12.

_____ "Snowbanks North of the House." The American Poetry Review, 4:1 (1975), 1,

_____ "Strips of August Sun." An Alternative Press Postcard. Detroit, Mich..

_____ "Suffocation." Choice: A Magazine of Poetry and Photography, 3 (1963), 111.

_____ "The Testament." Poetry, CIV:6 (Sept., 1964), 367-368.

_____ "Thinking of Troubles." Kayak, 1 (Autumn, 1964), 30.

Bly, Robert. "Unanswered Letters." Poetry, CIV:6 (Sept., 1964), 365.

_____ "Vietnam." Something, 2:1 (Winter, 1966).

_____ "Waking Up in a Car." The Iowa Review, 2:1 (Winter, 1971), 22.

_____ "Walking Near a Pasture." Kayak, 1 (Autumn, 1964), 30.

_____ "Walking to a Good Friday Service in New York at Night." Audience, 8:3 (Winter, 1962), 71.

_____ "What We Have Inherited From the Intellectual Leadership of New England." The Paris Review (Spring/Summer, 1959), 72.

_____ "Writing Again." The Tennessee Poetry Journal, 2:2 (Winter, 1969), 10.

B   Poetry Magazines Edited by Robert Bly

Bly, Robert, ed.. The Fifties, 1 (1958), 2-3 (1959).

_____ The Sixties, 4 (1960), 5 (1961), 6 (1962), 7 (1964), 8 (1966), 9 (1967), 10 (1968).

_____ The Seventies, 1 (1972).

C   Books Edited and/or Translated by Robert Bly

Bly, Robert, ed.. Leaping Poetry: An Idea with Poems and Translations. Chosen by Robert Bly. Boston, Mass., 1972,

Ekelöf, Gunnar. I Do Best Alone at Night. Translated by Robert Bly. Washington, D. C., 1968.

_____ Late Arrival on Earth. Translated by Robert Bly. London, 1967.

Hamsun, Knut. Hunger. Translated by Robert Bly. New York, N. Y., 1967.

Ignatow, David. Selected Poems. Introductory Notes and an Afterword by Robert Bly. Middletown. Conn., 1975.

Issa. Ten Poems. English versions by Robert Bly. 1972.

Kabir. The Fish in the Sea is Not Thirsty. Versions by Robert Bly. Northwood Narrows, N. H., 1971.

Lagerlöf, Selma. The Story of Gösta Berling. Translated and with an Afterword by Robert Bly. New York, N. Y., 1962.

Lorca and Jiménez. Selected Poems. Chosen and translated by Robert Bly. Boston, Mass., 1973.

Martinson, Ekelöf, and Tranströmer. Friends, You Drank Some Darkness. Chosen and translated by Robert Bly. Boston, Mass., 1975.

Rilke, Rainer Maria. Ten Sonnets to Orpheus. Translated by Robert Bly. San Francisco, Calif., 1972.

Tranströmer, Tomas. Twenty Poems. Translated by Robert Bly. Madison. Minn., 1970.

D   Prose Articles by Robert Bly Published in Periodicals

Bly, Robert. "Eugenio Montale: Ascending." The New York Times Book Review (Nov. 9, 1975), "The Guest Word."

_____ "For Alden Nowlan, with Admiration." The Tennessee Poetry Journal, 4:1 (Fall, 1970), 6-10.

_____ "Growing up in Minnesota." The American Poetry Review, 4:1 (1975), 4-6.

Bly, Robert. "My Counsel: Stop War" (Acceptance of 1968 Poetry Award). The American Dialog, 5:2 (1968-69), 29.

———— "Note on Prose vs Poetry." Choice: A Magazine of Poetry and Photography, 2 (1962), 65-80.

———— "On Pablo Neruda." The Nation (March 25, 1968), 414-418.

———— "Poetry in an Age of Expansion." The Nation, CXCII (April 22, 1961), 350-354.

———— "Poetry - What is it Saying and to Whom? Artists and Indians." The American Dialog, 5:2 (1968-69), 28.

———— "The Problem of Exclusive Rights." The American Poetry Review, 2:3 (May/June, 1973), 48-50.

———— "Reflections on the Origins of Poetic Form." Field, 10 (Spring, 1974), 31-35.

———— "Some Thoughts on Rescue the Dead." The Tennessee Poetry Journ 3:2 (Winter, 1970), 17-21.

———— Speech at a symposium for editors of American little magazines The Carleton Miscellany (Spring, 1966), 20-22.

———— "Voznesensky and His Translators." Kayak, 9 (1966), 46-48.

———— "The War Between Memory and Imagination." The American Poetry Review, 2:5 (Sept./Oct., 1973), 49-50.

E   Writings on Robert Bly's Poetry in General

Baker, A. T.. "Poetry Today: Low Profile. Flatted Voice." Time (July 12, 1971), 61-69.

Binni, Francesco. "'Esterno' e 'Interno,' nell' 'Image Poetry' di Robert Bly e James Wright." Nuova Corrente, 59 (1972), 352-381.

Browne, Michael Dennis. "Robert Bly Gets Up Early." A poem. Crazy Horse, 12 (Autumn, 1972), 8-9.

Friberg, Ingegerd. "Modersmedvetandets arketyp." Tärningskastet, 2 (1977) 54-55.

———— "Robert Bly: En livsnära diktare." Tärningskastet, 1 (1976), 35-53.

Gitlin, Todd. "The Return of Political Poetry." The Commonweal, XCIV:16 (July 23, 1971), 375-380.

"Letters" (to the editor). The American Poetry Review (Jan./Febr., 1974), 53-55.

"Letters" (to the editor). Kayak, 13 (1968), 12-21.

Libby, Anthony. "Fire and Light. Four Poets to the End and Beyond." The Iowa Review, 4:2 (Spring, 1973), 111-126.

Lundkvist, Artur. "Ett krig ger bismak åt källvattnet." Dagens Nyheter (May 6, 1974), 4.

Mueller, Lisel; Knoepfle, John; and Etter, Dave. Three Essays on Midweste Poetry in Midcentury. La Crosse, Wis., 1971.

"The National Book Awards." By the editors of The Nation (March 25, 1968) 413-414.

"19th National Book Awards Stir Controversy in N. Y.." The Library Journa 93:7 (April 1, 1968), 1395-1396.

Ossman, David. The Sullen Art. Interviews with modern American Poets. New York, N. Y., 1963.

Reinhold, Robert. "Captain Bly and the Good Ship Lollipop." The Smith, 22-23 (July 4, 1973), 60-79.

Sullivan, Dan. "Minnesotans Publish Magazine to Boost Bright Young Poets." St P. P. P. (Dec. 13, 1959).

The Tennesse Poetry Journal, 2:2 (Winter, 1969). A special Robert Bly issue.

True, Michael D.. "Robert Bly, Radical Poet." Win, IX:2 (Jan. 15, 1973), 11-13.

Zweig, Paul. " The American Outsider." The Nation, (Nov. 14, 1966), 517-519.

F   Reviews:

a) Of Silence in the Snowy Fields and of The Lion's Tail and Eyes

Bergonzi, Bernard. "New Nature Poets." The Guardian (March 3, 1967).

Blackburn, Thomas. "Three American Poets." The Poetry Review (London, Autumn, 1967), 255-259.

"Chained to the Paris Pump." The Times Literary Supplement (March 16, 1967), 220.

Clunk. Review of Silence in the Snowy Fields. Burning Deck, 1 (Dec. 26, 1962).

Colombo, John Robert. "Poetry Chronicle." The Tamarach Review (Toronto, Winter, 1963), 86-95.

Cox, C.B.. "Ox, Mule and Buzzard." The Spectator, 24 (March, 1967), 342-343.

Cuscaden, R.R.. Review of Silence in the Snowy Fields. Elisabeth , V (March, 1963), 17-18.

Derleth, August. " Books of the Times." The Capital Times (Madison, Wis., Jan. 17, 1963).

Fines, C.O.. Review of Silence in the Snowy Fields. Thin Line, 1 (Spring, 1963), 26-30.

Friedman, Norman. "The Wesleyan Poets - III: The Experimental Poets." The Chicago Review, 19:2 (1967), 52-73.

Fowlie, Wallace. "Not Bards so Much as Catalyzers." The New York Times Book Review (May 12, 1963), 36.

Guest, Barbara. "Shared Landscapes." Chelsea, 16 (March, 1965), 150-152.

Gunderson, Keith. "The Solitude Poets of Minnesota." Burning Water (Fall, 1963), 57-61.

Gunn, Thom. "Poems and Books of Poems." The Yale Review (Autumn, 1963), 135-144,

Hamilton, Ian. "On the Rhythmic Run." The Observer (March 26, 1967), 23.

Hogan, Sheila. "Book Reviews." Quarry (Winter, 1965), 52-53.

Horton, Jane C.. "Poetry Volumes of Varying Worth." The Atlanta Journal (Jan. 6, 1963).

Howard, Richard. "Poetry Chronicle." Poetry (June, 1963), 182-192.

Jacobsen, Josephine. Review of Silence in the Snowy Fields. The Baltimore Sun (March 13, 1963).

Jerome, Judson. "A Poetry Chronicle - Part I." The Antioch Review (Spring, 1963), 109-124.

K., J. K.. Review of The Lion's Tail and Eyes. Thin Line, 1 (Spring, 1963), 30-31,

May, Derwent. "Lions and Fauns." The Times (April 6, 1967), 9.

Mc Grath, Thomas. Review of Silence in the Snowy Fields. The National Guardian (March 28, 1963).

Mc Pherson, Sandra. "You Can Say It Again. (Or Can You?)" The Iowa Review, 3:3 (Summer, 1972), 70-75.

"Notes on Current Books." The Virginia Quarterly Review (Winter, 1963) XXII.

Oberbeck, S. K.. "A Poet Who Listens." The St. Louis Post Dispatch, (March 24, 1963), 4.

Offen, Ron. "Poetry." The Literary Times (Chicago, Ill., March, 1963), 4.

Ray, David. "Notes, Reviews, Speculations: Robert Bly, Silence in the Snowy Fields." Epoch (Winter, 1963), 186-188.

Review of Silence in the Snowy Fields. The Beloit Poetry Journal, 14:2 (Winter, 1963-64), 39.

Review of Silence in the Snowy Fields. The Booklist and Subscription Books Bulletin, 59:7 (Dec. 1, 1962), 274.

Review of Silence in the Snowy Fields. The Irish Times (March 17, 1967).

Review of Silence in the Snowy Fields. The Virginia Quarterly Review (Winter, 1963).

Smith, Ray. Review of Silence in the Snowy Fields. The Library Journal (Nov. 1, 1962), 4025.

Stepanchev, Stephen. "Eight Poets." Shenandoah, XIV (Spring, 1963), 58-65.

_____ "Singer of Silence." The New York Herald Tribune (August 11, 1963).

Stitt, Peter. "Robert Bly's World of True Images." The Minnesota Daily, Ivory Tower (April 8, 1963), 29 and 47.

Taylor, W. E.. "The Chief." Poetry Flórida and ..., 1:3-4 (Summer, 1968), 12-16.

Thorpe, Michael. "Current Literature 1967: I. New Writing: Poetry." English Studies, XLIV:3 (June, 1968), 277.

Tulip, James. "The Wesleyan Poets - II." Poetry Australia (Dec., 1966), 38-41.

Wheat, Allen. "Solitude and Awareness: The World of Robert Bly." The Minnesota Daily (Oct., 1967), 19-23 and 44.

White, Robert. Review of Silence in the Snowy Fields. Blue Grass (Winter, 1963), 37-38.

Williams Ward, May. Review of Silence in the Snowy Fields. The Wellington News (Febr. 22, 1966).

b) Of The Light around the Body and of The Teeth Mother Naked at Last

Birney, Adrian. "Impure Poetry." The Pequod, 5 (Spring, 1970), 59-61.

Bland, Peter. "Poetry: Bly, MacCaig, Mahon." The London Magazine (Dec., 1968), 95-98.

"Bookmarks," The Prairie Schooner, XLV:1 (Spring, 1971), 92-93.

Bostick, Christina. From "The Individual and War Resistance," The Library Journal (March 15, 1972), 1142.

Brownjohn, Alan. "Pre-Beat." The New Statesman (August 2, 1968), 146.

Burns, Gerald. "U. S. Poetry 1967 - The Books that Matter." The Southwest Review (Winter, 1968), 101-106.

Carruth, Hayden. From "Critic of the Month." Poetry (Sept., 1968), 423.

D., M.. Review of The Teeth Mother Naked At Last. The Prairie Schooner Review (Summer, 1971), 186.

Davison, Peter. "New Poetry: The Generation of the Twenties." The Atlantic Monthly (Febr., 1968), 141-142.

Delonas, John. Review of The Light around the Body. The Library Journal, 92 (Oct. 15, 1967), 3647.

_____ Review of The Light around the Body. The Library Journal Book Review (1967), 403.

Dodsworth, Martin. "Towards the Baseball Poem." The Listener (June 27, 1968), 842-843.

Goldman, Michael. "Joyful in the Dark." The New York Times Book Review (Febr. 18, 1968), 10 and 12.

Halley, Anne. "Recent American Poetry: Outside Relevancies." The Massachusetts Review (Autumn, 1968), 696-713.

Hamilton, Ian. "Public Gestures, Private Poems." The Observer (June 30, 1968), 24.

Hammer, Louis Z.. "Moths in the Light." Kayak, 14 (April, 1968), 63-67.

Hefferman, Michael. "Brief Reviews." The Midwest Quarterly XII:3 (Spring, 1971), 353-356.

Kalstone, David. "Poetry Has Made Friends With Everyone." The New York Times Book Review (Febr. 13, 1972), 3, 16, and 18.

Katz, Bill. Review of The Teeth Mother Naked at Last. The Library Journal Book Review (1971), 350-351.

Lask, Thomas. "Books of The Times: The Public Mind and the Private Mind." The New York Times (August 22, 1967), 37.

Leibowitz, Herbert. "Questions of Reality." The Hudson Review, XXI (Autumn, 1968), 553-563.

Mazzocco, Robert. "Jeremiads at Half-Mast." The New York Review of Books (June 30, 1968), 22-25,

Meiners, R. K.. From "The Way Out: The Poetry of Delmore Schwartz and Others." The Southern Review (Winter, 1971), 314.

Miles, Josephine. "The Home Book of Modern Verse, 1970." The Massachusetts Review (Autumn, 1971), 689-708.

Naiden, James. "Vietnam Everyone's Fault? Poetry Protesting War 'Crashing Bore.'" The Minneapolis Star (March 30, 1971), Section 1, B, III.

"Notes on Current Books: The Light around the Body, by Robert Bly." The Virginia Quarterly Review, 44:1 (Winter, 1968), XVIII.

Review of The Light around the Body. The Booklist and Subscription Books Bulletin, 64 (Oct., 1967), 231-232.

Review of The Light around the Body. The Kirkus Reviews, 35 (June 15, 19

Review of The Light around the Body. The South Dakota Review, 5:3 (Autumn 1967), 68.

Rexroth, Kenneth. "The Poet As Responsible." The Northwest Review, (Fall Winter, 1967-68), 116-118.

Ruffin, Carolyn F.. "From the Book Reviewer's Shelf: Three Poets of the Present ...." The Christian Science Monitor, LIX (Oct.9,1967)

Simpson, Louis. "New Books of Poems." Harper's Magazine (August, 1968), 73-77.

Smith, Ray. Permanent Fires. Reviews of Poetry, 1958-1973. Metuchen, N, 1975. 11-13, and 125.

"Special Pleading." Review of The Light around the Body. The Times Literary Supplement (August 15, 1968), 867.

Symons, Julian. "New Poetry." Punch or The London Charivari (July 24, 19 136.

Tulip, James. "The Poetry of Robert Bly." Poetry Australia (Sydney, August 1969), 47-52.

Zinnes, Harriet. "Two Languages." The Prairie Schooner Review, 42 (Summer 1968), 176-178.

c) Of Jumping Out of Bed, of Sleepers Joining Hands, and of Old Man Rubbing His Eyes

Cavitch, David. "Poet As Victim and Victimizer: Sleepers Joining Hands." The New York Times Book Review (Febr. 18, 1973).

Chamberlain, J. E.. "Poetry Chronicle." The Hudson Review, XXVI:2 (Summer 1973), 388-404.

Cooney, Seamus. Review of Sleepers Joining Hands. The Library Journal Book Review (1972), 363.

Cotter, James Finn. "Poetry's New Image of Man." America (June 9, 1973), 533-535.

Dawe, Charles. "Sleepers Joining Hands." The Boston Phoenix (April 10, 1973), section 3,

Foster, Michael. "On Sleepers Joining Hands." The Shore Review, 11 (Fall, 1973), 52-55.

Garrison, Joseph. Review of Old Man Rubbing His Eyes. The Library Journal (April 1, 1975), 674.

Gilder, Gary. "Books in Brief." The Kansas City, MO. Star (April 22, 1973)

Hyde, Lewis. "Let Other Poets Whisper.... You Can Hear Bly." The Minneapolis Tribune (Febr. 25, 1973), 10D-11D.

Keating, Douglas. "Bly Collection Is Noteable Achievement in Verse." The Philadelphia, PA. Bulletin (Sept, 16, 1973).

Klotz, Neil. "20th Century Survival." The Mess (=The Manitou Messenger) (March 2, 1973), 10.

Metro, Jim. Review of Sleepers Joining Hands. The Montgomery, Ala. Advertiser (Oct. 7, 1973).

Miller, Vassar. "Poetry." The Houston, Texas Post (April 29, 1973).

Mohr, William. "Robert Bly." Momentum (May, 1974), 59-61.

Murrey, Michele. "Talent Will Out, Right?" The National Observer, 12 (March 3, 1973), 21.

Naiden, James. "Echoes Don't Lessen Poet Bly's Strength." The Minneapolis Star(Nov. 20, 1973), 2B II.

"New and Recommended (Fiction and Poetry)." The New York Times Book Review (Febr. 25, 1973).

Nicolai, Peter. "Poetry." The Minnesota Daily (Febr. 5, 1973).

Oppenheimer, Joel. "A Newspaper Reader's Garden of Verses." The Garden City, N. Y. Newsday (Aug. 5, 1973), 16 and 20.

Piccione, A.. "Bly: Man, Voice and Poem." The Ann Arbor Review (August 15-16, 1973), 86-90.

"'Pilgrim Fish Heads.'" Review of Sleepers Joining Hands. The National Observer, 12 (June 9, 1973), 23.

Review of Sleepers Joining Hands. The Kirkus Reviews, 4:20 (Oct. 15, 1972), 1217.

Review of Sleepers Joining Hands. The New York Times Book Review (June 10, 1973), 41.

Review of Sleepers Joining Hands. Poetry Americana. Grand Rapids, Mich., 1973.

Reviews of Jumping Out of Bed and Sleepers Joining Hands. Choice (May, 1974), 434.

Reviews of Sleepers Joining Hands. Book Review Digest (May, 1973), 120.

Shapiro, Karl. "The New Poetry: Still Echoing the Agony of the '60's." The Chicago, Ill. Tribune (March 25, 1973).

Skelton, Robin. "Robert Bly's New Book." Kayak, 33 (Nov., 1973), 66-69.

"Sleepers Joining Hands." Editor's Note. The Marquette, Michigan Mining Journal (March, 1973), 2 and 13.

Stenberg, Mary. "New Work Based on Poet's Theories." The Escondido, Calif. Times - Advocate (Febr. 4, 1973).

Walsh, Chad. "Wry Apocalypse, Revolutionary Petunias." The Book World of Washington Post (April 1, 1973), 13.

Weber, R. B.. "Robert Bly: His Energy is Flagging." The Louisville, KY. Courier - Journal (March 3, 1973).

Zinnes, Harriet. "Images Plunging Inward." The New Leader (July 9, 1973), 19.

d) Of Books Edited and/or Translated by Robert Bly

Benedikt, Michael. Review of I Do Best Alone at Night. Poetry (Dec., 1968), 211-212.

Clark, Leonard. "Motions of the Heart." The Poetry Review (Summer, 1968), 109-111.

Clayre, Alasdair. From "Books & Writers." Encounter (Nov., 1967), 78-79.

Coleman, Alexander. "Two Latin American Poets and an Antipoet." The New York Times Book Review (May 7, 1972), 4 and 40.

Coxe, Louis. "Poets as Crusaders." The New Republic (Nov. 14, 1970), 26-2

Fraser, G. S.. "The Unfinality of Translation." The Partisan Review, XLI·2 (1974), 289-295.

Garrison, Joseph. Review of Friends, You Drank some Darkness: Three Swedi Poets. The Library Journal (April 1, 1975), 674-675.

Gullans, Charles. "Poetry and Subject Matter: From Hart Crane to Turner Cassity." The Southern Review (Spring, 1970), 488-505.

L., J.. "Reviews" of A Poetry Reading Against the Vietnam War. The South Dakota Review, 4:4 (Winter, 1966), 89.

Meyer, Michael. "The Call of the Deep." The Times Literary Supplement (Oc 31, 1975), 1287.

Mills, Jr., Ralph J.. "Five Anthologies." Poetry (Febr., 1967), 345-350.

Mojtabai, Ann G.. Review of The Sea and the Honeycomb. The Library Journa Book Review (1971), 350.

Moore, Stephen. "Literary Studies and Literature: The Return of History. The Michigan Quarterly Review, XII:3 (Summer, 1973), 285-290).

Murray, Philip. "Perilous Arcady." Poetry (August, 1972), 304-312.

Nelson, Cary. "Whitman in Vietnam: Poetry and History in Contemporary America." The Massachusetts Review (Winter, 1975), 55-71.

Review of Friends You Drank Some Darkness. The Kirkus Reviews, XLIII:5 (March 1, 1975), 268.

Review of Lorca and Jiménez. Choice (March, 1974), 98.

Review of Neruda and Vallejo: Selected Poems. Choice, 9 (April, 1972), 220

r., m.. Review of A Poetry Reading Against the Vietnam War. El Corno Emplumado, 23 (July, 1967), 148-151.

r., m.. Review of The Sea and the Honeycomb. El Corno Emplumado, 21 (Jan., 1967), 111.

Root, William Pitt. "Anything But Over." Poetry (Oct., 1973), 34-41.

R., W. G.. Review of Lorca and Jimenéz: Selected Poems. The Prairie Schoo Review, 48:1 (Spring, 1974), 91-92.

Taylor, Henry. "A Gathering of Poets." The Western Humanities Review (Autumn, 1971), 367-372.

Vendler, Helen. "False Poets and Real Poets." The New York Times Book Review (Sept. 7, 1975), 6-18.

Waring, Walter W.. Review of Forty Poems Touching on Recent American History. The Library Journal Book Review (1970), 441-442.

Young, Vernon. "Lines Written in Rouen." The Hudson Review, 24:4 (Winter, 1971-72), 669-686.

G   Articles on Modern American Poetry

Donadio, Stephen. "Some Younger Poets in America." Modern Occasions. New York, N. Y., 1966.

Garrett, George. "Against the Grain: Poets Writing Today." American Poetry Edited by Irvin Ehrenpreis. London, 1965.

Hoffman, Frederick J.. "Contemporary American Poetry." Patterns of Commit-ment in American Literature. Edited by Marston La France. Toronto, 1967.

Kelly, Robert. "Notes on the Poetry of Deep Image." _Trobar,_ 2 (1961), 14-16.

Rexroth, Kenneth. "The New American Poets." _Harper's Magazine_ (June, 1965), 65-71.

Shapiro, Karl. "The Poetry Wreck." _The Library Journal,_ 95 (Febr. 15, 1970), 632.

Simpson, Louis. "Dead Horses and Live Issues." _The Nation_ (April 24, 1967), 520.

Welland, Dennis. "The Dark Voice of the Sea: A Theme in Modern American Poetry." _American Poetry._ Edited by Irvin Ehrenpreis. London, 1965.